# STRATEGIC HUMAN RESOURCE MANAGEMENT AND DEVELOPMENT

# STRATEGIC HUMAN RESOURCE MANAGEMENT AND DEVELOPMENT

DR. ANURADHA PATHAK
PROF. PRIYANKA S. KASKAR

REGAL PUBLICATIONS
New Delhi

STRATEGIC HUMAN RESOURCE
MANAGEMENT AND DEVELOPMENT

ISBN 978-81-8484-366-8



*Typeset by*
RAHUL COMPOSERS
New Highway Apartments, Lakshmi Niwas
760, Pocket-D, Lok Nayak Puram, New Delhi - 110 041

*Printed in India at*
MAYUR ENTERPRISES
WZ Plot No. 3, Gujjar Market, Tihar Village, New Delhi - 110 018

*Published by*
REGAL PUBLICATIONS
F-159, Rajouri Garden, New Delhi - 110 027
Phone : 45546396, 25435369
E-mail : regalbookspub@yahoo.com, regaldeepbooks@yahoo.com

# Contents

# Preface

Debates in the early 1990s suggested the need to explore the relationship between strategic management and HRM more extensively and the emerging trend in which HRM is becoming an integral part of business strategy. The emergence of SHRM is an outcome of such efforts. Its purpose is to ensure that HRM is fully integrated with the strategy and strategic needs of the firm; HR policies are coherent both across policy areas and across hierarchies; and HR practices are adjusted, accepted and used by line managers and employees as part of their everyday work.

SHRM therefore has many different components, including HR policies, culture, values and practices. Strategic HRM is a multidimensional process with multiple effects. Such writing also highlights the growing proactive nature of the HR function, its increased potential contribution to the success of organisations and the mutual relationships (integration) between business strategy and HRM.

Strategic HRM is concerned with the relationship between human resource management and strategic management in the firm. Strategic HRM refers to the overall direction the organization wishes to pursue in order to achieve its goals through people. It is argued that, because intellectual capital is a major source of competitive advantage, and in the last analysis it is people who implement the strategic plan, top managernent must take these key considerations fully into account in developing its corporate strategies. Strategic HRM is an integral part of those strategies.

Strategic HRM addresses broad organizational issues relating to organizational effectiveness and performance, changes in structure and culture, matching resources to future requirements, the development of distinctive capabilities, knowledge management and the management of change. It is concerned with both meeting human capital requirements and the development of process capabilities, that is, the ability to get things done effectively. Overall, it will consider any major people issues that affect or are affected by the strategic plan of the organization. 'The critical concerns of HRM such as choice of executive leadership and formation of positive patterns of labour relations, are strategic in any firm.'

Strategic HRM focuses on actions that differentiate the firm from its competitors. It develops declarations of intent which define means to achieve ends, and it is concerned with the long-term allocation of significant company resources, and with matching those resources and capabilities to the external environment. Strategy is a perspective on the way in which critical issues or success factors can be addressed, and strategic decisions aim to make a major and long-term impact on the behaviour and success of the organization.

Completion of this work would not have been possible without reference to the authentic publications on the subject—Indian and Foreign. We shall, therefore, like to record our sincerest thanks to the authors and publications houses of those publications. Although every effort has been made to offer the most authentic position on the subject, claiming hundred per cent accuracy will be too tall a claim. Any error, omission and suggestions for the improvement of the book brought to our notice shall be thankfully acknowledged and incorporated in the next edition.

First of all, we heartily thankful to Almighty God. We acknowledge the inspiration and blessings of our parents from the core of our heart and extend thanks to our family members for their moral support which helped us in successful completion of this book.

At last, we extend our sincerely thanks to Regal Publications for motivating guidance during preparation of this book on several aspects.

DR. ANURADHA PATHAK
PROF. PRIYANKA S. KASKAR

# An Introduction to Strategic Human Resource Management (SHRM)

## INTRODUCTION

Liberalization and industrialization has created pressure on organizations in India to create opportunities for technology upgradation and sophistication, high growth and buoyant environment where there is unrestricted trade and economic activities. Thus there is huge responsibility on HR department and HR specialist to bring large scale professional changes in their organizations.

SHRM is a concept that blends traditional HR management practices within a firm's overall strategic planning and implementation program. Nowadays increased interest in HRM is also because of the perceived connection between HRM activities and production. Strategic human resource management (SHRM) enhances productivity and effectiveness of organizations. Their implementation in organizations has proven that when organizations employ such personnel practices they are more able to achieve their goals and objectives in a far better way.

### Strategy

Strategy is multidimensional concept which goes beyond traditional competitive strategy concepts. "It is the direction and scope of an organization over long term which achieves advantage for the organization through its configuration, to meet the needs of markets and to fulfill stakeholders expectations." The concept of SHRM is based on the notion that HR strategies should be integrated with corporate strategies.

The most important reason for the increased interest in the HRM by Indian Business is the realization of the connection between HR activities and productivity. As a result of this realization, more and more Indian companies are trying to acquire the status of global organizations, for, e.g. Wipro, Aditya Birla Group, Ranbaxy and Infosys. They are using best management and HR practices that aim at cutting costs, improving product quality and services and developing in-house technology as well as improving quality of their employees. They have adopted modern innovative managerial tools, methods and processes like TQM, QCS, JIT, benchmarking, teamwork, etc. to improve their efficiency and effectiveness.

## Evolution of Concept

In today's intensely competitive world, competitive advantage lies not just in differentiating a product or service or in becoming a low cost leader, but in also being able to capture company's special skills or core competencies, as well as rapidly responding to customer's needs and competitor's moves.

The concept of SHRM was developed in 1984. This term was first coined by Fombrun, Tichy and Devanna. They suggested that HR systems and organizational structures should be managed in such a way that is congruent with organizational strategy. SHRM is the result of two major radical shifts, first the shift from old Personnel Administration to Human Resource management. This change is based on the belief that people are an important asset in organizations that can be managed systematically by coordinating the shape and the substance of several traditional policies and practices. Second major shift is the reorientation of generic strategic models to the modern concept of SHRM. This reorientation is based on the philosophy that in addition to coordinating HR policies and practices with each other, this also needed to be coordinated with the needs of the organization.

Major impetus in the field of SHRM came in the mid-1990s when Huselid (1995) published his landmark study demonstrating statistically significant relationship between HRM practices and corporate performance. Also in the same year, MacDuffies industry focused study illustrated how particular bundles of HR practices when aligned with an organizational logic lead to plant level performance. Thus, all over the world HR practitioners have realized that in addition to personal and developmental aspects, there is urgent need to use strategic management concept too. This reorientation of generic strategic models to internal aspects of the organizations became a focal point for strategic HRM.

An important aspect of SHRM is employee development. This is possible when the company has employed effective recruitment and selection technique. Human beings are the most important asset of an organization. Motivated human resource can help the organization to achieve unimaginable heights of success. So, it is necessary to invest in the development of the employees. SHRM is essential in both large as well as in small companies. In small companies, it can be a simple process as owner or manager takes very little time everyday to observe, assist and assess employees and provide regular reviews. Large companies can have a whole department in charge of human resource and development.

Let's understand some terms which are used in SHRM:

*Core competencies*: A unique capability in the organization that creates high value and differentiates organization from its competitors.

*Mission Statement:* It explains the purpose and reason for existence, it is usually broad but does not go beyond couple of sentences and it serves as a foundation for everything that organization does.

*Strategy*: It is the company's plan for how it will balance its internal strengths and weaknesses with external opportunities and threats in order to maintain a competitive advantage.

## IMPORTANCE OF SHRM

HR management can play a role in environmental scanning i.e. identifying and analyzing external opportunities and threats that may be crucial to the company's success. Similarly, HR management is in a unique position to supply competitive intelligence that may be useful in the strategic planning process. HR also participates in the strategy formulation process by supplying information regarding the company's internal strengths and weaknesses. The strengths and weaknesses of a company's human resources can have a determining effect on the viability of the firm's strategic options.

By design, the perspective demands HR managers become strategic partners in business operations playing prospective roles rather than being passive administrators reacting to the requirements of other business functions. Strategic HR managers need a change in their mindset from seeing themselves as relationship managers to resource managers knowing how to utilize the full potential of their human resources.

The new breed of HR managers need to understand and know how to measure the monetary impact of their actions, so as to be able to demonstrate the value-added contributions of their functions. HR professionals become strategic partners when they participate in the process of defining business strategy, when they ask questions that move strategy to action and when they design HR practices that align with the business strategy. By fulfilling this role, HR professionals increase the capacity of a business to execute its strategies.

The primary actions of the strategic human resource manager translate business strategies into HR priorities. In any business setting, whether corporate, functional, business unit or product line a strategy exists either explicitly in the formal process or document or implicitly through a shared agenda on priorities. As strategic partners, HR professionals should be to identify the HR practices that make the strategy happen. The process of identifying these HR priorities is called organizational diagnosis, a process through which an organization is audited to determine its strengths and weaknesses.

Translating business strategies into HR practices helps a business in three ways. First, the business can adapt to change because the time from the conception to the execution of a strategy is shortened. Second, the business can better meet customer demands because its customer service strategies have been translated into specific policies and practices. Third, the business can achieve financial performance through its more effective execution of strategies.

In brief, a strategic perspective of HRM that requires simultaneous consideration of both external (business strategy) and internal (consistency) requirement leads to superior performance of the firm. This performance advantage is achieved by:

- Marshalling resources that support the business strategy and implementing the chosen strategy, efficiently and effectively.
- Utilizing the full potential of the human resources to the firm's advantage.
- Leveraging other resources such as physical assets and capital to complement and augment the human resources-based advantage.

## PROCESS OF STRATEGIC MANAGEMENT

The strategic management process defines the organization's strategy. It is also the process which helps managers make a choice of a set of strategies for the organization that will enable it to achieve better performance. Strategic management is a continuous process that appraises the business and industries in which the organization is involved, its competitors; and fixes goals to meet all the present and future potential competitors and then reassesses each strategy.

Strategic management process has following five steps:

1. **Mission and Goals:** The first step in the strategic management begins with senior managers evaluating their position in relation to the organization's current mission and goals. The mission describes the organization's values and aspirations; and indicates the direction in which senior management is going. Goals are the desired ends sought through the actual operating procedures of the organization. It typically describe short-term measurable outcomes.
2. **Environmental Scanning:** Environmental scanning refers to a process of collecting, scrutinizing and providing information for strategic purposes and helps in analyzing the internal and external factors influencing an organization. After executing the process, management should evaluate it on a continuous basis and strive to improve it.
3. **Strategy Formulation:** Strategy formulation is the process of deciding best course of action for achieving organizational objectives. After conducting environment scanning process, managers formulate corporate, business and functional strategies.
4. **Strategy Implementation:** Strategy implementation implies putting the organization's chosen strategy in to action and making it work as intended. Strategy implementation includes designing the organization's structure, distributing resources, developing decision making process, and effectively managing human resources.
5. **Strategy Evaluation:** Strategy evaluation which is the final step of strategy management process involves: appraising internal and external factors, measuring performance, and taking remedial/corrective actions. Evaluation assure the management that the organizational strategy as well as its implementation meets the organizational objectives.

These steps are carried by the businesses, in chronological order, when creating a new strategic management plan. Present businesses that have already created a strategic management plan will revert to these steps as per the situation's requirement, so as to make essential changes.

## APPROACHES OF THE SHRM

There are two approaches to SHRM. First approaches of the SHRM, attempts to link Human Resource activities with competency based performance measures (Havards approach) and second one attempts to link Human Resource activities with business surpluses or profit (Michigan approach). These two approaches indicate two factors in an organizational setting.

The first one indicates human factor, their performance and competency and the second one indicates business surplus. Both factors are equally important for gaining competitive advantage. An approach of people concern is based on the belief that human resources are uniquely important in achieving persistent business success. Michigan approach attempts to integrate business surplus to the human competency and performance. The way in which people are managed, motivated and deployed, and the availability of skills and knowledge will all shape the business strategy. The strategic orientation of the business then requires the effective orientation of human resource to competency and performance excellence.

## BENEFITS OF SHRM

SHRM provides a host of benefits to the organizations.

1. Identifying and analyzing external opportunities and threats that may be crucial to the company's success.
2. Providing clear business strategy and vision for the future.
3. Supplying competitive intelligence that may be useful in the strategic planning process.
4. Recruiting, retaining and motivating people.
5. Developing and retain of highly competent people.
6. Ensuring that people development issues are addressed systematically.
7. Supplying information regarding the company's internal strengths and weaknesses.
8. Meeting the expectations of the customers effectively.
9. Ensuring high productivity.
10. Ensuring business surplus thorough competency.

## BARRIERS OF SHRM

Barriers to successful SHRM implementation are complex. The main reason is the lack of growth strategy or failure to implement one. Other major barriers are summarized as follows:

1. Inducing the vision and mission of the change effort.
2. High resistance due to lack of cooperation from the bottom line.
3. Interdepartmental conflict.

4. Lack of commitment of the entire senior management team.
5. Ineffective plans that integrate internal resource with external requirements.
6. Limited time, money and the resources.
7. Resistance of employees.
8. Resistance of senior level managers to take up strategic steps.
9. Diverse work-force with competitive skill sets.
10. Fear towards victimization in the wake of failures.
11. Improper strategic assignments and leadership conflict over authority.
12. Ramifications for power relations.
13. Vulnerability to legislative changes.
14. Resistance that comes through the legitimate labour institutions.
15. Presence of an active labour union.
16. Economic and market pressures influencing the adoption of strategic HRM.

## HR PRACTITIONERS' ROLE

HR managers should act as strategic partners and be proactive in their role than being mere reactive, passive spectators as they have key role in the effective planning and implementation of the policies and decisions of the organization. The HR managers should, therefore, understand how far their decisions contribute to business surplus incorporating human competency and performance to the organization. A crucial aspect concerning SHRM is the concepts of fit and flexibility. The degree of fit determines the human resource system's integration with organization strategy. It is the role of HR Managers to ensure this fit between Human Resource System with the Organization Strategy.

## HIERARCHY OF STRATEGY

Another aspect of strategic management in the multidivisional business organization concerns the level to which strategic issues apply. Conventionally there are three different levels of strategy—

1. Corporate
2. Business
3. Functional.

## CORPORATE-LEVEL STRATEGY

Corporate-level strategies address the entire strategic scope of the enterprise. Corporate-level strategy describes a corporation's overall direction in terms of its general philosophy towards the growth and the management of its various business units. This is the "big picture" view of the organization and includes deciding in which product or service markets to compete as well as in which geographic regions to operate. For multi-business firms, because market definition is the domain of corporate-level strategists, the responsibility for diversification, or the addition of new products or services to the existing product/service line-up, also falls within the realm of corporate-level strategy. Similarly, decisions like whether to compete directly with other firms or to selectively establish cooperative relationship strategic alliances falls within the purview corporate-level strategy. However, corporate level managers requires ongoing inputs from business-level managers. Critical questions answered by corporate—level strategists thus include:

1. What businesses should the firm be in?
2. How should the resources be allocated among existing businesses?
3. What level of diversification should the firm pursue; i.e., which businesses should the company enter and which businesses should be targeted for termination or divestment?
4. How diversified should the corporation's business be, i.e should it opt for related diversification; i.e., similar products and service markets, or unrelated diversification; i.e., dissimilar product and service markets. If related diversification is chosen, how will the firm leverage potential cross-business synergies, i.e. how will adding new product or service businesses benefit the existing product/service line-up?
5. How should the firm be structured? Where should the boundaries of the firm be drawn? Do the organizational components such as research and development, finance, marketing, etc. fit together? Are the responsibilities and accountability for each business unit clearly identified?

Thus, corporate strategies deal with plans for the entire organization and they initiate change as industry and specific market conditions warrant. Top management has primary decision-making responsibility in developing corporate strategies and these managers are directly responsible to shareholders. The role of the board of directors is to ensure that top managers actually represent these shareholders' interests. However, corporate strategists are paralyzed without accurate and up-to-date information from managers at the business-level.

## BUSINESS-LEVEL STRATEGIES

Business-level strategy deals with decisions and actions pertaining to each business unit, the main objective of a business-level strategy being to make the unit more competitive in its marketplace. They are similar to corporate-strategies. But corporate strategies focus on overall performance, while, business level strategies focus on only one rather than a portfolio of businesses.

Business-level strategies are thus primarily concerned with:

1. Coordinating and integrating unit activities so they conform to organizational strategies.
2. Developing distinctive competencies in each unit.
3. Identifying product or service-market niches and developing strategies for competing in each.
4. Monitoring product or service markets so that strategies conform to the needs of the markets.

In a single-product company, corporate-level and business-level strategies are the same. Thus, in single-business organizations, corporate and business-level strategies overlap to the point that they should be treated as one united strategy. However, the product made by a unit of a diversified company would face many challenges and opportunities faced by a one-product company. As for most organizations, business-unit strategies are designed to support corporate strategies, the focus for business-level strategies is on the product or service and not on the corporate portfolio.

Business-level strategies thus support corporate-level strategies as these strategies are concerned with aligning their activities with the overall goals of corporate-level strategy while simultaneously, navigating the markets in which they compete in such a way that they have a financial or market edge—a competitive advantage-relative to the other businesses in their industry.

Although business-level strategy is guided by 'upstream' corporate-level strategy, business unit management must craft a strategy that is appropriate for its own operating situation. In the 1980s, Harvard Business School's Michael Porter developed a framework of generic strategies that can be applied to strategies for various products and services, or the individual business-level strategies within a corporate portfolio. Porter made a significant contribution to our understanding of business strategy by formulating three competitive strategies: cost leadership, differentiation; and focus on a particular market niche. Cost-leadership strategies require firms to develop policies aimed at becoming and remaining the lowest cost producer and/or distributor in the industry. Note here that the focus is on cost leadership, not price leadership. Differentiation strategies require a firm to create something about its product that is perceived as unique within its market. Focus, the third generic strategy, involves concentrating on a particular customer, product line, geographical area, channel of distribution, or market niche.

Miles and Snow (1984) have identified four modes of strategic orientation: defenders, prospectors, analyzers and reactors. Defenders are companies with a limited product line and where the management focus is on improving the efficiency of their existing operations. Prospectors are companies with fairly broad product lines and where the management focus is on product innovation and market opportunities. This orientation makes senior managers emphasize 'creativity over efficiency'. Analyzers are companies that operate in at least two different product market areas, one stable and one variable and, as such in this situation, senior managers emphasize efficiency in the stable areas whereas innovation in the variable areas. Reactors are companies that lack a consistent strategy—structure—culture relationship. In this reactive orientation, senior management's responses to environmental changes thus tend to be piecemeal strategic adjustments.

## FUNCTIONAL-LEVEL STRATEGIES

Functional-level strategies are concerned with coordinating the functional areas of the organization (marketing, finance, human resources, production, research and development, etc.) so that each functional area contributes to individual business-level strategies and the overall corporate-level strategy. This involves coordinating the various functions needed to design, manufacturer, deliver, and support the product or service of each business. Functional strategies are primarily concerned with:

- efficiently utilizing specialists within the functional area.
- integrating activities within the functional area (e.g., coordinating advertising, promotion, and marketing research in marketing; or purchasing, inventory control, etc. in production/operations).
- assuring that functional strategies fit with business-level strategies and the overall corporate-level strategy.

Strategies for an organization may be categorized by the level of the organization addressed by the strategy. Corporate-level strategies involve top management and address issues of concern to the entire organization. Business-level strategies are generally developed by upper and middle-level managers and are intended to help the organization achieve its corporate strategies. Functional strategies address problems commonly faced by lower-level managers and deal with strategies for the major organizational functions (e.g., marketing, finance, and production) considered relevant for achieving the business strategies.

| *Level of Strategy* | *Definition* | *Example* |
|---|---|---|
| Corporate strategy | Market definition | Diversification into new product or geographic markets |
| Business strategy | Market navigation | Attempts to secure competitive advantage in existing product or geographic markets |
| Functional strategy | Support of corporate strategy and business strategy | Information systems, administrative and human resource practices, as well as production processes that facilitate achievement of corporate and business strategy |

## STRATEGIC HRM AND BUSINESS STRATEGY

The need to integrate business strategy and HRM strategy has received much attention from the HR academic community, and it is to this discourse that we now turn.

- It is a common experience that a strategy turns out to be 'good' if it is the one suggested by its people.
- One of the driving factors behind the evaluation and reporting of human capital data is the need for better information to feed into the business strategy formulation process.
- In majority of organizations people are now the biggest asset. The knowledge, skills and abilities have to be deployed effectively if the organization is to create value.
- The intangible value of an organization which lies in the people it employs is gaining recognition by the stakeholders, and, today, it has been generally accepted that human resource helps the organization have the advantage of long term sustained performance.

- It is therefore too simplistic to say that strategic human resource management stems from the business strategy.

## APPLICATION OF STRATEGIC HRM CTICES APPLIED

Strategic human resource management often is viewed as a set of decisions regarding the acquisition, allocation, utilization, and development of human resources that affect organizational performance. It has been found that training and development proves to be the most important strategic HRM practice by managers to enable employees to fit in cross cultural diversities existing within the organization. Organizations have started spending huge amount after cross-cultural training of employees. Training is also imparted to employees as it is seen as a critical and effective tool to ensure product and service quality and standards.

In multinational corporations, training is the keystone for localization of top and senior managers. Trained , throughout the globe, have successfully replaced expatriate managers at the corporate and department levels. In Ericsson China Ltd., for example, out of 12 senior managers at the corporate level, nine are local Chinese. Also, out of 25 department directors, 21 are Chinese managers.

In an environment where almost all welfare benefits come with full-time employment and where the newly established social security system provides only minimal protection, job security has become very important for all employees.

It has now become a popular practice in many firms to have clearly defined duties, roles and responsibilities of all employees which are evaluated regularly to determine his/her level of compensation. Job analyses with the detailed job descriptions and job specifications have become crucial these days. A strict performance appraisal system is adopted in many organizations. Job responsibilities, professional skills and qualifications, the ability to innovate and to accomplish goals form the basis for performance appraisal. The recent studies highlight the fact that appraisal has positive impacts on employee performance ranging from moderately effective to very effective.

While recruiting and retaining qualified professionals, such as technical, marketing, and managerial staff, (especially the young staff) it is necessary to provide adequate opportunities for career and personal development. More and more companies provide opportunities for development and continuous learning in return for high performance and productivity during an employee's stay.

An important part of the ownership reform seen in many organizations today is employee ownership (i.e., some stock of the company is sold to employees), thus linking the benefits of the employees with company performance. Ownership reform helps to increase the overall organizational efficiency and reduce financial debt.

## ROLE OF STRATEGIC HUMAN RESOURCE MANAGEMENT (SHRM)

Strategic human resource management (SHRM) represents a relatively new transformation in the field of human resource management. SHRM is concerned with the role of human resource management systems, especially, focusing on the alignment of human resources as a means of gaining competitive advantage. Organizations are becoming aware that successful human resource policies and practices may increase performance in different areas such as productivity, quality and financial performance.

## HUMAN RESOURCES AS A SOURCE OF COMPETITIVE ADVANTAGE

The concept of competitive advantage was formulated by Michael Porter. Porter believes that competitive advantage arises when firms create value for its customers. Porter emphasized on the importance of 'differentiation', i.e. making the product unique in the market and on 'focus' i.e. seeing a particular buyer group or product market 'more effectively or efficiently than competitors who compete more broadly'. He thus developed his framework of three generic strategies—cost leadership, differentiation, focus that organizations can use to gain competitive advantage. Porter asserts that the environmental determinants largely affects a firm's performance. Resource-based view, on the other hand, asserts that the basis for a competitive advantage of a firm lies primarily in the application of the bundle of valuable resources at the firm's disposal. Competitive advantage, according to this view, differs from the environmentally focused strategic management paradigm. In that its emphasis is on the links between the internal resources of the firm, its strategy and its performance.

The resource-based view suggests that human resource systems can contribute to sustained competitive advantage by focusing on the development of competencies that are firm specific. The sustained superior performance of many companies has been attributed to unique capabilities of the organizations in managing human resources successfully to gain competitive advantage. Failure to do so results in to organizational vulnerability and competitive disadvantage.

In the closing years of the twentieth century, management has come to accept that people, not products, markets, cash, buildings, or equipment, are the critical differentiators of a business enterprise. All the assets of an organization, other than people, are inert and passive. The key to sustaining a profitable company or a healthy economy is the productivity of the workforce.

One fact that has been observed in recent years is that success through human resources can be sustained but can never be imitated by competitors.

The reason being that the success that comes from managing people effectively is often not as visible or transparent as to its source. How people are managed, and the effects of this on their behavior and skills, sometimes seen as the "soft" side of business, are occasionally dismissed. Even when they are not dismissed, it is often hard to comprehend the dynamics of a particular company and how it operates in a particular system. It is easy to copy one thing but much more difficult to copy numerous things.

HRM needs to achieve the following strategic goals in order for the organisation to gain and sustain competitive advantage:

- to invest in people through the introduction and encouragement of learning processes designed to increase capability and align skills to organizational needs;
- to ensure that the organization identifies the knowledge required to meet its goals and satisfy its customers and takes steps to acquire amd develop its intellectual capital;
- to define the behaviours required for organizational success and to ensure that these behaviours are encouraged, valued and rewarded;
- to encourage people to engage wholeheartedly in the work they do for the organization; and
- to gain the commitment of people to the organizations' mission and values.

## THE STRATEGIC ROLE OF HUMAN RESOURCE MANAGEMENT

The human resource management has consistently faced a battle in justifying its position in organizations. At good times when there are enough budgets, firms easily justify expenditures on training, staffing, rewards and employee involvement systems, but when faced with financial difficulties, such HR systems get the earliest cutbacks. The advent of the subfield of strategic human resource management

(SHRM), devoted to exploring HR's role in supporting business strategy, provided one opportunity for demonstrating its value to the firm. The birth of the field of strategic human resource management can be dated back to 1984, when Devanna, Fombrun and Tichy extensively explored the link between business strategy and human resources.

HRM discipline has witnessed a great deal of change over the past 25 years. These changes represent two major transformations. The first is the transformation from being the field of personnel management to being the field of human resource management. The second is the transformation from being the field of human resource management to being the field of strategic human resource management. The first transformation incorporated helped the recognition that people are an important asset in organizations and can be managed systematically. The second transformation has built on the preceding knowledge base of the discipline. This transformation is based upon the recognition that, in addition to coordinating human resource policies and practices with each other, they need to be linked with the needs of the organization. Given that these needs are reflected in the strategies of the firm, this transformation of "human resource management" came to be known as "strategic human resource management".

Strategic human resource management is based upon the recognition that organizations can be more effective if their human resources are managed with human resource policies and practices that deliver the right.

Researchers in the field of SHRM have increasingly relied on the resource-based view of the firm to explain the role of human resource practices in firm performance. Resource based view of strategy is that the strategic capability of a firm depends on its resource capability, especially its distinctive resources. Indeed, theoretical research on SHRM has suggested that systems of HR practices may lead to higher firm performance and can be sources of sustained competitive advantage because these systems of practices are often unique, causally ambiguous, and difficult to imitate. HR practices can enhance firm's performance when they are internally aligned with one another to manage employees in a manner that leads to competitive advantage. HR practices can create value for a firm when the individual practices are aligned to develop critical resources or competencies.

## IMPACT OF SHRM ON ORGANIZATIONAL PERFORMANCE

Many organizations face a volatile market situation. In order to create and sustain competitive advantage in this type of environment, organizations must continually improve their business performance which is highly based on the performance of human resource. Linked to this, more and more organisations are relying on measurement approaches, such as workforce scorecards, in order to gain insight into how the human resources in their organisations add value.

The relationship between HRM and firm's performance has been a hotly debated topic over the last two decades, with the great bulk of the primary scientific research coming from the USA, and, to a lesser extent, the United Kingdom. Both organizations and academics are striving to prove that HRM has a positive impact on bottom line productivity.

## CONCLUSION

Since it is clearly understood from academic research that human resources are a source of sustained competitive advantage, while, traditionally, the costs associated with the development of HR strategy have been regarded as an operating expense, these costs would be better considered as an investment in capital assets.

The way an organization manages its HR has a significant relationship with the organization's results, a revelation that supports the resource-based view, where business competitiveness is related, at least in part, to the investments in company's specific assets. Although the published research generally reports positive statistical relationships between the greater adoption of HR practices and business performance, it should also be kept in mind that many other factors besides HR practices could influence organizational performance. Also, it is possible that there are complex relationships between HR practices and other resources of the firm.

The causal linkage between HR and organizational performance will enable the HR managers to design programmes that will bring forth better operational results to attain higher organizational performance. The focus of the HR management should be to understand organizational performance processes and design HR practices that influence process and outcome variables.

Today global business competition management needs to be oriented towards the strategic use of human resources. Strategic human resources management helps organizations improve productivity and achieve their objectives. Integrating the use of personnel practices into the strategic planning process enables an organization to better achieve its goals and objectives. This can have a substantial effect on the ultimate success of the organization. To manage future operations effectively, it is essential that companies produce "business leaders" and "innovators" through SHRM Approach.

# 2 Traditional HR *v.* Strategic HR

## INTRODUCTION

The radical change taking place in the workplace and the work force has necessitated the shift of traditional human resource management into strategic human resource management. The days of the strict and rigid administrative human resource function are over. HR management is now considered as a critical strategic partner and is expected to contribute to the overall objectives of the company.

The distinguished characteristic of strategic HR management is its focus more on strategic rather than operational issues. However, the ·dministrative work is not ignored altogether.

Strategic HR management necessarily involves making the function of managing people the most important priority in the organization, and integrating all human resource programs and policies within the framework of a company's strategy.

Strategic HR management recognizes the fact that all decisions on finance, marketing, operations or technology are made by an organization's people. And hence, the success or otherwise of any organization can be accorded to its people.

Mello states that strategic HR management involves the perfect integration of practices, programs, and policies in order to facilitate the achievement of the organization's objectives. It considers the implications of corporate strategy for all HR systems within an organization by translating company's objectives into specific people management systems.

The most important consideration of strategic HR management is that there is no one best way to manage people and hence it demands high element of flexibility.

Therefore, the specific approach and processes will vary from organization to organization, and also from time to time as the organization advances. It may even vary in an organization with clearly defined business units or functional areas. However, all HR programs and policies must be consistent and must therefore be integrated within a larger framework, leading to the facilitation of the organization's vision and its objectives. The traditional outlook fails to cater to these present needs.

Human resource management has been traditionally defined as the set of philosophies, processes and procedures a firm uses for the following four basic tasks:

- **Managing the entry and exit process:** The traditional HR function looks for recruiting people the organization would need in the future. Therefore, manpower forecasts are made and a corresponding plan is made. HR managers have also been involved in the exit or separation process. This is normally done by retirement or by having the employee fired.
- **Managing the growth and development process:** There are traditional HR tasks such as orientation or socialization, training and development, and performance appraisal. Processes are designed in the manner that employees understand the overall scope and direction of the organization.
- **Managing the reward and recognition process:** Rewards come through the administration of compensation and benefits, and recognition comes in the form of promotion, job assignments and rotation. However, the process of rewards and recognition includes the countermeasures of demotions and disciplinary action. Performance appraisal is also used to determine the reward and recognition system or otherwise.
- **Managing the overall organization climate:** In the highly competitive and rapidly changing business environment of today, it is necessary to foster a climate that challenges employees to better levels of performance. Of course, the organizational climate is not a variable to be managed or designed and hence, it is tough to make organizational climate congenial.

However, it is necessary for all the organization's processes and procedures, to be aligned and integrated from its compliance with the law to its new strategic initiatives.

In the shift from traditional HR to strategic HR, there are a number of issues which HR practitioners must consider. The first is whether the main responsibility for management programs should rest with staff specialists in the corporate HR department or with the line managers who are the ones most in contact with the workers.

Traditional HR assumes the role of handling transactions as they arise, involving the series of activities such as compliance with changing laws, recruiting and screening applicants for current needs, rectifying problems between supervisors and subordinates, and basically responding to events after these happen.

Strategic HR is much more transformational and realizes that the success for any organization for growth, adaptation, or change within the organization is dependent upon the employees who either adopt or adapt to change. HR, therefore, plays a transformational role by assisting the organization in identifying and meeting the larger challenges it faces in its external environment by ensuring that the internal mechanisms that facilitate change are in place.

Traditional HR departments must, therefore, rethink, redefine and reevaluate their roles. HR managers must learn to operate their departments more like a business. Businesses must have clear strategies, outcomes, and vision to attain specific objectives which are aligned to the corporate objectives. HR practitioners must answer the following questions:

- **What is the HR Strategy?** : Strategy defines how a business positions itself and allocates resources to products to deliver value to customers.
  An HR strategy articulates the purposes of HR within the firm, the deliverables or outcomes from HR work, and the services delivered by the HR department.
- **What are the Products or Services of HR?** : Many typologies of HR work exist to describe types of HR processes. The new HR typologies will identify new HR products or services required to meet changing business needs. Its main products are the flow of intellectual capital and knowledge within a firm. It also aims at ensuring the development of a new generation of leaders within a firm.
- **How should HR be Organized to Ensure that the**

**Strategy is Executed?** : Increasingly, organizations are being defined less by structure and more by how capabilities are acquired and developed. The tremendous growth of outsourcing is clear evidence of this development. As HR functions articulate clear strategies, products or services, they identify the organizational choices that ensure that capabilities, even across organizational boundaries, meet strategic goals.

It is clear that strategic management of human resource has become inevitable. The central idea behind strategic HR management is that all initiatives involving how people are managed need to be aligned with, and, in support of the organization's overall strategy. No organization can expect to achieve its goals if it has people management systems that are at odds with its vision. And hence, to understand how to strategically manage human resources, it is necessary to understand the process of strategic management.

# 3 Dimensions of Strategic HRM

Many theorists have identified a number of important themes associated with strategic HRM. These are:

## RE-ENGINEERING AND STRATEGIC HRM

Both 'hard' and 'soft' normative models of HRM lay emphasis on the importance of organizational and job redesign. Much of the literature on the 'soft' HRM model is concerned with job design which covers the vertical and horizontal compression of tasks, worker autonomy and self-control or accountability. A new buzz word for the redesign of work organizations is 'Business Process Reengineering' (BPR).

Hammer and Champy (1993) popularized the concept named 're-engineering' with over 2 million copies of their book sold worldwide since it was published in 1993. Hammer and Champy define BPR as: The fundamental rethinking and radical redesign of business processes to achieve dramatic improvements in critical, contemporary measures of performance, such as cost, quality, service, and speed.

Hammer and Champy argued for a new and improved approach to organizational design, work processes, and management. *First,* many middle-management positions give way to 'enabling' information technology and self-managed work teams which removes the hierarchy of the corporation and its structure gets flattened.

*Second*, according to Champy work is redesigned into self-managed teams and managerial accountability is shifted to the 'front line': 'Whatever supervisory capacity those middle managers might have had now passes to the people who work in teams or have become increasingly more self-managed'.

*Third*, information technology allows organizations to do work in 'radically' different ways. *Fourth*, senior management make an 'unwavering' commitment to radical change process by including cultural change, set ambitious goals, and initiate the re-engineering process. Thus, elimination of many middle-management positions, the vertical and horizontal compression of job assignments, as well as introduction of self-managed work teams draws attention to 'strong' leadership and corporate culture, and the critical role of HRM. In essence, BPR puts the HRM techniques that seek to make workers' behaviour and performance more compatible with the organization's culture and goals. *Finally*, re-engineering is a social construct which displays the inherent power of corporate leaders to shape and define reality.

Champy's candid observation also reveals the 'darker side' to re-engineering and further tensions between 'hard' and 'soft' HRM models. The 'hard' version of HRM might be a necessary prerequisite before the 'soft' version of HRM is put to work in the re-engineered workplace.

## LEADERSHIP AND STRATEGIC HRM

During the last 25 years, human resource strategy has grown and changed considerably—from functional strategies in the 1980s and capabilities strategies in the 1990s to today's result-oriented strategies. Such strategic shifts in HR reflects changing labor markets and new business philosophy. Research suggests that in the future there will be a need for increased contributions from HR business strategy, including ethical and cultural leadership. In the immediate future, strengthening HR strategic leadership is one of today's most critical goals.

In the management texts, leadership has been defined in terms of traits, behaviour, contingency and power of an administrative position. Most definitions assumes that leadership involves a process whereby an individual exerts influence upon others in an organizational context. Leadership is by nature dialectical: it is socially constructed through the interaction of both leaders and followers. After a comprehensive review of the leadership literature, Yukl (1998) affirms that any definition of leadership is 'arbitrary and very subjective' and goes on to define leadership as:

> The process wherein an individual member of a group or organization influences the interpretation of events, the choice of objectives and strategies, the organization of work activities, the

motivation of people to achieve the objectives, the maintenance of cooperative relationships, the development of skills and confidence by members, and the enlistment of support and cooperation from people outside the group or organization.

TABLE I

**Strategic HR : New Roles in Today's Workplace**

| *Traditional HR Roles* | *Today's Strategic Roles* |
|---|---|
| Reactive | Proactive |
| Employee advocate | Business partner |
| Task focus | Task and enablement focus |
| Operational issues | Strategic issues |
| Qualitative measures | Quantitative measures |
| Stability | Constant change |
| How? (tactical) | Why? (strategic) |
| Functional integrity | Multi-functional |
| People as expenses | People as assets |

*Source* : Holbechke, L. (2001). Aligning human resources and business strategy. Woburn, MA: Butterworth-Heinemann.

Morgan argued that leadership is not simply a process of behaving or a process of manipulating rewards, it is a process of 'power-based reality construction'. Within the literature of leadership, there is a continuing debate over the alleged differences between a manager and a leader. For example, Bennis and Nanus proposed that 'managers are people who do things right and leaders are the people who do the right thing'. Kotter stated that managers develop plans whereas leaders create a vision and a strategy for achieving the vision. Also, Kotter proposed that managers and leaders differ in their methods of execution. Managers organize and engage in a process of controlling and problem-solving, while leaders involve in a process of alignment and seek to motivate and inspire. It indicates that an individual can be a manager without leading, and an individual can be a leader without being a manager (for example, an informal group leader or elected trade union leader). Kotter argues that a balance of management and leadership is necessary for effective operation of the work organization.

The concept of leadership is the main aspect for developing a 'strong' organizational culture and building a high level of worker commitment and cooperation. Of the many management gurus, Peter

Senge makes the most explicit link between strategic HRM, workplace learning, and leadership when he writes that 'leaders are designers, stewards, and teachers' and that a learning organization will remain only a 'good idea, an intriguing but distant vision' until the leadership skills required are more readily available. Thus, leadership competencies would seem to be a key constraint on the development of a resource-based SHRM model and a 'learning organization'. Barney emphasizes that the resource-based SHRM requires leaders that develop the organization's 'rare and non-substitutional' human assets. Unlike technology assets, organizations cannot readily purchase human sustainable competitive advantages on the open markets and therefore 'managers are important in this model, for it is managers that are able to understand and describe the economic performance potential of a firm's endowments. Without such managerial analyses, sustained competitive advantage is not likely'.

'Transformational' leaders exalt to employees the need for working beyond contract for the 'common' good. This leadership style emphasizes the importance of vision building and the ability to communicate this vision and, simultaneously, enthuse subordinates to make their vision a reality: 'to innovate, to change and indeed to conquer new frontiers in the marketplace or on the shop floor'. In contemporary parlance, the transformational leader is concerned with empowering workers. The transformational model shifts the focus away from the hierarchical nature of work organizations, towards the individualization of the employment relationship, and the development of individual leadership qualities or traits.

Legge states that even though the new leadership paradigm emphasize 'shared leadership' and empowerment among 'core' workers, they represent a 'unitary' frame of reference on employment relations and are squarely aimed at 'bottom-line' results.

## Workplace Learning and Strategic HRM

Within most formulations of strategic HRM, employee development has been regarded as a key 'lever' that can help management achieve the effectiveness in operations. Beer states that 'employee development is a key strategy for organizational survival and growth'. Many others believe that investment in employee development has become a 'litmus test' of whether or not employers have adopted the HRM model.

In recent years, the concept of the 'learning organization' or 'workplace learning' has attracted many academicians and corporate leaders. Workplace learning is that part of the management process that attempts to facilitate work-related continuous learning at the individual, group and organizational level. For workers and managers, the assumptions about workplace learning capture the essence of the American Dream, the opportunity for progress or growth at work based on individual achievement.

Workplace learning is the main aspect in the 'soft' resource based SHRM model. Individual, team, and organizational learning enable organization to increase its 'core competencies' and thus act as the engine for sustainable competitive advantage.

An organization's investment in workplace learning acts as a powerful signal of its intentions to develop its 'human assets'; this can help develop commitment to the organization rather than compliance. Most advocates of Japanese or 'lean' production systems emphasize the importance of investing in human capital and the processes of workplace learning.

Kochan and Dyer advise those firms adopting a 'mutual commitment' strategy to gain competitive advantage to make the necessary investment in their workforce and adopt the concept of lifelong learning. The relationship between learning and worker commitment, flexibility, and quality has also been subject of discussion.

Some of the writers emphasize how 'cultural control' can be reinforced through workplace learning and how the training of 'competencies' can render work more 'visible' in order to be more manageable . Coopey argues that workplace learning theory assumes a unitarist perspective in which goals are shared. However, he ignores conflict occurring from inherent tensions in the employment relationship, and that political activity by organizational members is likely to impede learning. He argues that likely effect of workplace learning is to strengthen the power of senior management, those at the 'apex of the organization'.

'High quality', 'flexible specialization' and 'functional flexibility', is the assumption of a well-trained 'high quality workforce'. However, empirical data shows that in most Anglo-North American companies there is a growing trend in 'non-standard' forms of employment (for example, part time and contractors). The validity of this data and the plausible insight that 'peripheral' workers tend to receive the lowest level of training, would create a gap between the theory and practice of strategic HRM models.

## Trade Unions and Strategic HRM

The new HRM model depicted as 'unitary'; assumes that management and workers share common goals, and differences are treated and resolved rationally. According to the theory, if all workers are fully involved into the business they will identify themselves with their company's goals and management's problems. The result will be that they would consider themselves as an inseparable part of the company. What is good for the company and management will be perceived by workers as also being good for them. Critical to achieving this goal is the concept of worker 'commitment' to the organization. This HRM goal has led writers to argue that there is a contradiction between the normative HRM model and trade unions. In the prescriptive management literature, the argument is that the collectivist culture, emphasizing group orientation, fits uncomfortably with the HRM goal of high employee commitment and the individualization of the employment relationship including individual contracts, communications, appraisal and rewards.

Critics argue that new HRM model is inconsistent with traditional industrial relations and collective bargaining, albeit for very different reasons. HRM policies and practices are designed to provide workers with a false sense of job security and obscure underlying sources of conflict inherent in employment relations. According to Godard, historically a major reason for managers adopting 'progressive' HRM practices has been to avoid or weaken unions. However, he does concede that 'it would also be a mistake to view progressive practices as motivated solely or even primarily by this objective'. Yet many other industrial relations scholars, have argued that independent trade unions and variants of the HRM model cannot only coexist but are even necessary to its successful implementation and development. They argue that trade unions should play a proactive role promoting the more positive elements of the 'soft' HRM model. Such a union strategy would create a 'partnership' between management and organized labor resulting in mutual gains for both the organization and workers. It is clear from the above discussion that HRM discourse has been strongly influenced by political-legal developments and the decline in trade union membership and power in the organizations over the last few years.

## HRM AND ORGANIZATIONAL PERFORMANCE

Although most HRM models provide no evidence for any HRM- performance link, the models tend to assume that an alignment between business strategy and HRM strategy will improve organizational performance and effectiveness. The resource-based SHRM model assumes a chain of 'soft' HRM policies of empowerment, team working and workplace learning, employee commitment, synergy and improved organizational performance. A core assumption of this approach is that committed workers are more productive. The importance of commitment to organizational efficiency and competitiveness is emphasized by Beer in following words: 'Increased commitment can result not only in more loyalty and better performance for the organization, but also in self-worth, dignity, psychological involvement, and identity for the individual' . In the late 1990s, demonstrating that there is indeed a positive link between HRM and performance has become 'the dominant research issue' in the HRM field.

The major empirical questions on this topic asked are: What types of performance data are available to measure the HRM–performance link? Do 'commitment-type' HRM systems produce above-average results than 'control-type' systems? Do work organizations with a better 'fit' between HRM practices and business strategy have superior performance (Cappelli and Singh)?

Measuring the links between workforce issues and economic performance is well defined in the field of industrial relations. Although the 1960s and 70s saw research on the effects of such management initiatives as employee involvement schemes on various outcomes (attitudes, job satisfaction and productivity), Purcell wrote that if it were possible to prove that 'enlightened or progressive' HRM was invariably associated with higher productivity and lower costs 'life for the... HRM executive would be easier'. As it is, there is little conclusive evidence. A similar point is made by Legge when she comments on the absence of 'few, if any, systematic evaluations' of 'high commitment' management practices on organizational performance. Guest (1997) examines the weaknesses in the current theoretical HRM models with regard to the HRM—performance link. Knowledge in this area is still incomplete, but North American scholars, have recently provided important information on these empirical questions. American academics Ichniowski gave a comprehensive review of some of the methodological challenges researchers face in identifying the connection between HRM practices and performance and review the findings from a body of US research using different research designs. Betcherman provide evidence on the HRM-organizational performance relationship using Canadian data. Both Betcherman and Ichniowski research suggests that innovative HRM practices can increase organization performance.

Let us look at some of the methodological challenges with this type of research.

## METHODOLOGICAL ISSUES

There are two main types of workplace research designs, surveys and case studies. Surveys of business establishments provide a vast amount of quantitative data that can test theories and allow a statistical analysis of HRM practices. However, the results cannot hope to provide an accurate picture of the subtleties and intricacies of the way work is structured and actually performed, and the dynamics of the employment relationship. Case studies, on the other hand, can provide rich data on workplace activities and can also suggest ways of testing hypotheses. Case studies provide for the opportunity to test for the accuracy of the source of the information. For example, a mail questionnaire asking respondents to indicate, in quantitative terms, extent of changes in skills resulting from self-managed work teams, can be done by researchers gathering data from managers and workers affected. Another important point is the choice of research design. The information received from mail questionnaires tend to be biased as there is only one respondent per establishment, typically personnel managers. 'Any idiosyncratic opinions or interpretations of the questions can distort the results'. The value of talking both to managers and workers is emphasized by Nichols: 'a study which systematically samples both managers and workers is always likely to provide at least some snippets of information that rarely surface in other accounts and to suggest different lines of interpretation'. However, it is questionable how far researchers can generalize from case study results. Whatever the research design, the data might not provide a full account of HRM-organizational performance.

Measuring the HRM–organizational performance relationship poses some other reasons: first, databases tend to estimate individual HRM practice rather than an entire 'system'. Second, research on the outcomes of new HRM practices requires management participation and, most important of all, many managers are unwilling or unable to disclose commercially sensitive information to an independent researcher. The researcher therefore, is compeled to use 'intermediate' performance indicators such as accident, absenteeism and grievance rates. Third limitation in the regression equation, is that innovative HRM practices is based on subjective judgements. Researchers and respondents might define a 'self-managed team' in different ways, with or without team 'leader'. A fourth challenge is how to isolate external variables. For example, exchange rates which significantly affect financial outcomes, makes it difficult to measure accurately the impact of HRM practices.

Even if the appropriate indicators are made available to the researcher and the external variables isolated, the problem of identifying the causal links remains a major challenge. However, it is difficult to confirm whether certain HRM practices allow firms to become superior or do superior, performing firms adopt certain HRM practices? In short, the implication of HRM choices for organizational performance is difficult to conclude with complete confidence. A combination of both survey and case studies can probably provide the great confidence about the direction and magnitude of the performance effects of the new HRM practices.

## RESEARCH FINDINGS

The work by Ichniowski *et al.* reviews a varied body of research on HRM–firm performance link and further research carried by Betcherman and his Canadian colleagues provides new evidence on the subject. Longitudinal case studies, in a Californian-based auto assembly plant and a US paper mill, document the reconfiguration of traditional work structures to the 'team concept' and subsequent improvements in productivity and quality performance. A cross-sectional comparative case study of two clothes factories found that 'team-orientated' work structures produced a 30 per cent advantage in overall production costs over a traditional work structure.

Of the case studies examined, over 75 per cent of those that reported changes in economic outcomes also reported that these were positive. The results do need interpreting with some caution. The performance measures differ across studies and so are not comparable. Further, access to performance data may suggest that the more successful firms are overrepresented. The findings from four industry studies—steel making, automobile assembly, clothes manufacture and metalworking—reveals that different work configurations and employee empowerment arrangements associated with the new HRM model have positive effect on output and quality performances.

Another important investigation is Arthur's investigation into the performance effects of two labour management taxonomies: 'control' (traditional personnel management) and 'commitment' (new HRM). His regression results indicate that, at least in the context of a high-tech mass production plant, commitment type HRM practices were 'associated with both lower scrap rates and higher labour efficiency than control'-type HRM practices.

Integrated HRM innovations have a greater effect than individual HRM practices. Also the findings from cross-industry analyses show similar results on the HRM-firm performance link. Ichniowski *et al.* concluded from the empirical evidence which presents a consistent picture; HRM innovations can improve organizational productivity and the magnitude of performance effects is 'large'.

Study of the Canadian companies by Betcherman provides a statistically significant association between the new HRM approach and unit costs, and the result from the regression analysis confirmed that organizations that operated under more strategic and participation-based HRM model experienced outcome trends that were superior than those organizations that operated under a traditional employment model. The more intangible corporate 'ideology' variables—'progressive decision-making' and 'social responsibility'—appear to have a more significant impact on performance outcomes than team-based programmes or incentive pay plans. These results suggests that 'innovative [HRM] practices and programmes on their own are not enough to substantially improve performance. What seems more important is that they be introduced into a supportive work environment'.

This obvious paradox may result from the long-term investment costs associated with the resource-based approach to strategic HRM and the pressure mounting on individual managers to achieve short-term financial results.

# Barriers to Strategic Human Resources

## INTRODUCTION

The people in the organizations interact with the customers to generate revenue. They introduce the small and significant innovations that move the company forward. They set the strategic direction for the organizations and then put those strategies into operation. Human Capital is thus the most valuable asset. It is unfortunately undervalued in most organizations today.

Helping the organization recognize human capital as a valuable asset and as competitive differentiator is the strategic role of human resources.

Human Resources must generate maximum ROI from human capital investments. Human Resources guide the alignment of employee roles, job functions, talent, and individual performance with business results and goals. It finds, engages, assesses, develops, and retains the talent that drives the business. It manages administrative requirements such as payroll, benefits, the recruitment process, policy standards, and holiday and sick leave tracking.

Three critical barriers prevent human resources fulfilling its strategic role and hamper it typically.

## BARRIER I : LACK OF INFORMATION IN DEFINING AND SELLING THE ROLE AND BUSINESS VALUE OF HUMAN RESOURCES

Senior management expects every business unit to generate reports and data that measure performance against plan. Human resource management works on the same lines. Experts opine that better human capital practices lead to higher financial returns and have a direct impact on share price. Investors, for example, scrutinize headcount and salary or wages ratios. Historically, however, human resources has focused more on managing administrative requirements than on communicating—and selling—the business value of human capital management.

While managing administrative requirements is essential, there are certain other critical strategic aspects of managing human capital too. To achieve the same it is necessary that human resources understand the strategic objectives of the business, translate these into job skill requirements and individual capabilities, and designs an appropriate performance tracking process. Human Resources should first assign a value to each human capital asset, and by communicating this value, underline the importance of managing its performance:

*Base Salary expense + Recruiting expenses +*
*Transfer expenses + Training expenses +*
*Bonus/incentive expenses +*
*Stock options grant value (Estimate)*

---

*Human Capital asset investment*

It is possible to better manage human capital assets by asking the following questions. What is the quality and value of the employee/ employer relationship? What are the training and development needs of the employees? How should we provide incentives and motivation for employees? Answers may come from reports on staff turnover, manning tables, high performer retention rates, head-count growth, role definitions, job productivity and individual performance monitoring.

Assessing comparative productivity ratios such as revenue to head-count also helps manage resource requirements; both short term and long -term. This information spots and demonstrates the asset's strategic business value to the organization. Lack of such information or failure to communicate this information properly impairs human resources' ability to fulfill its strategic role.

## BARRIER 2: LACK OF VISIBLE AND CONSISTENT HUMAN RESOURCES PRACTICES

The credibility and business value of Human Resources is often compromised by a lack of consistency in decisions and by insufficient information. This allows an informal network to bias the selection and promotion of employees. As a strategic partner in the business, human resources should understand and define the factors defining success for employees. Does the business depend on customer services, or on innovation, or on low cost? Based on this understanding, human resources can initiate practices that guide employees toward consistent and measurable milestones, creating a structured process.

Implementing visible and consistent practices requires quality information. It is not possible to achieve the consistency needed if policy documents, performance reviews, career objectives, and compensation assessments are not combined and positioned within a larger structure. Consistency requires a well-defined and structured process shared across the organization.

Clarity of well defined processes for collecting Human Resource Information is needed. Other such information needed is how should this data be stored and retrieved? Can this mostly qualitative information be analyzed usefully, and synthesized into a metric framework etc.? With such a synthesis, Human Resources gain the ability to compare and contrast different performance drivers. Identifying, managing and retaining talented individuals is a key competitive requirement. The consistent information and management practices allow the company to achieve this.

## BARRIER 3: HUMAN RESOURCES HAVE A NATURAL ALLY IN IT BUT DOES NOT FULLY LEVERAGE THIS ASSET

Both Human Resources and IT strive to position themselves within an organization as driving business value instead of expense. They can be seen as two sides of the same coin.

Human Resources is responsible for job design and ensuring that the right skills and competencies are developed or acquired to fill these jobs. In turn, performance in these jobs is defined and measured against goals and objectives. In this sense, Human Resources' information needs to mirror the performance to be monitored, analyzed and planned for in a given jobs. Both Human Resources and IT must understand how software tools and skills drive greater productivity. As performance management information becomes more consistent and reliable, it will also enhance the performance and compensation process for which Human Resources is responsible.

# Integrating Human Resource Strategy with Business Strategy

## INTRODUCTION

Developing a human resource (HR) strategy to support the business plan requires human resource management (HRM) planning to be recognized as a fundamental part of the business planning process. Integrating HR strategy and strategic planning is fundamental to achieving business excellence.

There are four underpinning themes to this concept: first, that achieving business excellence is more than a simple accumulation of a series of best practices; second, that achieving excellence in corporate business strategy (process and inputs) is the single most important factor in achieving vision, mission and goals; third, this provides a unique opportunity to view the organization holistically, with the principle focus being on the 'total organization' and the 'total team' as the underpinning concepts; and fourth, that people tend to do two things well, i.e. the things they regard as important and/or enjoy and those things that the boss regards as important and will check.

Recent years have witnessed the decline of organizations that ought not to have failed on account of their inability to meet the challenges of merger or acquisition. Despite the search for better ways of doing business and the adoption of survival strategies including business process re-engineering and total quality management (TQM), some organizations continue to struggle to retain their competitive edge. Organizations may seem to 'weather the storm' short-term (e.g. Rover at Longbridge), but ultimately have not learned the 'excellence' lesson as once again they become vulnerable to acquisition. The long-term failure of companies, who have reengineered or attempted TQM, is often regarded as an implementation failure rather than a fundamental conceptual failure. Alternatively, there is the view that the long- term organizational stress that goes with sustained improvement effort is too much for some organizations. As a result, more emphasis is placed on the quick fix solutions and short-term financial gains.

Organizations have now to face greater risk whilst operating in an imperfect internal and external climate. They have to respond to these changes very quickly. The shift has been towards the knowledge economy, information management, global trading and the employment of people for their creativity and knowledge. This has emphasized the importance of investment in employee development as the means of retention and reward, rather than crude pay, and a total realignment in mind-set about HRM, motivation, reward and development strategies. If we extrapolate these trends we have valuable evidence as to what will succeed in the future. Integrating human resource strategies with business strategies has become the necessity of the time.

## STRATEGIC DECISION-MAKING

Strategic decision-making begins with the identification of vision and mission and their articulation to all stakeholders. In order to make the mission and vision a reality, the organizations require the identification of processes in which they must excel if they are to add value. The process by which business strategy is developed and defined is the highest level process the organization can engage in, and is the starting point for realizing vision and mission, then excellence in business strategy becomes the single most critical issue.

Clear and relevant vision, mission and objectives are fundamental and have to be articulated at all levels to foster commitment, ownership and involvement. Organizations are likely to fail at this first hurdle for two reasons: first, the intellectual capacity to understand the 'umbilical cord' that connects each level of strategy is not harnessed at organizational level-rather, senior managers tend to remain committed to their own functional missions; second, the absence of leadership competence, as opposed to management, fails to articulate the mission and vision at all levels. This means that the organization and its people have no shared sense of purpose or direction as against the belief of Taylor's principle. Consideration of the barriers to TQM will help to identify the more common problems in order to deal with them.

The clarity of vision, mission and objectives helps to identify the routes an organization needs to take in order to achieve them. The key questions are what the critical success factors are (the key processes that will enable maximum leverage and customer satisfaction) and how to address these to achieve tangible benefits in profit and customer and employee satisfaction.

Quality and quality improvement play a vital role in the companies and hence one of the key activities is to identify a total quality improvement process. Without having a reputation for supplying quality goods or services the organizations would find it extremely difficult to operate in their respective markets.

The strategic planning process is in reality a process of honest self-assessment that clearly identifies what business the organization is in, how it should improve or reinvent itself and how it intends to make the transformation. Self-assessment can help organizations build quality into their strategic planning activities. This calls for honest benchmarking internally and externally to gauge the enablers and results content of all activities. Only by objective examination of the current status of processes and performance can an organization identify how and what to improve in the short- and long-term. For the most part there are few examples of real self assessment, perhaps because few organizations can sustain such capacity for direct, accurate self-assessment.

Successful strategic planning is about releasing the potential of the whole organization, the success of leadership is about inspiring people to share in the vision so that they both embrace it and seek to fulfill it. In strategic planning, it is essential to take a holistic approach to identifying future market trends and identifying the realistic goals. Too many strategic planning processes make its implementation complicated. Additionally, organizations do not put enough effort into making the strategy a reality. Self-assessment bridges the gap between strategy and action.

In the holistic view a shared vision of the future is addressed and reinforced by ownership and mutual support. It seems obvious that if employees feel comfortable with change, they will at least embrace it or at worst not obstruct it. Ownership accommodates the most effective 'comfort zone' available.

## HRM IN TODAY'S CONTEXT

SHRM is all about the harnessing of the intellectual capacity of the organizations, attracting them and keeping the best people by adequate reward system and performance appraisal. It is also about enhancing skills in order to accelerate performance.

It can be argued that the successful exploitation of technology in a dynamic environment depends crucially upon a skill base capable of identifying opportunities for, and managing technological development.

Many companies today fail to have strategic approach to HRM, especially in identifying current and future staffing needs and providing necessary training and development skills as and when necessary.

The companies, many times, rely on identifying needs based on existing staff profiles and loose projections for new business. Their ability to react to change is thus limited. Time spent on identifying needs at an organizational level would facilitate a more strategic view of requirements. Companies employ different strategies to stimulate and maintain staff, including bonus schemes, share opportunities and support for leisure activities.

Some companies appear to be addressing the question of management development for the senior team within their overall consideration of planning. Building a team needs to reflect the organizational development priorities which may be a part of management development strategy within the strategic management process.

Harnessing intellectual capacity by truly involving all of an organization's people in the strategy formulation is critical to successful implementation, but it can introduce difficult and often uncomfortable analysis that may find managers adopting a defensive posture. Often managers confuse involvement with interference and fail to recognize the leadership opportunities this presents. Some still find involvement of employees threatening and this leads to a defense of the status quo. The total quality approach calls into question all the traditional approaches to HRM and argues for a more proactive people- focused approach in which HR professionals adopt total quality to become strategic partners in improvement and business planning. The really successful companies have used TQM to put the spectre of Taylorism behind them, recognizing that TQM could provide a holistic approach.

The introduction of an effective HR strategy aligned to strategic business planning is thus a prerequisite to ensure that underlying power structures, procedures, practices, values and norms are in place to facilitate the necessary pace of change that can be sustained within the psychological capacity of the business. There are many different ways of managing the improvement process, including a consultative approach through participation, intervention, education and communication. Even the style adopted has much to do with the nature of the change proposed, its pace and sustainability. The style of management and blend of skills play an enabling role in the development of strategies within small firms.

Of equal importance is the need to put in place appropriate reward systems linked to the process improvements required for excellence. Without a reliable performance appraisal through an performance assessment, it is impossible to relate rewards to performance in a way that is motivating. A holistic approach recognizes that business processes cut across functions, and hence, it is important to link reward systems to recognition of the accomplishment of teams rather than individuals. Performance goals then have to be tailored specifically to what the work team needs to accomplish and it is also important to link the goals of the individuals to those of the team. Team reward systems reduce the threat of conflict, increase the rewards to individuals who have a shared set of goals and produce more consistent behaviours than is evidenced in individuals alone. If this is the reality, then 'whole organization' reward becomes the preferred approach. Add to this the notion that in the new economy 'reward' embraces knowledge, acquisition and personal growth, and these beliefs begin to prescribe an approach to HR planning that supports rather than obstructs excellence. It prescribes a solution based on achieving a balance of individual, team and organization, a balance that allows for comfort zones within which employees can embrace true ownership.

## DISCUSSION

The process of carrying out change is not just confined to strategies and plans; it is also about relationships between people and the management, of workforce diversity in the context of the changing business environment. The contemporary management demands excellence through recognition of the individual and the team work that gives a balanced approach to HR planning pivotal to overall strategy achievement. Since strategy is related to what customer satisfaction means for an organization and to the ever-changing environment it operates in, there is no blueprint for choosing how to manage a company's resources, no best way that is appropriate under all circumstances. Strategic planning becomes a process of planning within a range of parameters rather than formal targets; the emphasis is on the overall direction and pace of change rather than detailed milestones.

There is a belief that if you tell people what is happening, what you expect from them, and, what is necessary in order to achieve excellence, then they will perform accordingly. Some education strategies have effected improvement this way but others have foundered because informing and involving people does not always guarantee the desired changes.

People have to believe in a strategy and this requires that leaders create the right environment for the change to occur and for making the people believe that it can. Human management systems must be tailored to fit each unique business. But to create business excellence with HRM processes that intrinsically add value, all organizations need to develop HR strategies in a way that the integration of business planning with business excellence becomes possible. A holistic approach nurtures proactive incremental change. It also avoids the sudden traumatic change that the organizations are not able to sustain.

## CONCLUSION

Excellence is not just about best practice or keeping pace or leapfrogging the competition on Monday to be caught again on Wednesday. Nor is it simply about fulfilling customers' requirements, though it cannot be ignored altogether. Excellence is all about having the individual intellectual capacity and the collective business intelligence to predict today what will happen tomorrow. Again, it demands the integration of organization's intellectual capacity with strategic business planning. It implies a balanced approach to excellence based upon a different interpretation of motivation theory, recognizing a new balance between financial and non-financial rewards. It calls for the personal growth and for organizational advancement, grabbing the opportunity for excellence wherever possible.

Successful strategic planning seeks input from all stakeholders, including the shareholders, customers, suppliers and people, to identify the part each has to play to ensure the success of the business strategy. The 'people' part of the strategic planning has its own significance, since the capacity of the organization to learn is fundamental to improvement. The learning component of HR strategy becomes the business's own learning strategy.

To harness intellectual capacity and to procure and maintain the best people, far more innovative approaches than performance-related pay are necessary. Organizations have to create fluid structures of employment. This may mean that it is prudent to accommodate employees' own business interests within the umbrella of the organization. The congenial organizational climate paving way for generation of new ideas from its 'people' needs to be fostered.

Whilst many organizations are investing heavily in employee development to retain the best, the future suggests more fundamental rethinking of the employee relationship. Knowledge and intellectual capacity are likely to be the tradable commodities of the labour market (in higher education they already are). They will also be the competitive edge in organizations where they are the only tangible asset.

# 6 Competencies-based Approaches and Model

## INTRODUCTION TO COMPETENCIES

Competencies and competency-based human resources management (CBHRM) are not much prevalent in Indian private sector. While organizations have used the idea of competencies for over fifty years, the expansion of the competency movement within the private sector and, now, into the public one, has resulted in a proliferation of definitions, tools, models and applications. Different authors have different opinion and they lack uniformity. But this has been accepted by most that CBHRM is more effective when competencies are linked closely to proven strategic planning processes and measurable organizational performance standards. In the current planning environment of the public sector, there is a concern that CBHRM may reinforce inappropriate HRM approaches and, therefore, not support the broader objectives of the government in the areas of globalization, social diversity, governance, and the knowledge economy.

There is much confusion with respect to the use of competencies in both the private and public sectors. It is necessary to discuss these issues and an exploration and clarification of their respective roles in the strategic management of human resources is also essential.

## COMPETENCY DEFINITIONS AND TERMINOLOGY

In studying the competency area, one is immediately struck by the lack of uniform definitions, terminology, and the resulting misunderstanding. The difficulty appears to stem from drawing very fine lines of definition distinction with terms such as competence, competency, competencies, and competences.

**Boyatzis** states that "a job competency is an underlying characteristic of an employee—i.e., motive, trait, skill, aspects of one's self-image, social role, or a body of knowledge—which results in effective and/or superior performance in a job."

**Dubois**, a leading expert in the applied competency field, defines competence as "the employee's capacity to meet (or exceed) a job's requirements by producing the job outputs at an expected level of quality within the constraints of the organization's internal and external environments."

According to **Zemke,** "Competency, competencies, competency models, and competency-based training are all Humpty Dumpty words meaning only what the definer wants them to mean. The problem comes not from malice, stupidity or marketing avarice, but instead from some basic procedural and philosophical differences among those racing to define the concept and to set the model for the way the rest of us will use competencies."

**The American Compensation Association** defines competencies as "An individual's performance behaviours that are observable, measurable and critical to successful individual or corporate performance". Defining competency fully is not as simple as addressing the individual application.

Organizational competence and core competency link an organization's essential values and business to those of its employees. Core competency can refer to either an organization or an individual and resource-based analysis. There is a tight link between individual and organization core competencies and can help organizations to achieve sustained competitive advantage.

**Fogg** defines organization core competency as "those few internal competencies at which you are very, very good, better than your competition, and that you will build on and use to beat the competition and to achieve your strategic objectives."

Differences in definitions notwithstanding, **Hendry and Maggio** suggest that when competencies are linked to the broader goals of an organization, the following common elements emerge as outcomes of a comprehensive competency model:

- Identification of characteristics and behaviours that differentiate top performers from others in relation to their contribution to strategic objectives;
- Clarification, communication, assessment, and development of characteristics that focus individuals on core organization goals; practical observation help prescribe and validate behavioural descriptions that achieve the desired results: and

- Description of skills, attitudes, traits, and behaviours that can be attached to pay, performance measurement, hiring criteria, training, organizational staffing, career development, and succession planning.

## ORIGIN OF COMPETENCY PROFILING

**Furnham** states that "the term competence is new and fashionable, but the concept is old. Psychologists interested in personality and individual differences, organizational behaviour and psychometrics have long debated these questions of personality traits, intelligence and other abilities."

Competency-based methodology was pioneered by Hay-McBer company founder David McClelland, a Harvard University psychologist in the late 1960's and early 1970's. McClelland set out to define competency variables that could be used in predicting job performance and that were not biased by race, gender, or socioeconomic factors. His research helped identify performance aspects not attributable to a worker's intelligence or degree of knowledge and skill.

McClelland's competency methodology can be summed up in two factors: "Use of Criterion Samples" or systematically comparing superior performing persons with less successful persons to identify successful characteristics and "Identification of Operative Thoughts and Behaviours that are Causally Related to Successful Outcomes" or the best predictor of what persons can and will do in present and future situations is what they have actually done in similar past situations.

## COMPETENCY PROFILING

A competency profile is generally composed of five to ten competencies but can include as many or as few as are required to accurately reflect performance variations in the position. For example, a competency model for a public servant might include initiative, cooperation, analytical thinking, and a desire to help the client. Competency-based models are used to recruit, select, train, and develop employees. Unfortunately, the aforementioned lack of rigour in terminology can lead to loosely defined and improperly implemented CBHRM.

Competency profile development can be handled in a number of ways, two of which are the top-down and bottom-up approaches. The top-down approach generally involves picking, based on a strategic analysis of the organization's performance objectives, an array of competencies from a dictionary of competencies and assessing those for a particular position or class of positions. The shortcoming associated with this approach is that the competencies survey is carried out as an additional step separate from the creation of the profile. The top-down process has the potential to reduce the applied face validity of the profile and, subsequently, reduce employee buy-in.

The bottom-up approach on the other hand involves exploratory checklist surveys and subsequent confirmatory interviews to derive the competencies from employees, thereby increasing the face-validity and simultaneously developing the assessment questions to tap into them. In addition to these potential benefits, bottom-up approaches may result in employees being directly involved in the development of competency profiles that will describe behaviours that are relevant to their tasks. This is useful for gaining employee understanding of, input to, buy-in, and loyalty to the process.

## COMPETENCY-BASED HRM MODELS

### Defining Models in General

According to Forcese & Richer, "a model is an imitation or an abstraction from reality that is intended to order and simplify our view of that reality while still capturing its essential characteristics". It is a logical structure. Models can be either implicit or explicit. Implicit models do not clearly specify the interrelationships involved in the model but merely assume or imply their presence and, to this extent, are based on intuition. By contrast, an explicit model forces the individual to think clearly about and account for all the important interrelationships involved in a problem.

In good model design it is crucial that both the model and the individual relationships involved be tested or validated. This objective is not met when there is complete reliance on intuition and the results may not be reliable. As a result, explicit models are preferred to implicit ones.

## DEFINING COMPETENCY MODELS

**Dubois** in defining competency models states that they 'provide the adhesion or 'glue' that is necessary among the elements of an organization's human resource management system." Thus, competency models help organizations take a unified and coordinated approach to designing the human resource management system, including job design, hiring, performance improvement, employee development, career planning or pathing, succession planning, performance appraisals, and the selection and compensation systems for a job. The competency models, thus, help organizations beyond the benefits of simply HRD purposes.

Competency model enable the organizations to capture those competencies that are required for satisfactory or exemplary job performance within the context of a person's job roles, responsibilities, and relationships in an organization and its internal and external environment and is generally very detailed and might include, for example, a description of the job setting, the job tasks and activities, the job outputs, the employee competencies that are required for the job tasks, and the quality standards for outputs, etc. The contents of the competency model (models) are then converted, in a highly systematic manner, to a curriculum plan.

**Dubois** suggests the following minimum standards for effective results of competency models:

1. Competency models that result from the research and development processes must be aligned with the organization's strategic goals and business objectives.
2. Research and development methods used should produce valid and reliable competency models.
3. Organization leaders must advocate the use of a competency-driven approach for the success of organization's strategy.
4. Competency models must be sufficiently comprehensive to identify the competencies that distinguish exemplary employee performance.
5. Outputs from the competency model must be technically reliable and valid and acceptable to the client.

## COMPETENCY-BASED HRM—ADVANTAGES

A well framed competency-based HRM models can produce a number of positive outcomes. For example, CBHRM models can:

- align individual competencies to organizational strategies and goals;
- frame competencies profiles for specific positions or roles and match them with correct individuals in the organization;
- enable continual monitoring and modification of competency profiles;
- assist organizations in ranking competencies for compensation and performance management;
- facilitate employee selection, evaluation, training, and development;
- assist employers in hiring individuals with rare or unique competencies that are difficult and costly to develop.

## COMPETENCY-BASED HRM—DISADVANTAGES

However, these models have some serious limitations as discussed below:

- Competencies so developed may be vague or inappropriate if goals and strategies are not clearly communicated.
- They can be expensive and time-consuming to administer.
- They are difficult to preserve the organizational status quo and equally difficult to make provision for and procure soft, integrative and/or innovative competencies such as intercultural or cross-cultural competency.
- They add nothing in organizations that have difficulty in differentiating between successful and unsuccessful performance especially when the competencies are too "generic".

## COMPETENCY EXPERIENCE—GENERAL

The American Compensation Association (1996) conducted a major survey of 217 mid to large size organizations to determine their applications and experience with competencies. According to the survey there was vast difference in the degree of rigour and application of competencies. The major findings were as under:

- Communicating, valued behaviours and organizational culture (75% agreed competencies have a positive effect).
- "Raising the bar" of performance for all employees (59% agreed).
- Emphasizing people (rather than job) capabilities as a way to gain competitive advantage (42% agreed).
- Encouraging cross-functional and team behaviour (34% agreed).

The survey highlights the fact that HR applications are not applied according to the expectations of senior HR practitioners. Majority of competency-based compensation systems were in development or still in their first year of implementation.

The report points out that competency-based HR applications are evolutionary rather than revolutionary, in that they are treated as add-ons to existing HR practices. They have not, in fact, replaced the old methods.

Today the senior management, high performers, and functional experts are the top three sources of information to develop competencies. These competencies tend to highlight organizational behaviours rather than job-related skills. Application of appropriate competency model is of utmost important here.

The use of competency-based human resource models by banks, insurance companies, management consulting firms, technology companies, transportation companies, utility companies, delivery companies, retail eating outlets, manufacturing industries, and mining companies have increased tremendously in recent years. Industry publications suggest ongoing use of competencies in the private sector, but the extent of use remains uncertain.

## COMPETENCY EXPERIENCE IN PUBLIC SECTOR

As we know a wide variety of generic competency models are available for performance improvement in both the private and public sectors. These models typically link organizational core competencies with employee core competencies, as distinguished from employee job-specific competencies, in order to establish a direct linkage between the organization's priorities and employee behaviours. Creating effective linkages is a tough task. Besides, competency approach has advantages and disadvantages of its own. Bryson describes several methods by which public sector and non-profit organizations can identify their organizational core competencies as a significant output of the strategic planning process. For example, a strategic consideration of a public sector organization's strengths and weaknesses can identities its organizational core competencies in concrete terms. Improvement of organizational core competencies can then be achieved through coordinated adjustment of HRM administrative policies and practices covering all, or selected, personnel functions. But here it is necessary that competency models are explicitly future oriented rather than implicitly historic, and that it identify levels of superior strategic performance rather than signifying levels of threshold, or minimum, operational performance.

Using a top-down approach, Dror's (1997) generic strategic analysis of the alternative roles of senior civil services links the core capacities of the organization with the attributes of its individual members. These are equivalent to organizational core competencies and employee core competencies, respectively. Dror's recommended future-oriented core capacities (organizational core competencies). It includes: intervening in history, energizing, adjusting social architecture, risk-taking, handling complexity, making harsh tragic choices, and mobilizing support for constructive destruction.

A similar typology of functions unique to the public sector provided by Carroll (1997) includes: reconciling differences, achieving agreement, and using legitimate authority to carry agreements into effect. Dror suggest that these core capacities can be actualized through utilization of six attributes—super-professionalism, innovation-creativity, merit listing, virtuous, autonomous but subordinated, and mission-oriented—employee core competencies of the senior executive cadre. Dror believes that these executive core competencies are required to carry out higher order tasks which have strategic importance in determining the relative success of government in an era of globalization and rapid change.

Another, complementary, description of competencies which distinguishes the public sector from the private sector is provided by Sherwood (1997)—acceptance of the legitimacy of the democratic process and elected officials, an ethic of responsibility to the public at large, and respect for the expertise of other professionals. Taken together and extended, these competencies provide an alternative to the simple emulation of private sector competency models and profiles.

To evaluate the potential for success of the competency movement in the public sector, it is necessary to relate inputs to outputs. Presently, it seems that the competency movement will be less effective in public sector than the private one. An overall environment of optimism and the rigorous attempt at all levels is required which seems to be far from real at least at the presents point of time.

## PUBLIC SECTOR HRM ADMINISTRATIVE PRACTICES ON COMPETENCIES

Some important criticism of public sector HRM administrative practices on competencies are discussed below:

1. One of the main criticisms of the current HRM system in the federal public sector is the lack of effective internal integration among the sub-disciplines of the personnel function. Another main criticism is the uneven quality of strategic flexibility of the sub-disciplines (e.g., training is flexible, compensation is inflexible). Internal integration of HRM is possible when all personnel work in the pursuit of corporate strategy. Here competency at individual level does not work effectively.

   Career-based HRM, on the other hand, is more effective when individuals spend most of their career with the same organization, such as the military, police forces, religious organizations, and, to a lesser extent, the foreign service. To date, most successful applications of competency-based approaches have been in the area of human resources development—i.e., staff training—oriented to organizational performance improvement.

2. Some authors suggest caution in the application of competency-based approaches to other HRM practices. Others note the limited diffusion, even in the private sector, of economically viable changes to compensation-related employment practices which result in high performance.
3. In addition to the limited evaluation of competency-based approaches to HRM, there are other barriers to implementation at the level of individual HRM sub-systems and practices. Senior managers are frequently under pressure to imitate practices in other organizations, without being sufficiently familiar with contextual differences and tacit aspects of implementation methods.
4. At times HRM managers are often poorly positioned within the organization to ensure the strategic linkages that are required for success . This means that the transfer of high performance technologies from one organization to another is a non-trivial affair.
5. Successful implementation demands considerable management attention, expertise, and local contextual confirmation, even when the competency-based approach has been well validated in the original organization. Strategic crisis, regulatory and social policy initiatives, and broad access to detailed contextual information all promote successful innovation of competency-based HRM administrative practices.

An effective competency-based staffing model in the public sector will require improved methods for designing and maintaining managerial assessment and selection tools appropriate to its function or transitional state. Consultative methods (e.g. joint consultation), effective documentation, and active strategic monitoring and maintenance is essential for the attainment and long-term viability of functionally appropriate competency-based staffing models in the public sector.

According to Austin, the framework based on values of fairness, technical adequacy, and feasibility as viewed individually and collectively by political entities, management, labour unions, system designers, and human resource managers can be effective in public sector. According to Donnellon a methodology that supports diversity and measures 'soft' competencies can be more useful in public sector.

The research and policy-based development of new competency frameworks for staffing developed by Dror is not yet widespread in public sector organizations, due to some inbuilt constraints on strategic planning. The main reason for the lag in development of competency-based staffing is the difficulty of assessing non-managerial and work group contributions to organizational core competencies in public sector organizations. The problem arises due to difficulty in measuring results and performance and in attributing improvements to changes in competencies, as opposed to other factors.

Joint consultative approaches could be used for developing competency models and assessment methods, for quantitative measurement of performance at individual, team and organizational levels of analysis. For example, staff union input, among others, to the development of competency-based assessment processes has been shown to be effective in optimizing conflicting goals for the design of a public sector selection system in the United States.

## THEORETICAL ISSUES IN COMPETENCIES

The Recent CBHRM programs have raised a number of troubling questions. For example, most competency programs in the private sector have been developed around the notion of a firm developing a sustainable or durable competitive advantage—as manifested by larger profit margins or market share—over its competitors. One cannot copy or imitate HR systems of other organizations and, as such, each organization needs to develop HR system with attributes unique and synergistic. The same is not the case with competency programs. And hence it is easy for other organizations to imitate exactly the competency programs of the others and thus obtain the same competitive position. This limitation make this long-term success a matter of chance, even in the private sector.

Further analytical work is required to adapt these competitive concepts and to accomplish the objectives. Public sector and private sector have distinct objectives. Likewise, different political ideology (such as capitalist economy, socialist economy, mixed economy) have different objectives. The analysis cannot be done with a single stereotype method. Different strategic, accounting and accountability models have to be established to get reliable results.

The theoretical functioning of models sounds intersecting but there are many complexities in defining competencies, in designing the methods for their measurement, and for their use in decision-making. Thus, the application of competency-based models in organizations is quite complicated.

## CONCLUSION

Thus, this text provides a broad overview of the concept of competencies, its origins, and application in human resource management. A prime issue with CBHRM is that the approach, being relatively recent in the public sector, has not yet been assessed. Empirical data are, as yet, not available to measure program success and to validate underlying models, implicit or explicit. Some desirable characteristics of such programs, however, would be the establishment of clear linkages to strategic corporate objectives, the specification of the models in use, and the anticipation of the on-going need for self-correcting.

# Strategy Planning in SBU's, MNCs and Transnational Companies

## INTRODUCTION TO STRATEGIC PLANNING

Strategic planning is a management tool. Any management make use of strategic planning for following three important reasons—to focus on its energy, to ensure that members of the organization are working toward the same goals, to assess and adjust the organization's direction in response to a changing environment. In short, strategic planning is a disciplined effort to produce fundamental decisions and actions that shape and guide what an organization is, what it does, and why it does it, with a focus on the future.

Being strategic, thus, means being clear about the organization's objectives, being aware of the organization's resources, and incorporating both into being consciously responsive to a dynamic environment.

The process is about planning because it involves intentionally setting goals (i.e., choosing a desired future) and developing an approach to achieving those goals. The process is disciplined in the sense that certain order and pattern has to be followed. The process raises a sequence of questions that helps planners examine experiences, test assumptions, gather and incorporate information about the present, and anticipate the environment in which the organization will be working in the future.

Finally, the process is about fundamental decisions and actions because choices must be made in order to answer the sequence of questions mentioned above. The plan is ultimately no more, and no less, than a set of decisions about what to do, why to do it, and how to do it.

Because it is impossible to do everything that needs to be done in this world, strategic planning implies that some organizational decisions and actions are more important than others—and that much of the strategy lies in making the tough decisions about what is most important to achieving organizational success.

## STRATEGIC PLANNING AND LONG-RANGE PLANNING

Although many use these terms interchangeably, strategic planning and long-range planning differ significantly in their application. Long-term plans are generally considered to mean the development of a plan for accomplishing a goal or set of goals over a period of several years, with the assumption that current knowledge about future conditions is sufficiently reliable to ensure the plan's reliability over the duration of its implementation. In the late fifties and early sixties, for example, the US. economy was relatively stable and somewhat predictable, and, therefore, long-range planning was both fashionable and useful.

On the other hand, strategic planning assumes that an organization must be responsive to a dynamic, changing environment. Long term planning assumes the environment to be more or less stable, whereas strategic planning assumes environment to be quite dynamic. Strategic planning, then, stresses the importance of making decisions that ensures the organization's ability to successfully respond to changes in the environment.

## STRATEGIC THINKING AND STRATEGIC MANAGEMENT

Strategic planning is only useful if it supports strategic thinking and leads to strategic management. Strategic thinking means asking, "Are we doing the right thing?" This can be answered using three key requirements about strategic thinking: a definite purpose be in mind; an understanding of the environment, particularly of the forces that affect or impede the fulfillment of that purpose; and creativity in developing effective responses to those forces. In short, strategic management is the application of strategic thinking to the job of leading an organization. Dr. Jagdish Sheth, a respected authority on marketing and strategic planning, provides the following framework for understanding strategic management: continually asking the question, "Are we doing the right thing?" It entails attention to the "big picture" and the willingness to adapt to changing circumstances, and consists of the following three elements:

- formulation of the organization's future mission in light of changing external factors such as regulation, competition, technology, and customers;
- development of a competitive strategy to achieve the mission; and
- creation of an organizational structure which will deploy resources to successfully carry out its competitive strategy.

Strategic management is adaptive and keeps an organization dynamic and adaptive to the changing times. Strategic planning is about fundamental decisions and actions, but it does not attempt to make future decisions.

Strategic planning involves anticipating the future environment, but the decisions are made in the present. This means that over time, the organization must stay abreast of changes in order to make the best decisions it can at any given point—it must manage, as well as plan, strategically.

Strategic planning is also not a substitute of leadership. Ultimately, the leaders of any enterprise need to sit back and ask, and answer, "What are the most important issues to respond to?" and "How shall we respond?" Just as the hammer does not create the bookshelf, so the data analysis and decision-making tools of strategic planning do not make the organization work—they can only support the intuition, reasoning skills, and judgment that people bring to their organization.

Finally, strategic planning, though described as disciplined, does not typically flow smoothly from one step to the next. It is a creative process, and the fresh insight arrived at today might very well alter the decision made yesterday. It is never exact. One needs to make frequent changes before arriving at the final destination.

## BENEFITS OF STRATEGIC PLANNING

Strategic planning serves a variety of purposes in organization, including:

1. Clearly defining and arriving at the realistic goals and objectives consistent with the mission of the organization, keeping in mind the time frame and the organization's capacity for implementation.
2. Communicating those goals and objectives to the organization's constituents.
3. Developing a sense of ownership of the plan.
4. Ensuring the most effective use of the organization's resources by focusing the resources on the key priorities.

5. Providing a base from which progress can be measured and establishing a mechanism for informed change when needed.
6. Making efforts to build consensus for important organizational decisions.
7. Providing clearer focus of organization and making efforts to increase efficiency and effectiveness of the organization.
8. Bridging staff and board of directors (in the case of corporations).
9. Building strong teams in the board and the staff (in the case of corporations).
10. Providing the glue that keeps the board together (in the case of corporations).
11. Producing great satisfaction among planners around a common vision.
12. Making efforts to solve major problems.

## WHEN SHOULD STRATEGIC PLANNING BE DONE?

The scheduling for the strategic planning process depends on the nature and needs of the organization and its immediate external environment. For example, planning should be carried out frequently in an organization whose products and services are in an industry but are subject to rapid changes. In this situation, planning might be carried out once or even twice in a year and may be done in a very comprehensive and detailed fashion (that is, with attention to mission, vision, values, environmental scan, issues, goals, strategies, objectives, responsibilities, time lines, budgets, etc). On the other hand, if the organization has been around for many years and is in a fairly stable marketplace, then planning might be carried out once a year and only certain parts of the planning process, for example, action planning (objectives, responsibilities, time lines, budgets, etc) are updated each year. Yet the following guidelines have to be kept in mind by strategic planners:

1. Strategic planning should be done when a new business has to be set up. Besides, it should be kept in mind that the strategic plan is usually a part of an overall business plan, along with a marketing plan, financial plan and operational/ management plan.
2. Strategic planning should also be done in preparation for a new major venture. For example, when a new department, division, unit or product line has to be set-up.
3. Strategic planning should also be conducted at least once in a year. Again, strategic planning should be conducted well in

time in order to identify the organizational goals to be achieved at least over the coming fiscal year, resources needed to achieve those goals, and funds needed to obtain the resources.

These funds are included in budget planning for the coming fiscal year. However, all the phases of strategic planning need not be fully completed each year. The full strategic planning process should be conducted every year if the organization is experiencing tremendous change. Besides, following precautions should be taken:

1. Each year, action plans should be updated.
2. Note that, during implementation of the plan, the progress of the implementation should be reviewed at least on a quarterly basis by the board.

Again, the frequency of review depends on the extent of the rate of change in and around the organization.

## MEANING OF STRATEGIC BUSINESS UNITS

Strategic business units are absolutely essential for multi product organizations. These business units are basically known as profit centres. They are focused towards a set of products and are responsible for each and every decision, i.e. strategy to be taken for that particular set of products.

Example of Strategic business units—The best example of strategic business unit would be to take organizations like HUL, P&G or LG in focus. These organizations are characterized by multiple categories and multiple product lines. For example, HUL may have a line of products in the shampoo category. Similarly, LG might have a line of products in the television category. Thus to track the investments against return, they may classify the category as a different SBU itself.

Strategic business units work on the principle of micro management. What if you have 10 different tasks in a day, and all 10 of them are important? You will divide the tasks and then perform each of them separately. This is the exact reason behind converting a product/brand into a SBU or to make them part of a separate SBU.

There are several reasons SBU's are used in an organisation. However, along with the reasons for using SBU's there are also some powers which needs to be inferred on an SBU. Planning independence, Empowerment and others are such powers which influence a SBU. Some of such features are discussed below.

(1) **Empowerment of the SBU manager**: Several times the empowerment of SBU managers is crucial for the success of the SBU/products. This is mainly because this manager is the one who is actually in touch with the market and knows the best strategies which can be used for optimum returns. Hence empowerment of the SBU manager is of utmost importance. This can, however, be possible if the organization is able to put trust and confidence on him.

(2) **Degree of sharing of one SBU with another**: Many times organizations face shortage of funds and resources, and the SBUs are bound to share them. This might not always be negative. If one SBU gains more profit then usual, this revenue might also become useful for the other SBU thereby promoting growth of both of them. This is where sharing actually plays a positive role.

(3) **Changes in the market**: An SBU absolutely needs to be flexible because it needs to adapt to any major changes in the market. For example—if an LCD manager knows that LED's are more in demand now, he needs to communicate to the top management that he would also like a range of LED products to make the SBU even more profitable. Thus by adding LED to its portfolio, the SBU can immediately become double profitable. The organization as a whole can become profitable thus.

Each and every change in the market, and its effect on SBUs is anticipated which is then taken into consideration. Hence, for a multi product organization, business management may actually mean product portfolio management or SBU management.

The key to Strategic business management is to have a strict watch on the investment and returns from each SBU. The SBU manager too plays a crucial role in this and hence he is recruited from the industry with extensive experience of that particular industry.

## IMPORTANCE OF STRATEGIC BUSINESS UNITS

There are several benefits of an SBU:

(i) **SBUs make you Organized**—The first principle of time management is to get organized. Similarly, one of the first things you need to do is to see your organization clearly. And that can happen only if you are organized. If one of the marketing managers is handling 3-4 different products, then definitely he is going to get confused with operating all of them. The strategies might be hazy, there will be no time for creativity or innovation and all the time will be spent in just handling the existing work rather then expansion. Thus the first thing SBU's do is they help you get organized.

(ii) **Micro manage:** Once you are organized, it is possible to do division of work, and to manage the work at micro level. Just take an example of large companies like HUL and P&G (the best examples of multi-product organizations). They have at least 30 different products at all times. Each of them requiring separate manpower, strategies, expenses and returns. Thus this needs micro managing of the highest aspect. One important aspect of SBU's is FOCUS. Micro managing helps you focus on each and every product and every aspect separately.

(iii) **STP:** The success of a product depends on its segmentation targeting and positioning. Each of these processes requires being continuously in touch with the market, receiving feedback, identifying your target market, targeting them and then positioning accordingly. Thus, there are multiple tasks if an organization has multiple products. Therefore, dividing products into SBU's helps the organizations stay in touch of the market separately for each and every product. Thus a marketing manager/sales manager may be assigned one product at a time and may be assigned responsibility for that product itself. Thereby he may give valuable contribution in maintaining the STP of a product in the target market.

(iv) **Decision making:** Many times, better performing units or products start going in slump. Sometimes, it may be temporary, or it may be on prolonged basis. However, if one of these revenue generating SBU's gets hit, how would an organization manage the cash crunch? Well these are decisions which need to be made and for them you need to have the figures for each type of product/SBU. Thus, SBUs also propogate the correct decision making. These decisions can be at the micro-level (as explained above—managing STP, strategies) or they can be at the macro level (investments from the corporate fund, whether to continue investing etc.?).

(v) **Investments:** The best reference for investments in SBU's can be the BCG matrix. In the BCG matrix, the SBUs are divided as per their market share and the market growth rate. Thus BCG matrix enables the organization to take investments decisions of each product individually. This is possible only if each product is treated as a completely different SBU. This SBU may be a composition of one category of product (such as shampoo) or in case of larger organizations it may even be one single type of product (such as LED or LCD televisions).

(vi) **Profitability**: Micro-managing helps the managers to get a holistic view of the organization. This view is also used in preparing the financial statements as well as to keep tabs on the investments and returns for the organization from each SBU. Thus the overall profitability of the firm can be decided.

Thus, these six reasons along with several others show us the importance of both Micro managing as well as macro managing a multi-product organization. Overall success of the organization is possible only if it knows how to run its product portfolio and this is exactly where SBU's come in play.

## FOUR GENERIC STRATEGIES THAT STRATEGIC BUSINESS UNITS USE

Even though an industry may have below-average profitability, a firm that is optimally positioned can generate superior returns. That is where strategic business planning comes in. The generic strategies that strategic business units generally use are discussed below.

### Competitive Advantage

A competitive advantage is one gained over competitors by offering consumers better value. This can be done either by lowering prices of the product or increasing benefits and services to justify the higher price.

Differentiation and cost leadership strategies search for competitive advantage on a broad scale, while focus strategies work in a narrow market. Sometimes, businesses look for a combination strategy to please customers looking for multiple factors such as quality, style, convenience and price.

### Cost Leadership Strategy

Cost leadership works well when the goods or services are standardized. The company can take advantage of economies of scale by addressing to the masses. That way, the company can sell generic acceptable goods at the lowest prices. A company either sells its goods at average industry prices to earn higher profits than its competitors or it sells at below-industry prices, trying to profit by gaining the market share. Wal-Mart is an example of a company with a cost leadership strategy:

### Differentiation Strategy

Differentiation strategy calls for a company to provide a product or service with distinctive qualities valued by customers. The organization has the edge over the competitors. The companies, however, need to resort to frequent scientific research, need to have a highly skilled and creative product development team; a strong sales and marketing team; and a corporate reputation for quality and innovation. Apple, for example, uses differentiation strategy.

### Focus Strategy

Focus strategy is just what it sounds like: concentrate on a particular customer, product line, geographical area, market niche, etc. The idea is to serve a limited group of customers better than your competitors who serve a broader range of customers. A focus strategy works well for small but aggressive businesses. Specifically, companies that do not have the ability or resources to engage in a nationwide marketing effort will benefit from a focus strategy. It involves focusing the cost leadership or differentiation on a small scale, and to take its competitive advantage.

## INTEGRATED COST LEADERSHIP-DIFFERENTIATION STRATEGY

Now-a-days, companies prefer integrated strategies to a single generic strategy to enable them to adapt quickly and learn new technologies. This strategy has the advantages of both- differentiation strategy as well as cost leadership strategy. A somewhat distinctive product that is mid-range-priced can be a bigger draw to customers than a cheap generic product or an expensive special one.

## STRATEGIC PLANNING IN MULTINATIONAL CORPORATIONS (MNCs)

As Multinational Corporations (MNCs) operate across borders, and hence, strategic planning plays a more critical part in relating the entire firm and its components to the goals and strategies chosen. Firms' long-term performance has been concluded to be a direct result of effective planning and control.

With a few exceptions strategic planning is first applied in a homogeneous political setting, and then expanded as the company expands. Business environment, domestic characteristics and cultural differences are not same in all parts where the business operates. Necessary modifications are made to accommodate to the new complexities of the international environment and foreign subsidiaries. Inputs to strategic planning can be rendered of dubious quality when they are altered through cultural differences.

The intention of this text is to consider the cultural assumptions that underlie strategic planning methodologies, and the extent to which those assumptions interfere with international planning effectiveness. Some means are proposed by which MNCs can bridge the gap, making strategic planning more effective and useful.

## STRATEGIC PLANNING AND CENTRAL EXPECTATIONS

It could be advantageous for MNCs to set headquarters for their separate units, and to keep them responsible for operations and functioning of these units. The strategic guidelines and controls are to be issued by the headquarters. Centralized planning and decentralized operations constitute a common means for running a worldwide business. A strategic plan is crafted for the central body or world headquarters, as well as for each foreign subsidiary. The local plan must mesh with and translate worldwide strategy into local requirements. Thus, local requirements at global fronts can be satisfied. Foreign subsidiaries participate in the process by receiving requests for data, information, and reports as input to either the planning or the performance measurement (control) cycle, and returning them in the proper format and on time. Accuracy, reliability, and comparability of data are essential elements for the process.

The expectations of the central planning staff are that each subsidiary will fulfill its planning-related tasks as requested, so that the process may be finalized. Doing what headquarters asks as part of the strategic planning task may be onerous but the legitimacy of the request usually is not questioned; but the ability and willingness to furnish what is requested may be influenced by factors quite separate from the legitimacy of the headquarters-subsidiary relationship.

### Co-Alignment of Home Office and Subsidiary

One of the influencing factors is the extent to which MNC and subsidiary share the same goals. MNC's normally continue to find ways to motivate subsidiary top managers to comply with corporate strategic decisions.

A second factor is the situations experienced locally and its consistency with the situations, practices and values of the MNC. Such a situation sees that no built-in conflicts occur between what headquarters wants and assumes to be forthcoming, and what the subsidiary is capable of giving.

Yet the reality is that the home country or the host country's culture and the business culture of the MNC are often in serious conflict. This disparity would not be so serious if the local subsidiary were staffed completely with expatriates from the home culture and the MNC, carrying and implementing those values into foreign lands. The co-alignment of home office and subsidiary is very much needed in today's times.

## SUBSIDIARIES' INPUTS TO THE STRATEGIC PLANNING PROCESS

Central staff needs local data in order to frame strategic planning, to allocate resources, to assess performance and to find out whether the standards set are appropriate or not. Normal periodic operating data, including financial and manufacturing reports; capital investment proposals; proposals for marketing initiatives; assessment of local subsidiary performance against MNC targets and against local competitors; long-term investment needs; long-term competitive assessment, etc. are some of the informations that central office needs on regular basis. Again, such data may be required to be returned in a format stipulated by headquarters' central planning staff.

The information has to be of high quality, reliable, and comparable across subsidiaries. It should facilitate easy analysis and interpretations. Mis-reporting and mis-representation should be strictly controlled. To the extent, the quality and reliability of such data is compromised; the integrity of the planning and controlling process too is compromised.

## CULTURAL DISTANCE, CONFLICT, AND UNIVERSAL MANAGEMENT TECHNIQUES

As the culture of MNC's home country and the subsidiary's host country differ; and as the operations are to be decentralized, conflicts become most obvious. Hofstede, Laurent, and Newman, among others, argue that Western management theories and techniques are inherently culture-bound and thus may not be fully transferable to other cultures. To that extent, strategic planning becomes defective and the human resources component becomes suspectable. Consider the magnitude of the MNC's task of rendering comparable the results of widely differing approaches to the basic strategic planning process.

If the crucial data come from cultures outside the cultural domain in which the technique was developed, and the data are the product of a local, culturally-derived process, how much confidence can the MNC have in its planning data and other inputs, not knowing how valid or comparable they are? What are those assumptions that are important to the effective use of strategic planning?

## SUGGESTIONS FOR RESOLVING CULTURAL DISCRIPENCIES

The first question that MNC executives need to work out is **"What"** can be done to short-circuit the negative effects that might be expected due to cultural differences? The answer to the question begins with anticipation. The executive must anticipate and expect that there is something hidden below the surfaces of the process and the inputs.

Beginning with the assumption that cultural effects exist, the question becomes, **"Where?"** The MNC executives need to have cautious in those parts of the process that are subject to interpretation or manipulation. More care should be taken to the specific actions, facts, or conclusions that stem from cultural inconsistencies with MNC planning processes.

The third question begins with **"patterns"**. Expecting culture-based problems and looking for weak spots allows the executive to draw comparisons across time, and across comparable subsidiaries. This will highlight the potential patterns that are inconsistent with other elements in the planning data or process. Likewise, the comparisons with similar subsidiaries may allow inconsistencies to be highlighted for further investigation.

The fourth question begins with, **"Who?"** Who is a proper resource with whom to discuss the implications or reality of the suspicious patterns found? That person may be an ex-expatriate with significant experience in the culture, preferably one who has moved on to other responsibilities. Or that person may be an outside expert in cross-cultural relations. But the fact that cannot be ignored is that the problem needs to be discussed to the right person.

The fifth question to be asked is, **"How?"** i.e. asking, "How cultural discripencies arise?" It is asked to the current head of the suspected subsidiary, and who is willing to discuss (and not defend or give unjustifiable explanation) of what the executive suspects. The question may also be asked to the head of a sister subsidiary which seems to have avoided the culture-induced pattern.

These discussions have the potential, if pursued diligently but not threateningly, to become major learning opportunities for subsidiary head and home office alike.

The sixth question is **"How may we as an organization learn from this?"** The answer should be gained through meetings and mutual discussions between subsidiary executives—expatriates and local hires alike—and home office personnel. Such discussions should be treated as problem-solving meetings, begun with insights into cultural issues and assumptions. Preferably, they should be conducted in small groups or task forces, the results of which include actionable items. Specifically, the agenda should be to open insights and to learn from mistakes, and the corrections should be such that they are possible of being imposed to strategic planning process.

The executives need to find out the sources of tension or temptation for bias. If the meeting becomes a one-way diatribe on doing things the way head office wants, then a useful opportunity has been missed to modify and make the process more effective, and also to receive the experience and participation of valued MNC members. The purpose of such meetings is to welcome recommendations, implement them if possible, and form a basis of new training programmes and exercises. Another intent is that changes may be to the strategic planning process, so that it may be made more consistent with MNC objectives, and not just on the basis of the assumptions and judgments of the central planning staff.

The seventh and final question is, **"How effectively have we accommodated local and home office culture, assumptions, and practices?"**

It is answered by (a) continuing discussions with subsidiary heads, (b) continuing the reviews of comparable subsidiaries' results and processes, and (c) analyzing the new results from all subsidiaries, and particularly the suspect subsidiaries, against their previous patterns derived over time in order to see if the process has been improved. The validity of the results, of course, must be verified carefully through normal follow-up and analysis.

## TRANSNATIONAL COMPANIES

Transnational corporations are those corporations which operate in more than one country or nation at a time -- have become some of the most powerful economic and political entities in the world today. Many of these companies have far more power than the nation-states across whose borders they operate.

For example, the combined revenues of just General Motors and Ford—the two largest automobile corporations in the world—exceed the combined Gross Domestic Product (GDP) for all of sub-Saharan Africa. The combined sales of Mitsubishi, Mitsui, ITOCHU, Sumitomo, Marubeni, and Nissho Iwai, Japan's top six Sogo Sosha or trading companies, are nearly equivalent to the combined GDP of all of South America. Overall, fifty-one of the largest one-hundred economies in the world are corporations. The revenue of the top 500 corporations in the U.S. equal about 60 percent of the country's GDP. Transnational corporations hold ninety percent of all technology and product patents worldwide, and are involved in 70 percent of world trade. More than thirty percent of this trade is "intra-firm"; in other words, it occurs between units of the same corporation.

The number of transnational corporations in the world jumped from 7,000 in 1970 to 40,000 in 1995. While global in reach, these corporations' home bases are concentrated in the Northern industrialized countries, where ninety percent of all transnationals are based. More than half come from just five nations: France, Germany, the Netherlands, Japan and the United States. But despite their growing numbers, power is concentrated at the top. i.e., the 300 largest corporations account for one-quarter of the world's productive assets.

The United Nations has justly described these corporations as "the productive core of the globalizing world economy." Their 250,000 foreign affiliates account for most of the world's industrial capacity, technological knowledge, international financial transactions, and ultimately the power of control. In terms of energy, they mine, refine and distribute most of the world's oil, gasoline, diesel and jet fuel, as well as build most of the world's oil, coal, gas, hydroelectric and nuclear power plants. They extract most of the world's minerals from the ground. They manufacture and sell most of the world's automobiles, airplanes, communications satellites, computers, home electronics, chemicals, medicines and biotechnology products. They harvest much of the world's wood and make most of its paper. They grow many of the world's major agricultural crops, while processing and distributing much of its food.

Given their dominance of politics, economics and technology, it is not surprising to find the big transnationals deeply involved in most of the world's serious environmental crises.

Transnational corporations exert significant influence over the domestic and foreign policies of the Northern industrialized government that host them. Surprise! Indeed, the interests of the most powerful governments in the world are often intimately intertwined with the expanding pursuits of the transnationals that they charter. At the same time, transnational corporations are moving to circumvent national governments. The borders and regulatory agencies of most governments are caving in (or being paid off) to the New World Order of globalization, allowing corporations to assume an ever more stateless quality, leaving them less and less accountable to any government anywhere.

These corporations, together with their host governments, are reorganizing the world economic structures—and thus the balance of political power—through a series of intergovernmental trade and investment accords. These treaties serve as the frameworks within which globalization is evolving—allowing international corporate investment and trade to flourish across the Earth. They include:

- The Uruguay Round of the General Agreement on Tariffs and Trade (GATT).
- The World Trade Organization, which was created to enforce the GATT's rules.
- The proposed Multilateral Agreement on Investment (MAI).
- The North American Free Trade Agreement (NAFTA).
- The European Union (EU).

These international trade and investment agreements allow corporations to circumvent the power and authority of national governments and local communities, thus endangering workers' rights, the environment and democratic political processes.

A legitimate question is: Is the World Trade Organization an arm of the United Nations?

In a "Substantive session", 16 July 1996, the United Nations provided a discussion and a "draft decision submitted by the President of the Council on the basis of informal consultations" on the topic of one item on their agenda, i.e. "Non-Governmental Organizations" (i.e. Transnational and National Corporations):

> "The Economic and Social Council, reaffirming the importance of the contributions of non-governmental organizations to the work of the United Nations, taking into account the contributions made by non-governmental organizations to recent international conferences, decides to recommend that the General Assembly examine, at its fifty-first session, the question of the participation of non-governmental organizations in all areas of the work of the United Nations, in the light of the experience gained through the

arrangements for consultation between non-governmental organizations and the Economic and Social Council."

In many respects, the logic is inescapable. If as few as 300 Transnational Corporations (TNCs) do indeed represent 51% of the largest one-hundred economies, then it is basic economic (and therefore political) logic that the TNCs should be represented at the United Nations. Or else, one needs to remove from the General Assembly all the smaller economies (countries). But then this also implies that at some point a TNC or two will become a member of the Economic and Social Councils, and then, perhaps, the General Assembly. And then, of course, the Security Council?

Is this altogether bad news? If we are replacing tyrannical, autocratic, or undemocratic member nations with TNCs (who are theoretically answerable to shareholders, and where anyone in the world can become a shareholder), then it might not sound so bad. However, there are shareholders and there are stakeholders. Holding a hundred shares of stock does not count for quite as much as holding ten million shares. And the reality is that if TNCs do become effectively sovereign nations, then it's inevitable that the rich shareholders will use their power to take over the TNCs and become the world's elite governing force. The fact that CEOs and high executive officers have been taking any and most all corporate shareholders to the cleaners for decades is just more fuel to the raging inferno of the lack of corporate accountability.

To counter this trend, Dave Hartley has suggested "four wisdoms of de-globalization":

> Think for yourself question authority globalize consciousness localize economies.

There is a slight problem, however. The TNCs and domestic major corporations already control the governments of the United States and most of the industrialized nations. This is done by Corporate Politics, and the wholesale purchase of politicians. Already in place is a Corporate State, which wields the economic power of Money. This, by the way, is not a new development. Even in the United States, the dye was cast by the Fourteenth Amendment to the Constitution for the United States of America, whereby private corporations were given the status of persons—and thus allowed to enjoy the benefits of the Bill of Rights, without the commensurate unlimited liabilities of life. In other words, it's pretty much a done deal.

The problem, of course, is not merely the greed, power-hungry, and irresponsible actions of certain CEOs and the elite of the TNCs—but also those who support them. The latter clearly includes bribed governments, but they also include the average person who buys the products and uses the services that these corporations provide. The fact that there is seemingly little choice—due to governmental intervention—makes it less of a charge of negligence to the average individual. But these same individuals also often take the path of least resistance, and choose the quality of life which includes telephones, Internet connections, utilities and services at their beck and call, easy transportation, vacations at remote locations, and so forth and so on. An intriguing discussion of this idea is included in One World Order—a conservation among several interested observers.

E.g., one highlight of the One World Order have made it clear that there are forces in the world (potentially for the last several hundred years) that control the destiny of the planet. That there's a Hierarchy which far transcends the mundane, worldly powers. These forces may have initiated all manner of questionable acts—from initiating wars and famines to encouraging plagues, etc. They have simply responded to these incidents, but in a way that mundane ethics and morality.

If we assume TNCs are simply a portion of the problem, that there are in fact powers far in excess to the corporate CEOs, and that these higher powers are intent upon a One World Order, for the better cause if one was in an overcrowded lifeboat, for example, and in order to save everyone else, the toughest dude in the boat tossed three of the weaker members overboard and allowed them to drown... what would you do?

Being in charge sometimes requires tough decisions. The key is the deeper intentions of whoever is in charge. If, for example, someone or some group has much more power than President Obama,.would this be all that bad? Would that perhaps be wonderful news? Doesn't it depend upon what the tougher dude's intentions are? And how those stack up to Obama's intentions.

Conspiracies do not generally have a great deal of credibility with the average individual. But there is just the possibility that the "Mother of Conspiracies" may be one that has an agenda that is not all that bad. Perhaps, in our Creating Reality, we can manifest exactly that sort of situation.

## TRANSNATIONAL BUSINESS STRATEGY

In the words of George Stonehouse, "A transnational business conducts operations in several countries with varying degrees of coordination and integration of strategy and operations." A transnational strategy combines global reach, coordinates operations and leverages unique advantages of local markets to drive sales, market share and profit growth.

## Basics

Transnational strategy involves operating in different world markets, designing responsive organizational structures and establishing value-added activities that exploit national similarities and differences. Stonehouse defines transnational strategic management as iterations of organizational learning and performance improvements. The foundation of a transnational strategy is a global vision, but with customized implementations for local markets and regions.

## Country Environment

The country environment is an important aspect of transnational strategy. In a March 2007 interview with Harvard Business School Working Knowledge writer Sean Silverthorne, Harvard Professor Richard H.K. Vietor suggests that countries with a sound fiscal and monetary environment, secure property rights and anti-corruption policies attract transnational companies. A small-business owner should select a country based on its current business environment and a reasonable estimate on what the business and political environment might be in three to five years. In an October 1999 interview with Harvard Business School Working Knowledge writer James Aisner, Harvard Professor Michael E. Porter discussed the importance of clusters in country selection. Clusters are geographic concentrations of competing and cooperating suppliers and service providers. Emerging nations should encourage transnational companies to build linkages with the local economy and become consumers of local goods and services. The development of skills training and support infrastructure are also important characteristics of countries that are appealing for transnational companies.

## Branding

Transnational businesses may use global brands or create specialized local brands. In an October 2007 Harvard Business School Working Knowledge article, Harvard professor John A. Quelch cites the cases of American and Japanese automakers to suggest that developing a marketing strategy around one set of brands is more efficient than having several different brands for different regions of the world. Global brands share certain characteristics, such as a focus on a single product category and consistent market positioning.

### Contingency Planning

Transnational strategy also includes contingency planning. Natural disasters, such as the March 2011 earthquake in Japan, can cause severe disruptions in the supply chain. Many times manufacturers and suppliers lack contingency plans and find themselves scrambling for alternatives when disaster strikes. Diversification of supply sources and having alternative distributors are some of the contingency planning options. However, management should consider whether customers would be willing to pay for the cost of establishing and maintaining these backup supply and distribution arrangements.

### Considerations

Although people use the terms interchangeably, global, multinational, international and transnational businesses have subtle differences. International is a generic term that applies to all businesses with foreign operations. A multinational business operates in several foreign countries, but it delegates strategic decision-making responsibility to its overseas subsidiaries which operate as autonomous businesses. A global business conducts activities in many countries but with an integrated worldwide strategy.

# Globalisation of Business and HR Challenges

## INTRODUCTION

Globalisation is widely used term since the nineties of the last century with the end of the cold war and the break-up of the former Soviet Union and the global wave towards the rolling ball. With increased reliance on the market economy and renewed faith in the private capital and resources, a process of structural adjustment spurred with the increased influences of the World Bank and other International organisations in many of the developing countries. Globalisation has brought in new opportunities to developing countries with greater access to developed country markets and technology transfer. But globalisation has also brought up new challenges like growing inequality across and within nations, volatility in financial market and environmental deteriorations. Also the major negative aspect of globalisation is that a great majority of developing countries are not included in the process. Till the nineties the process of globalisation in India was inhibited by the barriers to trade and investment; however, the liberalisation of trade, investment and financial flows initiated in the nineties has progressively lowered the barriers to competition and and paved way to globalisation

## DEFINITION

### Globalised World—What does it Mean?

Though the precise definition of globalisation is still unavailable a few definitions worth viewing, Stephen Gill defines globalisation as the reduction of transaction cost of transborder movements of capital and goods thus of factors of production and goods. Guy Brainbant says that the process of globalisation not only includes opening up of world trade, development of advanced means of communication, internationalisation of financial markets, growing importance of MNC's, population migrations and more generally increased mobility of persons, goods, capital, data and ideas but also infections, diseases and pollution

Globalization describes the interplay across cultures of macro-social forces. These forces include religion, politics, and economics. The process of globalization can erode and universalize the characteristics of a local group.

## IMPACT ON INDIA

India opened up the economy in the early nineties following a major crisis that dragged the economy close to defaulting on loans. The new initiated policy regime radically pushed forward in favour of a more open and market-oriented economy.

Major strategy measures initiated in the early nineties included scrapping of the industrial licensing regime, reduction in the number of areas reserved for the public sector and initiation of the privatisation programme, amendment in the monopolies and the restrictive trade practices act, reduction in tariff rates and change over to market determined exchange rates.

Over the years of steady liberalisation, more and more sectors opened up for foreign direct investments and portfolio investments facilitating entry of foreign investors in telecom, roads, airports, insurance and other major sectors.

The Indian tariff rates reduced sharply over the decade from a weighted average of 72.5% in 1991-92 to 24.6% in 1996-97. Though tariff rates went up slowly in the late nineties it touched 35.1% in 2001-02. India is committed to reduced tariff rates.

## INDIA IS GLOBAL

The increasing integration of India with the global economy have helped step up GDP growth rates, which picked up from 5.6% in 1990-91 to a peak level of 77.8% in 1996-97. However, a Global comparison shows that India is now the fastest growing country after China.

## GLOBALISATION AND POVERTY

Globalisation in the form of increased integration though trade and investment is one of the important reason why much progress has been made in reducing poverty and global inequality over recent decades.

Despite this progress, poverty remains one of the crucial international challenges we face. Of the developing world 4.8 billion people still live in extreme poverty.

However, the proportion of the world population living in poverty has been steadily declining and the number appears to have fallen in recent years despite strong population growth in poor countries. If the proportion living in poverty had not fallen since 1987 a further 215 million people would be living in extreme poverty today.

India has to concentrate on five important like technological entrepreneurship, new business openings for small and medium enterprises, importance of quality management, new prospects in rural areas and privatisation of financial institutions.

New prospects are growing for rural India. The growth of Indian economy to a large extent depends upon rural participation in the global race. With the implemention of the new economic policy the role of villages got its own significance because of its unique outlook and branding methods. For example food processing and packaging are the prospective areas where new entrepreneurs can enter. It may be organised in a collective way with the help of co-operatives to meet the global demand.

Understanding the current status of globalisation is necessary for setting future course of action. For all nations to reap the benefits of globalisation it is essential to create a level playing field. President Bush's recent proposal to eliminate all tariffs on all manufactured goods by 2015 will make it possible.

## INDIAN STAND IN TERMS OF GLOBAL INTEGRATION

India clearly lags behind in terms of globalisation. Number of countries have a clear lead. Among them are China, large part of east and far east Asia and eastern Europe. Lets look at a few indicators how much we lag.

- Over the past few decades FDI flows into India have averaged around 0.5% of GDP against 5% for China 5.5% for Brazil. Whereas FDI inflows into China now exceeds US $ 50 billion annually. It is only US $ 4 billion in the case of India.
- India's share of world merchandise exports increased from .05% to .07% over the past 20 years, whereas China's share has tripled which is almost 4%.
- India's share of global trade is similar to that of the Philippines an economy 6 times smaller according to IMF estimates.

- As some experts pointed out that India, as a geographical, politico-cultural entity has been interacting with the outside world throughout history and still continues to do so, it has to still adapt, assimilate and contribute.

## COMMON CHALLENGES FOR HR IN INDIA

Now lets have some insights into the common challenges our Indian colleagues face which may improve support and collaboration between managers in both locations. The common challenges are:

- Recruitment
- Attrition
- Salaries and bonuses
- Job Satisfaction
- Training

## RECRUITMENT

Recruitment is a function that requires business perspective, expertise, ability to find and match the best potential candidate for the organisation. The biggest challenge for HR professionals is to source or recruit the best people or potential candidate for the organisation.

In the last few years, the job market has undergone some fundamental changes in terms of technologies, competition in the market, etc. In an already saturated job market, where the practices like poaching and raiding are gaining momentum, HR professionals have to face and conquer various challenges to find the best candidates for their organisations.

The major challenges faced by the HR Professionals in recruitment are:

- **Adaptability to globalization:** The HR professionals are expected to keep in tune with the changing times, i.e. the changes taking place across the globe.
- **Lack of motivation:** Recruitment is considered to be a thankless job. Even if the organisation is achieving results, work of the HR department or professionals are not appreciated or recognized for recruiting the right employees and performers.
- **Process analysis:** Speed of the recruitment process is the main concern of the HR in recruitment. The process should be flexible, adaptive, cost effective and responsive to the immediate requirements.
- **Strategic prioritization:** The emerging new systems presents both an opportunity as well as a challenge for the

HR professionals. Therefore, reviewing staffing needs and prioritizing the tasks to meet the changes in the market has become a major challenge for the recruitment professionals.

## ATTRITION

Today's businesses are more dependent on their top performers to innovate and provide services that differentiate a company from its fierce competitors which suggests that corporations are reliant upon their human assets to survive and thrive.

Changing work force demographics, such as the shrinking of the most desirable labor pool (25-34 year olds) and downsizing , have led corporate America to search for answers to recruiting and retaining the strategic asset of the twenty-first century: **talented people**.

Retaining top talent was less an issue in the past, but the shifting tides of the unspoken employee/employer contract have created new trends in the workplace. The old contract expected employees to:

- work hard
- be loyal

In return, they would have:

- a job for life
- a home away from home
- regular salary increments
- a good opportunity for a promotion

But as the new contract is substantially different which states that employees must now work harder, doing not just their own jobs, but the jobs of their former co-workers who were "right-sized", job security is extinct, promotions are scarce, salary increases are modest, and the constant uncertainty of change is almost guaranteed; is it surprising that employee loyalty is on the demise and talented individual contributors feel less bonded to their organizations?

A Nasscom Hewitt-Associates Survey shows that the cost of attrition is 1.5 times the annual salary of an employee. Costs are due to loss of productivity, temporary replacement, and new recruitment and training.

The attrition rate is linked to a number of causes, one being the average age of the employee. 87 percent of the BPO employees are under the age of 30. In the article Managing attrition in BPO, authors Anirban Majumdar and Kamal Poddar of the Institute of Management in Kozhikode, Kerala, state that attrition is linked to career opportunities.

Only 10 out of every 100 people will ever make it to consultant level and one out of every 100 to line manager.

This shows that the job is stressful as employees are moved from one process to another and are given little time to adjust. The work environment has rigid rules and strict monitoring mechanisms by which employees become affected by sleep disturbances due to working irregular hours.

Last but not least, regular poaching by competitors contributes to employees leaving the organisation for a better career opportunities.

## SALARIES AND BONUSES

According to Gevrey of Trans works, "New hires are offered a competitive salary of anywhere between USD 200 and USD 300 a month, which is very interesting for Indian youngsters. Those who are capable and loyal to the company get a chance to move up within a reasonable period of time. There are financial bonuses for best performers. We recently gave a bonus of a scooter worth a USD 1000."

## JOB SATISFACTION

Job satisfaction is one of the most important links to retain employees. In order to manage the expectations of the recruit, it is important that the job description and role of the employee in the organization should be clearly understood when entering the organisation.

A Tesco employee segmentation survey in 2005 indicates that there are five broad attitude segments of people working within their workforce: 25 percent are work-life balancers; 18 percent are pleasure seekers; 25 percent want it all; 16 percent live to work whereas 16 percent work to live.

Thus, by understanding the drives and needs of each segment the organisation can tailor the employment proposition and improve retention.

## TRAINING

Gevrey thinks that the recruit's level of competencies and their job expectations can only be fully understood in the initial training programme. Interpersonal and intercultural training should also be included in the later stage of this program.

Once the employees move up the ladder they find very little time for training. If there is a lack of leadership training on the operational level then it is reflected on the work floor and consequently on the job satisfaction of the employee.

"In certain cases, when we have two candidates," says a Bangalore BPO manager, "one candidate may be technically very competent but low on soft skills and the second candidate scores very well on soft skills. So what we do is take the guy lower on the technical skills and give him intensive training on the job and assign him on to a leadership profile."

## THE RECRUITMENT PROCESS

Satish Seetharam, Manager at Bosch in Bangalore says, "We look at the business requirements first. We make sure that the job profile we are looking for not only matches with the skills and competencies but also the job expectations of the candidate. An open discussion with the candidate gives insight into how long he will be staying with us."

## PEOPLE-ORIENTED

The challenges for HR managers in India are truly different from challenges faced in the West. Though the attrition rate is high, Indian HR managers are very people-oriented, whereas their western counterparts are far more process and task-oriented.

According to Gevrey, Indian organizations value the happiness of the employee and consequently the well-being of his extended family.

The employee is given leave to take his mother to the hospital, or is allowed to attend the wedding of a neighbor or to mourn a family member on the other side of the country.

The well-being of the employee on a personal level is considered to be extremely important for the organisation. Western HR managers understand this and take this into consideration when working with Indian colleagues.

## THE SCENARIO IN INDIA

India has witnessed a revolution in the field of HR; from playing a supportive role to being a strategic partner in the growth of businesses. It has transformed itself from being merely Personnel Management—which maintained records and ensure statutory compliances, while doing the bare minimum to keep employees satisfied; to being an integrated part of the corporate.

The HR function of 21st century India has made a major transition from being 'behind-the scenes' supportive appendage to becoming the critical differentiator in business. Rapid globalization has made companies realize that people are the key to the growth of business. This has led to companies routinely using their innovative HR practices as their USP (Unique Selling Proposition) to keep up with the times of a rapidly changing labor scene.

**Employee Sourcing:** It is the most important aspect of human resource. A large part of the mind space of HR is committed head hunting. With the opening up of an economy which is both expanding at a frenetic pace, and maturing in terms of width and depth, the war for talent has reached a crescendo in terms of options available to professionals. Talent acquisition has become one of the crucial factors for recruitment professionals. In sectors like IT and BPOs, high attrition levels have become prevalent.

Quality of manpower is another issue of concern in India. While millions of graduates and post-graduates pass out of Indian universities each year, the actual number of employable talent is severely limited. So the challenge lies with the employers to adopt the innovative modes of recruitment and to ensure that it can separate the wheat from the chaff.

**Employee Motivation:** In a market where job-hopping has become the usual trend, keeping the workforce motivated is one of the key challenges for HR. Motivation no longer now comes from just a lucrative pay. Nowadays companies have to make employee feel special to ensure that he doesn't walk out into the arms of competition. Talent segmentation and segregation with performance appraisal and rewards is essential to a good team of workers. In other words, employers have to ensure that apart from the basic needs, employees also expect job satisfaction, learning and development facilities.

**Employee Engagement and Talent Retention:** Winning the hearts and minds of talent is of prime challenge in the current context as employees are no longer committed to their companies. Their focus is towards their own professional growth and careers. Employee engagement means that HR has its eyes and ears open to the ground realities that an employee faces in the job. Issues like work-life balance, fun and challenge and fun at work are considered part of the employee experience. Employee Satisfaction Surveys cannot just remain an exercise and results cannot be ignored. Specific ATRs (Action Taken Reports) have to be presented and acted upon as proof of developmental intentions of HR. Addressing employee grievances is another area that has to be made vigorous so that issues do no escalate.

Attraction, motivation and retention are the essence of HR deliverables. As the economy booms and increase in the expectations of industries as it matures—age old personnel management fundamentals do not apply practically. Creativity and innovation by HR function can make a big difference in how an employee can actually be attracted, motivated and retained.

## WORKFORCE DIVERSITY

During the past decades, the term "diversity" has been widely used to refer to the demographic composition of a team which is usually measured in empirical studies, using the compositional approach, which focuses on the distribution of demographic attributes—e.g. age, ethnicity, gender-within teams. Researchers studying team diversity and organizational demography both assess the extent to which members of an organizational unit are similar or dissimilar to each other. Also both use indices of variation (not central tendency) to assess the composition of organizational units (teams, departments, entire organizations)

## DEMOGRAPHIC CHANGES

In June 2009, U.S. President Barack Obama in a speech at a Wisconsin town hall meeting stated that the U.S. would have to take decisive steps to impart better education to its children or else suffer further economic damage. He added American students now compete with children from India and China, who "are coming at us hard, and...they're really buckling down."

The global economic meltdown is a subject of many conversations about how the world economy might steer itself back to health. In this context, it is surprising to see how Obama's remarks include any consideration of education, or of the quality and size of an educated population. And yet it's clear that if a country's colleges and schools are in good health and if a significant proportion of the population is graduating from them, the projection of economic growth are hopeful. To conclude, when conditions are right, large number of young workers have potential to drive a nation's growth to remarkable levels.

Theory known as the "demographic dividend," coined by demographer David Bloom, proposes that when young working-age adults comprise a disproportionate percentage of a country's population, the national economy is affected in positive ways. Indeed, when he and other demographers have referred to the periods of sustained economic growth around the world, they found that the effect of the demographic dividend was impressive. Bloom estimates that the dividend in the U.S., in the form of the baby boom generation, contributed 20 percent of the nation's GDP growth between 1970 and 2000. In Japan, the contribution during the same period, however was smaller because the dividend coincided with relaxed laws against abortion and birth control. But it still accounted for an estimated 10 percent. In East Asia as a whole, Bloom suggests, the demographic dividend drove one-third of the region's economic growth between 1965 and 1990.

The economic advantage coming from young workers is that they are very creative and imaginative. Also the added advantage of this dividend generation is that they don't have to spend their incomes on children, or they don't worry as much as previous generations about financial security and health expenses. Thus being free from major tensions, they may diverge from traditional career paths into more entrepreneurial activities, and when these risks pay-off, the results for the economy are innovation, productivity, and rapid growth. We can see a massive demographic dividend approaching in several countries and the country most likely to be affected, and presently already experiencing a dramatic boom, is India.

## TAKING THE DIVIDEND TO HEART

The underlying premise that growth depends first and foremost on people and their talents—feels simple and perceptive. The key parameters of some successful corporate tracks include the number of people recruited from colleges each year, and their powerful HR strategies like employee retention and productivity.

The idea that human capital drives growth has not always been popular. Unfortunately even, economists have underestimated the value of human capital and the impact of youthful energy. In India and China, for example, well into the 1970s and 1980s, people were viewed as more of a burden than an asset. The government of India promoted birth control, and appointed a demographer as its health minister, with the idea of reducing the population. In China, birth-control policies evolved to become more stringent, with the Communist Party's slogan transformed from "one is not many, two's just right, and three's too much" in the early 1970s, to "one is best, two's the maximum," and finally, to "it is good to have just one child."

However in India, attitudes are changing. A very young population is currently coming of age and entering the workforce. Consumer spending is booming. Thus population boom is increasingly seen as an asset as large portion of it has become productive.

India's democratically elected governments are in transition; its economic strength and demographics vary widely among regions. Its entrepreneurial sector, is one of the most prospective in the world. By looking at the business scenerio in emerging India, we can see the strategies, particularly those that involve talent, are used by the companies.

## EXPERIMENTAL ENTREPRENEURSHIP

Today's young generation is bringing forth new ideas especially in the field of marketing, distribution and networking. Within Indian firms such as ICICI Bank (India's largest private financial services company), Hindustan Unilever and Comat Technologies there are young, entrepreneurial leaders who are eager to experiment with new ideas and business models.

Banks in India are linking up with self-help groups and post offices so that it can reach the vast number of people who lack bank accounts and financial access. In urban areas, some banks are leveraging information technology and communication tools to serve their consumers.

Retailers are using unconventional methods to tap the rural consumer class and evade infrastructure constraints. They allow people pay with grain for consumer goods. Companies such as the Solar Electric Light Company (SELCO) are meeting the needs of unelectrified communities in the states of Tamil Nadu and Karnataka through solar lighting.

One major reason that global businesses are paying attention to India is this creativity and innovation. It might appear that India has attracted the attention of these businesses purely because of its huge and prospective consumer market, just as purchasing power in Europe and the U.S. But India's domestic economy includes more than passive consumers; valuable technological and business strategies. The youth in India are providing its markets with dual opportunities of the talent to build and sell products, and the consumers to buy them. This self-reinforcing circle is turning Indian economy into a force to be reckoned with.

## EMBRACING RISK IN A FEARFUL WORLD

Though the risk/reward ratios improved in global stock markets between 2008 and 2009, India has not been unaffected. The country's fiscal deficit has become more ominous, the construction and real estate sectors have taken hits.

The demographic dividend has a significant influence on a country's capacity for experimentation and entrepreneurship. Economists Gurdip Bakshi and Zhiwu Chen have noted, the demographic dividend confers the willingness to take risks. Conversely, in countries with aging and retiring populations—and many people becoming unemployed—people grow risk averse which dampens the country's productivity and growth.

Overall, the Indian economy looks far more optimistic than its global equivalent.

India can provide a buffer for economies now experiencing slow growth. Thus, India presents the opportunity for the developed world to cross-pollinate its risks. In fact, India's stock markets were home to more than 150 global pension funds from the United States, the European Union, Canada, among others.

In an era of globalization, demographic have more impact to local economies than such physical assets as land, resources, and even industrial bases. If we consider the case of United States, whose information technology and telecommunications industries drove rapid innovation and productivity gains during the 1980s and 1990s, it was the period of its demographic boom, when many baby boomers were in their most creative and unfettered period. Even after its dividend began to tail off, the U.S. continued to see gains. The reason for this could be attributed to its open immigration policies which paved way to hundreds and thousands of skilled foreign workers into U.S. industry and hundreds and thousands of foreign students into U.S. universities which is evident from the figures which states that more than 60 percent of advanced engineering degrees in the U.S. are awarded to immigrants, as are 40 percent of the patents. IT companies including eBay, Intel, Yahoo, Google, and Sun Microsystems were founded or cofounded by immigrants. If political proposals to tighten immigration laws, were adopted in the U.S., it could have been counterproductive—choking off talent when the country needed it most.

## STRENGTHENING THE WEAKEST SECTORS

The real gains of a population boom depend on policies that allow the young to attain high levels of education, find jobs, and contribute to the economy.

Even in developed economies bad policy can turn a talent advantage sour. Bloom has tracked a number of countries that did not cash in on their dividends. For instance, countries in Latin America stumbled during the 1980s. Similarly, Russia and Cuba failed to gain from their demographic positives. In India and countries with similar demographics, the failure to create opportunity can turn the dividend into a crisis. India experienced these problems throughout the decades of 1970s and 1980s, when unemployment and lack of income mobility were at apex in major cities.

Unless industry and government collaborate to build policies that make effective use of a country's young force, a demographic advantage can prove ineffective, and even counterproductive.

This suggests that businesses have to strategize while venturing into a country's market—considering not just profits but also those places where they can contribute to the growth of the whole economy, especially including those parts that would otherwise be weak. India, an emerging economy, has some obvious weaknesses in its institutions and market maturity. India dismantled its socialist framework in 1991, setting up its modern stock exchange and commodity markets and freeing businesses from rigid restrictions. Because the resulting economic infrastructure is so new, the demographic dividend will also place enormous pressure on natural resources, and this pressure is likely to intensify.

This environment presents corporations with several opportunities. Instead of relying solely on the growing middle class customers, many corporations have captured into the country's growing poor-but-aspirational consumer base. The advantage of doing so is two-fold: It expands markets in innovative ways, and it gives the bottom income earners a way out of poverty. The Tata Group's project of making urban housing available to the poor by offering homes starting at US $ 8,000 suggests the beginning of real estate developments.

Thus, the entrepreneurial private sector in India is providing services not yet provided by the government. And in this process, it is finding its entrepreneurialism reflected in a new sense of service and openness on the part of the Indian government. In India, where more than half the population lives without electricity, puts a low ceiling on productivity and potential GDP growth in many parts of the country. The challenges are compelling the Indian government to explore options beyond its traditional, coal-fueled electricity options, while including decentralized, diverse energy sources. Solar technology, wind power, biofuels, gas, and nuclear power offer India the opportunity for more equitable access to energy.

## TECHNOLOGY AND STRUCTURE ORGANIZATIONAL EFFECTIVENESS

To be effective, an organization must successfully respond to environmental factors. Various models of determining organizational effectiveness exist as organizations face different environments, their organizational members are made up of different kinds of people, and are at different stages of development. Each model is useful to an organization having a particular combination of these environmental and organizational attributes.

Two different underlying dimensions may be considered to develop models of organizational effectiveness. The first dimension is the organization's internal *versus* external focus and the second is the organization's emphasis on flexibility versus control. Flexibility allows faster change, whereas control allows a firm grasp on current operations. When these two dimensions are drawn result is the rational goal, open system, internal process, and human relations models.

An organization is effective to the degree it acquires inputs from its environment and has outputs accepted by its environment. The University of Alberta follows this model as it is concerned about the quality and number of students applying for admission and what jobs they receive on graduation.

The human relations model focuses on the development of the organization's personnel. The competing values model requires three sets of competing values. The first is the tension between internal *versus* external focus. The more the organization focuses on one; it loses its concentration on the other. For example, Apple Computer has focused externally on its customers making computers that are intuitive and easy to access. The second set of values in competition is flexibility *versus* control. Flexibility allows quick response to changing conditions and values innovation. Stability and predictability mean that routine activities are performed well but change is difficult to implement. The third set of competing values is the relative concern of the feelings, needs, and development of the people.

A private hospital, for example, is concerned about how patients are treated and the success rate of surgeries (the rational goal model). It is equally interested in how hospital procedures are performed (the internal process model) as well as with the skills and abilities of hospital staff (the human relations model). Finally, being a private hospital it must make a profit to survive, it also needs to take into account how many and what kinds of patients are admitted (the open system model). The hospital must balance the three sets of competing values to make it more effective.

Finally, organization would aim to at least minimally satisfy the most important constituents (or stakeholders) in its environment.

An organization seeking legitimacy survives by acting in a manner as being seen as legitimate by other organizations.

The organization adopting the fault-driven model of effectiveness seeks to get rid of traces of ineffectiveness in its internal functioning. The National Aeronautics and Space Administration (NASA) in the United States serves a good example whose systems are designed with backups to be reliable even if some components fail.

## ORGANIZATIONAL LIFE CYCLE

Does effectiveness of organization does vary with its stage of development? The answer to this question is obvious. As organizations pass through different stages of their life cycle; their structure, their basis of growth and their goals change. It should be remembered that organizations may not grow continuously but may remain at one stage of development for long periods.

It is interesting to know that some organizations are in operation for significantly fewer years than the average person lives. Failure is very common with new organizations. Restaurants, for example, are known to have high rates of startups and closures. It is called the liability of newness. Older organizations die, too, though it is very shocking. A recent example is Eaton's.

The first stage of an organization's development is the birth stage. The first crisis in this stage is that of leadership. Will the transition be made from being managed by the organization's founder to being managed by proficient managers?

The next stage of development is the organization's youth. The crisis in this stage is that senior managers may not wish to relinquish control to more junior managers by delegating tasks and authority to them.

At the organization's midlife, growth is through delegation and coordination and the structure becomes more bureaucratic and departmentalized. To transform from a red-tape bureaucracy to a collaborative team-oriented organization is the challenge that will eventually arise. At maturity this collaboration will be achieved. The major challenge at this stage is to avoid becoming stagnant and enduring a slow decline and eventual death. And finally, at the stage of decline and death some organizations cannot change because their management becomes a roadblock to change. Also, the organization's current structure presents a constraint on necessary change.

## ORGANIZATION STRUCTURE

The founder of an organization has to make a series of decisions about organization's goals and objectives, work to be performed to attain those goals, basis on which work is divided and coordinated, and who will do the work. These decisions may be interdependent if the organization is small. For example, the skills and abilities of the particular people hired into the organization will affect decisions about what the organization can do and how it will do it.

A small organization, for example, a shoe store, would have a simple structure where everyone, including the managers, is involved in selling. And for some specialized functions, such as accounting and advertising, bookkeeper may be contracted out and also an advertising agency.

Another example of simple form of organization would be a restaurant where structure has divided the staff into three groups: the bar, the food, and the service.

These simple forms could be much enlarged by adding more people to the basic structure. But as number of people increases in an organization, coordination becomes more difficult. The critical issue is that there often isn't enough time with the manager to deal with every person individually on every issue. To solve this problem, more vertical division of employees would occur.

As a business grows, more people are hired to do the basic work of the organization by which more jobs are created. It creates new departments to perform specialized services that used to be contracted out to other organizations or individuals. For example, a growing corporation that initially contracts its accounting to a public accounting partnership might set-up its own accounting department and hire an accounting manager as its head. Such specialized services are known as staff functions.

The opposite of staff is the line. Employees groups, and departments that are directly engaged in making or selling the organization's product, or managing those who do, are in the line. In a travel agency the travel agents are line personnel.

Besides accounting, other staff services include public relations, advertising, finance, and legal services. However, whether these activities are considered as staff or a line service depends on the basic work of the organization. For example, accountants working for a public accounting firm are line personnel, not staff.

Sometimes organizations are created large at the outset because size is an advantage or a necessity. For example, the owner of an independent supermarket does not open a small store and then grow larger as demand warrants. Instead, a large store is designed and built to deal with the expected number of customers in the neighbourhood. As an accepted fact, a small grocery store could not compete effectively in price and selection with other nearby supermarkets.

Few years back, Shawn Lowry and Lorne Fierbach, opened a web-based greeting card business in Los Angeles. The best part of their technology and structure is that it can handle up to 200,000 cards per day. Lowry says, "We didn't want to be a small card store where we took a few orders a day and personalized them and mailed them out. We built it like it was going to be a very successful company where we would be taking care of the nation's or North America's or the world's greeting card needs." Initial capital of $10 million was required to set-up the operation for large-scale activity.

Departmentation is the horizontal division on the basis of customer, product, geographic location, function performed or special knowledge, project, or a mixture of these components.

The division of the travel agency into corporate and holiday travel is a departmentation on the basis of customer.

A division by product-base is illustrated in the supermarket example where work is split into bakery, meats, dry goods, and produce. Employees would specialize in working with and knowing one type of product.

An organization can divide the work into different geographic areas where it has its operations. This arrangement is used when a large territory needs to be divided into parts of manageable size.

In a manufacturing firm functional departments typically include production, marketing and sales, and research and development, e.g. Production is responsible for making shoes; marketing and sales for advertising, distribution, and pricing; and R&D for exploring new designs and materials for shoes. Organizations often create a mixture, or hybrid, of the above-mentioned ways to departmentalize.

## TYPE OF STRUCTURE

Structure concerns about the reporting relationships between organizational members. These are the lines connecting the boxes, rules and regulations about how the work is distributed and performed and whether decisions are concentrated at the top of the organization or lower down. In order to compare one organization structure with that of another or to study the effectiveness of the organizational structure on the performance, we need to have consistent ways to measure structure. Three important structure measures are complexity, formalization and centralization.

Organization becomes more and more horizontally complex as more tasks are added to it and divided among individuals. As the vertical chain of command lengthens, more organizational layers are placed between top management and production workers. Thus, the organization becomes more vertically complex. Vertical complexity is often also called the tallness of the organization. Organizations today tend to move towards flatter structure by eliminating whole levels of middle management. This would result in downsizing and increase in the number of people supervised. Therefore, the span of control increases for the managers.

Formalization refers to the extent to which job activity is defined and controlled by rules. The more rules governing the work and the decisions, the more an organization is formalized. The best example is Police departments which very formalized as the activities of officers are strictly governed by rules that cover almost every situation that may arise. On the other hand, a campus radio station may be much less formalized, having just few rules governing the broadcasting actions of station members.

Centralization or decentralization concerns where in the organization decisions are made. When decision-making authority is reserved at top level, vertical centralization is high. Horizontal decentralization occurs when workers in different organizational units are allowed to make their work related decisions without referring to a more central authority.

These structural measures of complexity, centralization, and formalization may be combined to describe two categories of organizations : mechanistic and organic. Mechanistic organizations are those which operates as machines. They are characterized by highly specialized tasks which are rigidly defined, and communications that primarily take the form of instructions and decisions issued by superiors to subordinates. They have hierarchical authority and control. Thus, mechanistic organizations tend to be complex, formalized, and centralized. An automobile factory is an organization with mechanistic structure that uses a production line technology.

On the other hand, Organic organizations are more lively where the tasks are more interdependent and are continually adjusted and redefined through interaction with organizational members. An advertising agency needs to be highly flexible in dealing with customers and in creating concepts for television commercials and print advertisements.

## TECHNOLOGY

Technology is defined as the sequence of physical techniques, knowledge, and equipments used to turn organizational inputs into outputs. Joan Woodward conducted research to understand the connection between technology and structure. Her studies included 100 manufacturing firms in the southern part of England. She identified three types of technology.

The first was small batch. It included production of one or a few custom items by one person or a small team working closely together.

Woodward's second technology type was large batch/mass production. It included production of many units of an identical product. An example of large batch production is the making of beer, which in a brewery is made in large fermentation kettles that may each hold many thousands of liters. Each kettle holds one batch of beer.

Woodward's third type was continuous process. It included the production of a standard product without pause. An example of continuous process technology is a nuclear power plant as electricity is generated without pause for a long period of time. A few highly skilled technicians are required to monitor the nuclear reactor.

Woodward and her colleagues found that organizations were more effective when their technology coordinated the organization's structure. Organizations using a mass production technology were more effective when using a mechanistic structure, whereas an organic structure was best for small batch production because the production of custom items requires a good deal of informal communication and adaptation... The reason behind this was to have a control over complex repetitive process exerted by rules and regulations.

The concept that technology determines the best organizational structure is termed as technological imperative.

## GLOBAL SOURCING OF LABOUR

Global sourcing is a term which has grown popular in just few years.—It refers to the ability of business organization to perform critical business processes and IT functions anywhere in the world where the necessary concentration of skilled talent is available at the best value. Moreover, a comprehensive global sourcing model is often a means component of the distinctive capability that differentiates each high-performance business.

Accenture has found that leading organizations are increasing their pace of global sourcing strategies, especially in North America and Europe. Entering low cost countries and establishing their presence is a key contributor to the growing use of global sourcing. Parallel research which was conducted by Accenture in conjunction with the China Supply Chain Council concluded that business spending in low-cost countries has grown to 85 percent in the past few years.

The advantage of global sourcing is cost reduction. Companies that have applied global sourcing are pursuing more aggressive spending reduction targets than they were several years ago. Another major benefit of global sourcing is the ability to tap into skilled and motivated people anywhere in the world.

Many companies however, are finding common problems when global sourcing strategies are not accompanied by the optimal leadership, process, tools and infrastructure.

## GREATER REACH, GREATER VULNERABILITY

Indeed, the characteristics that give global sourcing its most important strengths can also represent weaknesses. With greater reach comes greater vulnerability: miscommunication, cultural misalignment, conflicts and the risks of work stoppages from political disruption or natural disasters.

To high performers, global sourcing is not just about off shoring to the low-cost location. It also means blending onsite, offshore and nearshore capabilities and is supported by industrialized methods strong leadership and communications, and effective change management.

## KEY TRANSFORMATION TOOL

According to Mindy Blodgett, a researcher with the Yankee Group, an IT and business analyst firm, "Companies not only are getting more comfortable with global sourcing, they are seeing it as a key tool for transforming their businesses."

Today organizations have realised that transformative value requires overcoming a number of challenges intrinsic in a globally sourced work environment, especially as one moves to multiple providers. For example, the shift from having control over a locally-based staff to managing a far-off network that includes both internal resources and external providers is an immense challenge.

In a study, two-thirds of respondents out of 200 US business executives surveyed, (whose companies had outsourced business processes or functions) said that they had experienced miscommunication problem within their global sourcing operations where the specific issues identified were differing communications styles varying approaches to conflict management, and decision-making styles that can vary from culture to culture.

The challenges and opportunities present in the global sourcing point to at least three capabilities to be mastered if an organization wants to achieve world-class status in the sourcing approaches and management techniques that contribute to high performance.

### Focus on Value and Results, not just Cost Reduction

In many of these cases, the problems can begin at the outset when, during contract negotiation, cost reduction prioritize over the value and results to be delivered.

According to Russell Taruscio, finance control and accounting procurement director for BP, "A buyer and a service provider have mutual interests. It isn't a buyer–supplier relationship like buying a house—where both parties walk away after the deal and grumble a bit because they didn't quite get what they wanted. It's a long-term relationship that requires that you have an open and honest mode of communication so that you can deal with the myriad environmental changes that will inevitably arise, or so that you just deal honestly with issues that arise in service delivery. This way, you can act constructively rather than simply pointing fingers at each other."

But this focus on value and results is more than just having a good relationship. Parties focusing on values mean they are more likely to take an end-to-end view of the process, so that all the parts of the value chain are involved to deliver a technical and a business result. Companies are not just managing an offshore component by itself or expecting that to be managed by the supplier. What's important is that all the sourcing machinery works end to end.

### Improve Cross-cultural Communications

The mastery of global sourcing involves dealing with a number of human factors that often intimidate to unravel the value of a global sourcing arrangement. Findings in one of the cross-cultural communication research suggest: Different ways of communicating, of completing work tasks and raising issues for discussion and resolving them, can derail a global project team.

Consider the cultural ramifications alone. Certainly human beings have a great deal in common, regardless of where in the world they live and work. Yet cultural and social influences are just different enough around the globe that bringing people together from different parts of Europe, North and South America, and the Asia Pacific region in a common but dispersed work environment can cause any number of misunderstandings, serious or otherwise.

For example, executives in some business cultures are generally discreet in their personal interactions. When they work with colleagues from a different culture, they are hesitant to express their feelings openly could prevent their legitimate concerns from being attended to quickly or properly. Another potential problem: People from some cultures may wrongly assume that their terminology and slang are universally understood, which could create confusion and mistakes.

A strong commitment to effective training with regard to cultural differences can create a huge difference.

### Provide Effective Transition and Change Management Services

Another critical success factor is ensuring that the transition to the new operating model is handled effectively, and that the offshore, nearshore and onshore teams have been trained to perform optimally in the new environment.

Yankee Group's Blodgett notes that transition services is a huge challenge for most of the companies. "Many companies complain about transition, and tend to blame the service provider if it doesn't go well," she says. "They want the service provider to provide transition guidance, but they don't want it to cost more."

According to Blodgett, companies that manage the transition best are the ones that centralize many of their processes and have industrialized as many of them as possible. Finding a provider with proven practices in transition services can be essential for realizing the business case for the sourcing model.

Transition is about more than technical knowledge. It is estimate that 75 percent of the entire transition effort should be dedicated to understanding business systems rather than technical systems. Companies can make a mistake by focusing their training on only technical software code and architectures. Infact, most of the service provider staff must be able to handle questions from the business people, not the IT professionals. If the company is an offshore center supporting an application, a client contacting the help desk won't be asking for C++ or COBOL tips; they will be asking to solve a particular business problem.

What does "Global Sourcing 2.0" look like? For high performers, it is a highly mutual and comprehensive environment which is focused on business transformation and on adding value that goes beyond the labor arbitrage benefits of offshoring work to a single, low-cost location. As organizations grows, management will need to develop more innovative, blended sourcing models. Those models need to be supported by advanced methods and tools, to overcome the considerable challenges of coordinating work across time zones, nations and cultures. Perhaps, successful global sourcing will require a new mindset—where companies seek to work with their service providers and their global workforces, so that the whole is always greater than the sum of the parts.

# Strategic Human Resource Assessment and Planning

## INTRODUCTION

In the era of competition, companies do not have any other choice but to compete better than their competitors. Human resource management plays a vital role in supporting the corporate strategic plan. All the HR functions contribute positively to achieve the objective. As HR department supports other departments, there is a critical need to get the best people in the right place at the right time.

HR forecasting helps to match the requirements and the availabilities of employees. There are two kinds of forecasting methods: qualitative as well as quantitative methods.

Miles and Snow typology could be used by companies as a tool to identify their positions. It discusses the importance of typology and forecasting for successful human resource management to function in a company.

Human resource planning is a process designed to predict and integrate the human resources response to an organization's strategic plan. Human resource planning enables the organization to:

- Have proper allocation of resources in a manner that will allow the organization to meet its goals.
- Prepare a framework for the organization's orderly growth and progress.
- Have a strategic base for making business decisions.
- Maximize organizational effectiveness by integrating the organization's mission, strategic plan, budget, technical knowhow and human resource needs.

Human resource planning also known as man power planning is a systematic process for identifying, acquiring, developing, and retaining employees to meet the needs of the organization. Thus, it is an comprehensive process, drawing together program management, strategic planning, budget, human resources, staff. It involves active collaboration and information sharing. Strategic planning sets direction for the organization and articulate measurable goals and objectives. Human resources provides tools for identifying competencies needed for recruiting, developing, training and motivating employees to build the human resource of the future.

Human resource planning is an effort to help an organization make decisions for both the short and long-term, at the same time allowing flexibility in the changing environment. HRP is intended to help solve staffing problems related to manage position movement into, around, and out of an organization.

Human resource planning ties human resource decisions to the organization's strategic plan. It allows HR decisions move away from piecemeal, individualized decisions to become part of the larger, more strategic goals of the organization.

It is important that a human resource plan must reflect the management environment of the organization for which it is developed. In addition, organization culture is an important aspect to be considered in human resource planning. Organization culture consists of the patterns of shared values and beliefs shared by the members of the organization and also provide norms for acceptable and unacceptable behavior.

Questions to be considered by organizations:

- Are there certain occupational groups with increasing turnover?
- What are the factors influencing turnover?
- Has turnover reduced the skill set of a certain occupational group?

Answering these questions help organizations to develop plans for stable staffing, succession planning, and skill development. The process of human resource planning requires all parties to think away from preconceived notions and to seriously consider change. The members of the organization need to have a vision of what is to be accomplished. Participants should discard personal considerations to make the process effective.

Although different HRP (human resource planning) models exist, all varies widely. They all rely on identification of staffing levels as well as competencies needed in the future; an analysis of the present workforce; a comparison of the present work force to future needs to identify gaps and surpluses; the development of strategies for building the manpower needed in the future; and an evaluation process to assure that the manpower plan remains valid so that objectives are being met. An important consideration over here is there is no prescribed format for a human resource plan.

The approach selected by the organization must be flexible rather than a rigid process. There is no one "right" way to practice human resource planning for the organization.

## HUMAN RESOURCE PLANNING AND STRATEGIC PLANNING?

Planning begins with the organization's strategic plan. At any given time, there may be long-term goals, for e.g. opening of a new facility or reduced spending. There may be situations where the organization may be required to face sudden changes which may include increased demand for services or receipt of grant funding.

Given these varying situations, organization's leadership envisions various steps which must take place in order for the goals to become reality. Human resource planning offers a means to systematically line up organizational priorities with the budgetary and human resources requirements to accomplish them.

In the beginning of the planning process with identified strategic objectives, managers can develop human resource plans that will help them accomplish those objectives. These plans provide a sound basis for justifying budget and staffing requests, as there is a clear correlation between objectives, the budget, and the human resources needed to accomplish them.

HR planning must relate to other planning efforts of the organization. Human resource planning done in a vacuum cannot be successful. For the proper implementation of HRP, one must be aware of organizational direction. Also, achieving organizational goals requires a competent workforce.

Human resource planning combines employees and employee skill sets needed to achieve the organization's goals. Effective human resource planning provides for a flexible and proficient human resource to be able to adapt to the changing needs of the organization.

Because human resource planning addresses staffing implications of strategic and operational plans, it affects the full range of HR functions like recruitment, hiring, training, compensation, and retention.

Human resource planning should also consider other human resource functions like succession planning, employee development, career ladders, and organization development. Each aspect should be considered to be important in identifying critical skills, forecasting potential vacancies, and preparing employees and the organization to meet future needs.

Human resource planning includes elements of strategic planning, workload projections, legislative forecasts, and budget projections. Human resource planning forecasts the numbers of people and type of skills needed at the future period of time to meet the future needs by comparing the available human resource (gaps).

An organization's human resource policies must be aligned to support the mission, vision, goals, and strategies by which the organization has defined its direction and expectations of people with it. An organization's human resource practices should be implemented by the standard of how well they help the organization pursue this intent. Government should build a solid foundation in strategic planning , succession planning, recruiting and training the best possible talent, and establishing a performance culture–including appropriate performance measures and rewards–that steers employees toward the accomplishment of their organizational mission.

Human resource planning is critical because if the right people with the right competencies are not in place, it is difficult to effectively achieve the organization's strategic goals and objectives. Thus human resource plan highlights the "people factor" in achieving results.

Human resource planning naturally supports and is a follow-up to strategic planning. Just as strategic planning helps an organization outline its plans, a human resource plan lays out the specific tasks and measures needed to ensure that the organization has the necessary man power to accomplish its mission.

A strategic plan charts broad mission-related targets and milestones. An understanding of organization's vision, mission, and measurable goals and objectives drive the identification of type of work needs to be accomplished.

When organizations effectively line up human resource activities with organizational strategy, activities fit strategically and reinforce one another.

This "strategic fit" approach produces several advantages:

(i) First, it creates consistency.
(ii) Second, human resource activities will strengthen and support the organization's business strategy.

(iii) Third, a good "fit" facilitates information exchange across activities.

(iv) Lastly, strategic fit approach eliminates redundancy and minimizes efforts being wasted.

Each of these activities reflects a fundamental decision made by the organization on preparing for tomorrow by investing in its people.

## MATCHING HUMAN RESOURCE REQUIREMENTS AND POTENTIAL HUMAN RESOURCE AVAILABILITY

Matching human resources with planned organizational activities presents some problems for the organization. Human resources have a certain degree of inflexibility in terms of their development and their utilization. It takes several months to recruit, select, place, and train the average employee; in large organizations, the process may take years. Decisions on personnel recruitment and development have long-lasting impact. Therefore, management must anticipate the demand and supply of human resources as a part of the organization's business planning processes.

Long-term business requirements, promotion policies, and recruitment (supply) possibilities have to be matched so that human resources requirements and availability estimates (from both internal and external sources) correspond sufficiently.

Establishing long-term human resources requirements is closely related to strategic business plans. Strategic business plans should provide a minimum base of information on which viable human resources plans can be built. On the other hand, management should consider labour availability when they establish strategic business plan because current and potentially available human resources affect the viability of strategic business plans.

## FORECASTING LABOUR DEMAND AND SUPPLY

Management needs to estimate future availabilities of labor that is, to assess the supply of labor, both within and outside of the organization. Also, they need to work out the future demand for specific numbers and types of employees.

Supply and demand analyses should be conducted separately. The reason behind this is that internal supply forecasts tend to rely heavily on organization-specific variables, such as turnover and retirement rates, transfers, and promotions, whereas, demand forecasts, depend primarily on variations in external factors like product or service demand. In sum, Cascio (1991) notes that, in contrast to forecasts of human resource supply, demand forecasts are beset with multiple uncertainties-in consumer behavior, in technology, in general economic environment, and so forth.

Two techniques are used to perform demand and supply forecasts: qualitative techniques and quantitative techniques.

## QUALITATIVE FORECASTING TECHNIQUES

Qualitative forecasts are essentially educated guesses or estimates by individuals who have some knowledge of previous HR availability's or utilization.

1. **Nominal Group:** Views regarding labor supply is taken from four to five participants. These views are written down, but are not discussed until all of the members have advanced their positions. The group then discusses the information presented and, subsequently, a final opinion poll is taken to determine its judgment.
2. **Delphi Technique:** This technique calls for a facilitator to seek written, expert opinions on labor forecasts. On the basis of responses received, a summary of information is developed and are distributed to the experts, who are then requested to submitted revised forecasts.
   Experts, in this technique, never meet face-to-face, but rather communicate through the facilitator.
3. **Replacement Planning:** Estimates of forecasting are based on charting techniques, which identifies current job incumbents and relevant information about each of them which includes a brief assessment of performance and potential, age, length of time in current position, and overall length of service.
4. **Allocation Planning:** This technique entail judgments about labor supply or demand by observing the movement of workforce through positions at the same organizational level.

## QUANTITATIVE FORECASTING TECHNIQUES

There are several quantitative methods for determining labour supply and demand (Duane).

1. **Regression Model:** Fluctuations in labour levels are worked out by using relevant variables, such as sales.
2. **Time-Series Model:** Fluctuations in labor levels are worked

out by isolating trend, seasonal, cyclical, and irregular effects.

3. **Economic Model:** Fluctuations in labour levels are predicted using a specific form of the production function.
4. **Linear Programming Model:** Fluctuations in labor levels are analyzed using an objective function as well as organizational and environmental restraint.
5. **Markov Model:** Fluctuations in labor levels are worked out by using historical transition rates.

## CHOICE OF A FORECASTING TECHNIQUE

Forecasters can choose either the qualitative or quantitative techniques or can combine them. In choosing an appropriate forecasting technique, the following factors should be considered:

1. **Organization's environment:** Jackson and Schuler observe that organizations operating in fairly stable environments may be able "to quantify the expected values of variables in their models, which means they can use statistical forecasting models." On the contrary, firms operating in unstable environments use quantitatively based predictions, since "both the variables and their expected values are difficult to specify accurately by replying on historical data".
2. **Organization size:** Stone and Fiorito suggest that larger organizations tend to use more sophisticated, quantitative techniques than do smaller ones. According to them, this relationship is particularly strong among government, mining, forestry, transportation, communications, and utilities organizations, which traditionally have had high internal stability due to low turnover among their employees.
3. **Perceived uncertainty in labour markets and economy:** In particular, "more sophisticated techniques will be discontinued if perceived uncertainty increases to a point where techniques are no longer feasible, or if perceived uncertainty decreases to a point where techniques are no longer needed". (Stone and Fiorito)
4. **Competition.** Organizations in industries that are regulated, operate within predictable product markets, and acquire resource slack tend to use similar forecasting techniques.

Thus, these factors indictae that different types of organizations must approach human resource planning differently. Considering organization's environment and size, seeming uncertainty in labor markets and economy, and competition, the Miles and Snow typology can be used to determine appropriate forecasting techniques in an organization.

## MILES AND SNOW TYPOLOGY AND FORECASTING

Miles and Snow (1984) identify three organizational types: defender, prospector, and analyzer.

## FORECASTING IN DEFENDER ORGANIZATIONS

Environmental conditions for the defender are comparatively simple. An industry that currently faces such type of situation is the electric utility industry in the United States, Lincoln Electric, McDonald's, New York Power Authority, etc. It generally has characteristics of predictable product market, high barriers of entry, and little product variation, thus allowing it to engage in less environmental scanning and more long-range forecasting and planning. Therefore, as Fiorito suggests, this low level of industry volatility allows organizations to use sophisticated or quantitative technique such as regression analysis to forecast labour demand and supply. There is an emphasis on internal labour-market forecasts. This explains the ability of defenders to pursue low-cost operations. Main reason behind success of defenders is production efficiency and tight business controls. The jobs within a defender organization tend to be highly specialized, as few resources are devoted to basic research and investments are usually made to streamline operations.

Coordination of work is brought about by formalization and specialization, thereby making the defender the stereotypical bureaucratic structure.

## FORECASTING IN PROSPECTOR ORGANIZATIONS

The prospector competes in a dynamic environment, with a rapid rate of technologies, product development, and market shifts, for example, Paramount, Reebok International, entrepreneurial firms, etc. As a result, it becomes very difficult for the organization to go for long term planning and forecasting. The environmental constraints on prospectors limit demand-forecasting process and forecasting labor supply becomes equally difficult. Therefore, labour demand and supply forecasts are based on qualitative techniques such as nominal groups and Delphi technique. There is an emphasis on external labour-market forecasts.

The emphasis on innovation and adaptation compel prospectors to be incompetent, particularly when compared with defenders. Success of prospectors depends on investments in research and development, with the objective of earning large profit margins on uniquely design products. For this, prospectors must assume an organic structure, avoiding the rigidities associated with formalization. Moreover, they tend to be highly decentralized, delegating decisionmaking authorities to appropriate personnel so that quick, intelligent responses can be made to dynamic market conditions.

## FORECASTING IN ANALYZER ORGANIZATIONS

The analyzer configuration combines the features of both the defender and prospector. This configuration seeks efficiency of operation like the defender, but, at the same time, it is like the prospector with an interest in new products and markets.

In coordinating its work, the analyzer faces a unique problem of separating the innovative activities (e.g., Research and Development (R&D) activities) from the formalized ones (e.g., production). It can resolve this problem by establishing two separate organizations, one structured around the characteristics of the prospector, while the other similar to that of the defender.

Another option for the analyzer is to focus on the innovative side, while contracting out the other organization's the production side.

Forecasting plays an important role in success of the organization. By forecasting the number of employees needed and their quality, a company would get the best people for the right places and at the right time. This function is crucial if a company wants to compete in the global market.

# 10 Human Resources Practices in India

India is the world's favourite outsourcing destination. India's share of the global offshore outsourcing market for software and back-office services is 44%. According to the National Association of Software Companies (Nasscom), India's premier trade body of the IT software and services industry, technology and IT services exports in India were worth $17.2 bn (£9.5 bn) in the year ended March 2005, a rise of 34.5% over the previous year. A further expansion of 30% in exports is predicted in the next twelve months, to reach $22.5 bn. The US accounts for 68% of Indian exports.

## CURRENT OUTSOURCING TRENDS WORLDWIDE

1. Outsourcing in traditional areas like customer care, financial services, manufacturing, IT etc. is growing.
2. Large multinational companies are investing in captive BPO units in supplier countries in different locations, to reduce risk and maintain control over quality.
3. Outsourcing has become more challenging. Customers are looking for business process excellence, speedy access to market, improvement in quality, benchmarking to world-class standards.
4. In the increasing scenario of global competition there is pressure mounting on margins from emerging lower-cost outsourcing destinations.
5. Risk factors involved in outsourcing like terrorism and war, disaster and disease make formulation of contingency plans a necessity.

6. For the past two decades, China has been growing at an astonishing 9.5% a year and India by 6%. They are influencing the global economy and leading the outsourcing revolution.

## FUTURE OUTSOURCING TRENDS WORLDWIDE

1. Outsourcing expenditure will continue to rise.
2. More countries will find attractive outsourcing options, creating a multi-polar world. The European Union markets will expand their offshoring programs, while Japan will increasingly look to China for its needs, whereas leading on the front will be UK and US.
3. Clients will have greater hold over driving and designing deals.
4. The interlinking of the supply chains as a result of outsourcing will create stability as companies pressurize governments to avoid wars.
5. Unexpected occurrences like war, terrorism, disease, natural disasters and economic disruption can throw a wrench in the works.
6. The rising price of oil will cause oil consuming countries like the USA to be less competitive relying more on India and China for outsourcing.
7. India will show excellence in Services that require advanced English like Knowledge Process Outsourcing (KPO).
8. Political backlash over outsourcing is likely to reduce over time as companies continue to reap the benefits of offshoring.
9. Technological power will shift from the West to the East as India and China emerge as big players in the global outsourcing market.
10. It is expected that by 2015 China will be No. 1, India No. 2 in the global top five outsourcing destinations.
11. Vendor focus will shift from basic skills, processes to domain knowledge, transition challenges, HR issues and governance.
12. Regional outsourcing hubs will develop to enable companies to minimize risk and leverage cultural and linguistic compatibility.

## OPPORTUNITIES FOR INDIA

### Near-shoring as a Business Strategy

India can collaborate with other countries to create the business environment while providing its domain knowledge and technological expertise for successful outsourcing. For example, TCS has a Latin American arm based in Mumbai, India which serves an insurance client in Chile with a center in Uruguay as a near-shore location.

## OPPORTUNITY AREAS

Knowledge Process Outsourcing (KPO) may soon be the biggest revenue generater in India as BPO companies move up the value chain in their service offerings. This includes:

### 1. Research and Development

- *Product Innovation:* Now Companies are investing more in innovation and new product development, examples include companies that have invested in R&D in India are Cisco Systems, Motorola, Hewlett-Packard, Google General Motors Corp. and Boeing Co among others.
- *Co-development:* In pharmaceuticals, India has the opportunity of co-development and ownership of new patented drugs through drug research, clinical trials and manufacturing. Indian pharma major Ranbaxy has an agreement with MNC GlaxoSmithKline to commercialize compounds they develop together.

### 2. Legal Outsourcing

India's qualified lawyers with experience in the British legal system and knowledge of English can offer paralegal support, legal support and patent services. Few Indian companies which are affiliated with American law firms are now able capture a tiny piece of the American market.

### 3. Engineering Outsourcing

India can provide high-quality engineering services in the fields of:

- *Mechanical and Electronic engineering*—analysis and design, embedded software.
- Plant Design, Process Engineering.
- Plant Automation Services.

### 4. Remote Infrastructure Management Services

India can offer management services for IT infrastructure, IT security and maintenance, thus, this sector presents great potential.

### 5. Accounting Services

We are in the initial stage where payroll processing and basic accounting task is being done for large American companies. However, in the latter stage soon a full range of accounting and tax services will be provided by Indian companies.

### 6. Outsourcing Options:

Outsourcing Options for India also exist in the field of Financial Research, content development, publishing, web services; human resource outsourcing: recruitment, training, education and many others.

## CHALLENGES FOR INDIA

### 1. Rising Competition

- In the coming years, China will replace India in the global ITES-BPO industry.
- India's appalling Infrastructure will continue to be a drag on the potential of India paving way to other countries for the competitive advantage.
- Other competing countries providing cheaper outsourcing options will provide tough competitors to India—East Europe, Latin America, South Africa.
- The education system needs to transform to enable people acquire skill sets that match industry needs.
- The transition to knowledge processing will be a much bigger challenge for the Indian companies as typical college graduates may not have knowledge or background to understand global issues required by this type of service.

### 2. Flexitime

Flexitime allows an employee to select work schedules while keeping in mind the organization's need to maintain work cover. It means an employee can choose working hours which are convenient, thus easing out the stress of commuting to work.

#### *Benefits of Flexitiming*

Indian employers are slowly realizing that allowing flexitime ensures that employee time is concentrated where the business actually needs it. The employees now are opting more and more for "flexitime". This flexible working strategy is vividly acknowledged as "no-more-late-excuses-to-boss". Flexitime let a person works according to its biological clock. It means that employees could go to the office from the time they fell doing so. Because of this privilege, employees could avail of some "breathing spaces" away from the pressure of office works and deadline and the psychological pressure of presence of their boss. Flexitime is deemed to be an important factor to prevent women's turnover and provide a useful "trick" for them to re-enter the labor force after giving birth or caring for an old parent.

### *Kinds of Flexitime*

#### *Flexitour*

Employees can select starting and stopping time for work independently and adhere to these timings regularly.

#### *Flexitime*

Employees can work during specified core hours, but can make up the rest of work hours as per their wish.

#### *Gliding Schedule*

Employees must meet the basic requirement of eight hours a day and 40/48 hours a week. Within that, you can opt to change your arrival and departure time every day.

#### *Variable Day*

Employees must meet the basic requirement of 40 or 48 hours (depending on the organization) a week but can vary the number of hours one may work each day.

#### *Maxiflex*

One can decide this kind of flexible work schedule which contains the least number of core hours and offers maximum flexibility.

### *Advantages of Flexitime*

#### *In Marketing*

Prudential ICICI has shifted its work time from 9 am - 6 pm to 11 am - 8 pm. "There is no point in calling employees at 9 am" says Vasant Sanzgiri of the Human Resources Department of the organisation. "Their work depends on customer convenience and actually begins only at 11 am. This way a lot more work gets done than by sticking to the 9 - 6 schedule."

#### *Creating Goodwill*

Sanzgiri claims that benefits of flexibility observed in terms of time are tremendous too, especially when most of the personnel in this department are female. "The staggered timing lets them avoid the rush hour and commute in comfort," he says. "And the late hours give them the flexibility to complete their housework before coming to work."

#### *In Media and Advertising*

In the field of media and advertising, flexitime has always been followed. A large number of public relations firms allow flexitime in India. One of these is Prahlad Kakker's agency, Genesis which has been following flexitime for years now. Kakker says that although the official time to start work is 9.30 am, very few of his employees come in before 11.30 am. "My office has people coming and going at different times of the day," he explains" each employee has his own individual responsibility to fulfill, for which he/she chooses his/her own time of working. I attract talent by maintaining flexibility. I have no objection to their schedules as long as they deliver the goods as and when I want."

*In Education*

Though not very popular in the field of education, the system is incepted in some educational institutions. Colleges like the SNDT at Ghatkopar, Mumbai, require teachers to put in six hours every day, as per thier convenience, any time between 8 am and 6 pm, thus giving a leeway of four hours. (Obviously, the actual lecture hours form the core hours when lecturers are expected to be around).

Flexitime, though though not very popular conept, and applied by selective companies, needs attention from the hardcore corporate sector, since many professions look upon extra hours as part of the job, especially at the senior level.

## 3. Downsizing

Downsizing refers to the planned elimination of positions or jobs with the intention to cut costs and to improve organizational performance. Also known as rightsizing, reorganization, restructuring, and rationalization downsizing, it is a technostructural organization development intervention, that ranges from a mere headcount reduction to a part of a continuous corporate renewal process through which the organization is reinvented. Reducing head count causes organizations to lose human capital, and be left with unhappy and overworked employees as the remaining employees have to do perform tasks for which they are not trained.

Downsizing remains an attractive option for many organizations since it creates the impression that decisions are made and actions are being taken.

Some experts believe that downsizing is handled in different ways. According to Hopkins and Hopkins (1999), while top management has a moral obligation to act in the best interests of the firm, they also have a legal obligation to protect the rights of employees. To achieve the latter end, the decision of downsizing should be communicated in a timely and appropriate manner with the provision of complete information.

Appelbaum and Donia (2001) suggest that organisations should minimize the negative outcomes of downsizing. They maintain that organisations should carefully review their decision to downsize: Indeed, this option should be resorted to only if other alternatives such as job sharing, pay freezes, wage cuts, and hiring freezes are not feasible. Moreover, the downsizing should be planned on a long term basis so that only those positions and functions that are clearly redundant are targeted. Thus, the .organization does not lose employees who are critical to its survival.

The.involvement of employees in the downsizing process cannot be compromised. Thus, two-way and honest communication must be practiced at all times.

# Employee Empowerment and Involvement

## EMPLOYEE EMPOWERMENT

The prime objective of empowerment is allocation of power between management and employees in such a way that employees' commitment can be enhanced. Managers in contemporary organisations advocate performance improvement through employee empowerment and decentralization.

Individuals feel empowered when they perceive and possess power to adequately cope with events, situations, or people they confront. According to Thomas and Velthouse (1990), an employee feels empowered due to a meaningful job, gaining confidence to perform the task, degree of autonomy in decision-making, and perceives that the job and individual performance have a positive and vital impact on the organisation.

Job autonomy is said to have significant and positive relation to organisational commitment and performance. Employee empowerment is reflected in job satisfaction, enhanced morale and improved performance which is ultimately in long-run interest of the organizations. The firms' objectives can be achieved easily.

Again, it is essential that employees are allowed to participate both at the shop floor and at higher levels. Participation improves communication and cooperation among members which contributes towards team-building. This results in self-directed work teams who work independently to solve problems or perform an assignment. These self directed work teams make decisions and then act on those decisions. Empowerment opportunities are more important in case of challenging work, rather than routine, repetitive production and service jobs because they create intrinsic motivation. Re-engineering of jobs is a major intervention of employee empowerment. Both work redesign and empowerment generate positive and direct influence on employees' commitment.

For an organisation to be effectively empowered, management must adopt high involvement practices where power, knowledge, information and rewards are shared with employees in the lower levels of the organisational hierarchy. Yukl and Becker (2006) have outlined a few facilitators for effective empowerment: informal organisational structure; flexible, participative and learning culture; reward and recognition system; non-routine and challenging jobs; access to resources and funds; degree of autonomy and selection of leader; leader as a role model; and mutual trust. If managed effectively, leadership can act as an important driver of the empowerment process.

Bogler and Somech (2004) identified six dimensions of empowerment such as: decision-making, professional growth, status, self-efficacy, autonomy and impact. They found professional growth, status and self-efficacy to be significant predictors of organisational and professional commitment.

According to Bramham (1994), a sense of commitment can be developed in employees through the process of de-layering and empowerment. Arnold, Arad, Rhoades and Drasgow (2000) have found that empowering team leaders are giving emphasis to coach, inform, lead by example, show concern, and encourage participative decision-making. Hence, empowered employees report higher job satisfaction, higher level of commitment and fosters innovation and creativity. Commitment has been examined as a determinant of job performance and organisational citizenship behaviour. In fact, the rationale for introducing HR policies is to increase the level of employee commitment so that positive outcomes can ensue.

Thus it can be concluded that work itself, supervision, co-workers as well as pay are found to be important elements that influence the level of employees' commitment. In the same way better career prospects and opportunities for training and education are found to be positively related to commitment. The management should try to focus more on these attributes to enhance commitment of employees.

## EMPLOYEE INVOLVEMENT

Employee involvement defines and describes how business units can improve their performance by cultivating employee interest and dedication. The following steps may be taken by the organizations to arouse employee involvement:

- **Collective Bargaining:** Collective bargaining may be described as a democratic decision making process and an institution for regulating bipartite relations in industry.
- **Joint decision making:** Spreitzer (2007) argued that decisions can better be made by involving those who are likely to be affected by the decision. Employees may participate in goal-setting, deciding the time required to complete a routine task, designing a job, scheduling a job etc.
- **Job enrichment:** Job enrichment is a widely practised empowerment mechanism in high performance organisations because it involves more effective use of skills and knowledge. It makes job more interesting and challenging.
- **Team effort:** Teams responsible for quality of products or services frequently collect data to find out whether performance is taking place in accordance with the standards set ,and, take corrective measures to ensure improved quality, thereby, gaining autonomy and discretion over their job.
- **Goal setting:** When members who have to work for the accomplishment of final goals set production targets and schedules, monitor customers' feedback, get trained for quality improvement and assume ownership, they feel empowered.
- **Employees' suggestions:** Ideas can be generated at any level. But the ones who have to practically work on to it are the best ones to give ideas and suggestions. Individual employees possess innumerable innovative ideas regarding improvement of work methods, material, cost-reduction and time-saving.
- **Periodic discussion with supervisors:** Regular meetings may be conducted at the workplace which provides a platform for the employees to voice their feelings and opinions. Employees should also be encouraged to ask questions and discuss day to day work related problems.
- **Encouraging initiative:** Care must be taken to reward and appreciate the initiatives taken by the employees even though they may not always be successful.
- **Training and development:** Training and upgrading new skills is the need of the hour. These are the means to assist

employees to increase their strength in one or more knowledge areas.

Besides, an empowering organisation emphasizes autonomy, recognition, rewards, management support and encouragement, proper information and individual participation for organisational excellence.

## EFFECTIVE EMPOWERMENT IN ORGANIZATIONS

Psychological empowerment in organizations is the perception by members that they have the opportunity to help determine work roles, accomplish meaningful work and influence important decisions. Over the past several decades an interest in empowerment can be seen in many areas such as motivation, leadership, group processes, decision making and organizational design. Many studies have examined aspects of leadership behavior or management programs that can increase empowerment, and some studies have examined the effects of such determinants on the perceptions of employees and on their performance. As discussed earlier, empowerment is considered important because of the potential benefits that can result from it, including increased commitment, better decisions, improved quality, more innovation, increased morale and increased job satisfaction.

This text will review what was learned about empowerment in the past half century. We will examine the use of empowerment programs by organizations and their effects on performance. We will suggest what needs to be studied in the future and discuss the practical applications of current knowledge for managers and administrators.

## PART I
## THE PAST :
## EMPOWERMENT THEORIES AND RESEARCH

Theories of psychological empowerment attempts to determine the essential components, why empowerment efforts will be successful, and the facilitating conditions in which people will actually experience empowerment at work. The theories cover various aspects as job design, participative leadership, organization structure, organizational culture, employee skills and traits, and leader selection and assessment.

### Components of Psychological Empowerment

Psychological empowerment is usually conceptualized as the enhanced task motivation that results from an individual's positive orientation to the work role. The four factors are meaningfulness, competence, choice, and impact (Thomas & Velthouse, 1990). These four defining factors are described as independent and distinct, yet related and mutually reinforcing.

Meaningfulness is "the value of the task, goal or purpose, judged in relation to the individual's own ideals or standards; the individual's intrinsic caring about a given task". It is analogous to the psychological state of meaningfulness in the job characteristics model of Hackman and Oldham (1980). In psychoanalytic terms, meaningfulness represents a kind of cathexis or investment of psychic energy.

Meaningfulness is described as the "engine" of empowerment, in that meaning energizes individuals to work. Within the empowerment construct, meaningfulness is characterized at the level of specific tasks or projects.

Competence is "the degree to which a person can perform task activities skillfully when he or she tries". The concept is analogous to Bandura's (1986) notion of self-efficacy or personal mastery. Competence refers to the individual's belief in his or her capability to perform work activities with skill. Competence captures the idea that the individual feels capable of successfully performing a particular task or activity.

Choice refers to the causal responsibility for a person's actions and whether behavior is perceived as self-determined. The concept is similar to locus of control. People with a strong internal locus of control orientation believe that events in their lives are determined more by their own actions than by chance, while people with a strong external locus of control orientation believe that events are determined mostly by chance or fate (Rotter, 1966). deCharms (1968) uses the term "locus of causality" and argues that perceiving one's own behavior as the origin (rather than pawn) is the fundamental basis for intrinsic motivation. Ryan (1989) uses the term "self-determination," which is the individual's sense of having a choice of initiating and regulating actions and one's own work. Liden and Tewksbury (1995) describes degree of choice in the work setting as the crux of empowerment. Thomas and Velthouse (1990) characterize choice as different from Rotter's locus of control (which also involves outcome contingencies); however, here we emphasize the similarities and overlap between the two concepts.

Impact is "the degree to which behavior is seen as "making a difference" in terms of accomplishing the purpose of the task, that is, producing intended effects in one's task environment". Impact builds on the concept of locus of control and the belief that one has an influence on organization-level decisions or policy and also on the notion of learned helplessness. Impact is analogous to the psychological state of knowledge of results in Hackman and Oldham (1980). Ashforth (1989) characterizes impact as the degree to which an individual can influence strategic, administrative, or operating outcomes at work.

## Job Design and Intrinsic Motivation

Empowerment opportunities are limited when employees perform routine, repetitive production or service jobs. There is more potential for meaningful work and self-determination in jobs that have complex tasks and are challenging. Thus, socio-technical systems designed with flexible technology encourage employee empowerment. Customer service jobs are more empowering when the business strategy allows customized and personalized attention and employees have longer interactions and continuing relationships with the same customers.

The job characteristics model believes that routine and overly specialized jobs are de-motivating. Jobs can be made more intrinsically motivating by redesigning work so that employees have control over tasks typically performed by supervisors. Five characteristics are essential to all jobs in order to have intrinsically motivating work. *Task identity,* i.e. the degree to which the individual performs a whole piece of work. *Task significance,* i.e. the degree to which the job has a substantial impact on the lives of others. *Skill variety,* i.e. the degree to which the job requires different skills of workers. *Autonomy,* i.e. the degree to which individuals feel personally responsible for their work. *Feedback,* i.e. the degree to which the job provides information on level of task accomplishment.

The five characteristics of jobs contribute to three critical psychological states in the individual: *experienced meaningfulness* of the work, experienced *responsibility for outcomes of work*, and *knowledge of the actual results of work* activities. Employees experience intrinsic motivation when the work generates these three psychological states. Outcomes of the job characteristics model include high internal work motivation, high growth satisfaction, high general satisfaction and high work effectiveness (Hackman & Oldham, 1980). Greater autonomy is linked to psychologically experiencing responsibility for work, which is linked to increased job satisfaction. Several decades of research investigating job characteristics in organizations have provided a great deal of support for this model; job characteristics are the most consistent situational predictors of job satisfaction in employees.

More than 90 percent of Fortune 1000 companies have made increases in job autonomy.

## Participative Leadership

Employees can be encouraged and facilitated to participate by involving others when making decisions that affect them. This may potentially improve the quality of decision making in the workplace, and help to improve the acceptance of decisions and employee satisfaction with the decision-making process. Besides, decision making skills of employees can be developed. Four basic types of decision procedures can be arranged on a continuum from no influence by others to high level of influence; these processes are autocratic, consultative, joint, and delegation. Autocratic decisions are made by the leader without asking for the opinions of others, so there is no participation. Consultative decisions are ones in which the leader asks others for opinions and ideas, i.e. subordinates are consulted but the final decision is taken by the superior alone, after considering others' views.

Joint decisions, as the name suggests, are made together by the leader and other relevant parties such as subordinates. Delegation means that the leader gives an individual or group the authority and responsibility to make a decision.

Even in participative leadership difference exists between the leaders who "tell" others of decisions made, and leaders who "sell" others by using influence tactics such as rational persuasion and inspirational appeals. Again, it should be kept in mind that there is a big difference between involvement in the decision process and true influence and empowerment. For example, we recall working with a manager who used a decision style that involved presenting hypothetical work situations, usually involving some demeaning or onerous task that was about to be imposed on his workgroup. Involving the team in the so-called decision process seemed transparently manipulative to team members, and contributed to employees feeling disempowered and unmotivated. Ultimately, many team members left the organization.

Despite the intuitive appeal of participative leadership, research fails to provide strong, consistent evidence that it improves the performance of a leader's unit. After 40 years of research, we can only conclude that sometimes participative leadership results in higher satisfaction, effort and performance at work, and sometimes it does not (Yukl, 2006). To explain why participative leadership is more effective in some situations than others requires a contingency model. The normative decision theory (Vroom & Yetton, 1973) identifies specific situations where participation can be effective. Five decision procedures are identified for decision making involving leaders and multiple subordinates: two types of autocratic decisions, two types of consultation and one type of joint decision making. The effectiveness of these decision procedures is contingent upon specific factors, such as the amount of information possessed by the leader, the likelihood that subordinates will accept the decision, and the extent to which the problem is unstructured and requires creative problem solving. The normative decision process model is one of the best supported theories of leadership, and it provides important and specific clues to developing empowerment.

### Organization Structure, Reward Systems, and Access to Information

Organizations with Centralization can limit the opportunities for managers to use job enrichment and delegation with direct reports. Organizations with formal structures and standardized rules and procedures for work performance also impede empowerment. Conversely, decentralized organizations that compete on the basis of customized products and services provide more opportunities for employees to take initiative in determining how to do the work.

Decentralization emphasizes on building more democratic organizations and redistributing power to all levels in the organizational hierarchy. Empowerment is increased by employee access to information, funds, materials, and facilities needed to do the work effectively. Employees that have more access to information about the mission and performance of the organization experience more empowerment. Successful empowerment may require management programs and systems that share information, knowledge, and rewards with employees at all levels (Lawler, 1996).

### Organizational Culture and Empowerment Values

Shared values, beliefs, and norms held by members of an organization are known as organizational culture. A supportive culture that values employees and their contributions to the organizational goals facilitates empowerment. Creative problem solving is supported by an organizational culture with strong values for information sharing, fair and constructive judgment of ideas, and reward and recognition for new ideas (Amabile, 1997). In contrast, a culture that only emphasizes traditional approaches and avoidance of mistakes discourages creative problem solving.

### Employee Skills and Traits

There is some evidence that employee characteristics are related to empowerment. The responsiveness of employees to opportunities for more responsibility and participation is greater when they have a high level of achievement motivation, high self confidence and self-efficacy, and an internal locus of control orientation (Argyris, 1998 Rotter, 1966).

In general, employees with higher levels of education, tenure and skill experience more feelings of empowerment. However, recent findings are somewhat contradictory. Some study says that sales employees with low levels of knowledge and experience benefited the most from empowering leader behaviors, while high-knowledge and experienced employees reaped no clear benefit. Similarly, Leach, Wall and Jackson (2003) found that an empowerment intervention increased job knowledge substantially in less experienced (rather than more experienced) machine operators. One potential benefit of empowerment is to "facilitate cognitive growth and awareness through the transfer of knowledge among individuals who might not otherwise share information". Organizations that invest in building employee skills, achievement orientation, and self confidence can increase the likelihood of successful empowerment.

### Leader Selection and Assessment

'Power corrupts, and absolute power corrupts absolutely' is applicable in most organizations. Thus, empowerment is more likely when leaders are elected for limited time periods, a practice often seen in voluntary organizations, professional associations, and democratic political units, such as city councils, school boards, and state legislatures. Such a practice provides another way to prevent leaders from accumulating too much power relative to subordinates. Private organizations seldom use this method, even though in many cases it would be feasible to appoint leaders for a specified time period or to use a hybrid form of selection. Regardless of the method of selection of leader, influence is greater (and more empowerment occurs) when members participate actively in assessing leader performance, especially when they are able to remove leaders with unsatisfactory performance.

## PART 2
## THE PRESENT : USE AND EFFECTIVENESS OF EMPOWERMENT PROGRAMS

In this section we will describe several different types of management programs used by organizations to increase empowerment. Yet, it may vary from country to country; and from organization to organization within the country.

### Employee Stock Ownership Plans

This is a revolutionary concept. In the United States, formal empowerment programs are found in many corporations which includes employee stock ownership programs, open-book management, and self-managed teams. To establish an employee stock-ownership plan (ESOP), a company creates a trust and contributes money or stock to it. These contributions are tax-deductible, and stock is allocated to individual employees based on seniority and compensation. Over eight million employees in over eleven thousand companies participate in such plans. ESOPs should not be confused with stock option plans that grant employees the right to buy company's shares at a specified price once the option has vested. Stock options can be given to as few or as many employees as the company desires, but ESOPs must include all full-time employees.

For ESOPs to promote empowerment, and be effective in real sense, employee shareholders must have a real voice in the way a company is being managed. One company that has achieved synergy between employee ownership and participation in decision making is Reflexite Technology Corporation, which manufactures reflective materials. At Reflexite employees are taught to understand financial terms so they can discern how company performance relates to bonus and dividend payments. Instilling ownership awareness at Reflexite also extends beyond teaching employees to read financial statements. All of the skill training is linked to owner-awareness training.

## Sharing Information

As a part of employee empowerment program, it is necessary to share information about business performance, plans, goals, and strategies. It is difficult to expect employees to make meaningful contributions to the success of the organization unless they have access to basic operating information. While organizations are making increasing efforts in this area, there is still a tremendous opportunity for greater sharing of business information with employees, particularly information about business operating results, competitors' performance, business plans and goals, and new technologies. Many public corporations, for example, provide only the financial information that the law requires tobe shared to shareholders in annual reports.

One more such program to empower employees through communication and learning is known as open-book management. As the name suggests, top management "opens the books" to employees to give them a clear understanding of financial information, such as revenues, profits, costs etc. For this type of program to be successful, however, it involves more than just sharing financial information with employees; it also requires training that will enable employees to understand, analyze and interpret the information and use it to improve company's performance. A good example is provided by Springfield ReManufacturing Corp. The CEO tries to ensure that all employees receive weekly financial information about the company and are able to understand it. Managers in each department provide informal training on a specific item and explain to employees how it is determined and how it affects the performance of the organization.

## Sharing Power through Parallel Structures

Empowerment of the employees through power sharing is the need of the hour. This process involves moving decision making downward in the organizational hierarchy. Problem solving activities and special meetings are typically held outside of normal work processes. Such empowerment activities are also known as parallel structures. Popular forms of parallel structures include quality circles, employee participation groups, quality-of-work-life groups, survey feedback, and suggestion systems.

In sharing power through parallel structures, employees are asked to provide input and recommendations though they are not typically given substantial power of decision making. This is a distinct limitation of this method. Recently, many organizations have started making use of such techniques. However, parallel structures are typically limited to fewer than half of the employees in the organizations that use them. The most successful parallel structures are survey feedback and employee participation groups. They are relatively easy to introduce and require no fundamental organizational change. As such they can produce positive results in many types of situations. There is some evidence that employee participation groups, survey feedback, and suggestion systems work better when they are part of an overall pattern of practices that involve employee empowerment.

## Self-managed Teams

Another type of program seen recently in the organizations, for increasing empowerment is the use of self-managed teams. Implementing this system requires more structural change in the organization than the parallel structures discussed above. Seventy-nine percent of Fortune 1000 companies and 81 percent of manufacturing organizations have implemented teams with some degree of self management (Nagle and Ward, 1997). Unlike traditional work units where a formal manager usually makes all the key decisions, members of self managed teams meet at regular intervals to determine how to do the work and who will do each task. The team has a leader to conduct meetings and coordinate activities, and this leadership role may be rotated among qualified members. The parent organization usually determines the mission, scope of operations, and the budget for self-managed teams. Of course, the amount of authority the team has for other types of decisions varies greatly from one organization to another, and in many cases, from time to time in the same organization. Each team is usually given authority and responsibility for operating decisions such as setting performance goals and quality standards, assigning work, dealing with customers and suppliers, determining work schedules, determining work procedures, making purchases of necessary supplies and materials, evaluating team member performance, handling performance problems of individual members and so on. For small expenditure for suppliers and equipment, the teams are usually allowed to make decisions without prior approval, but in most organizations any recommendations for large purchases must be approved by management. Sometimes self-managed teams are also given the primary responsibility for personnel decisions such as selecting, hiring and firing team members and determining pay rates (within specified limits).

Greater autonomy, variety of tasks, satisfied employees with lower turnover and absenteeism are major advantages of self-managed work teams. Having team members cross-trained to do different jobs increases the flexibility of the team in dealing with personnel shortages resulting from illness or turnover. Increased knowledge of work processes helps team members solve problems and suggest improvements. Employees who can make decisions and initiate changes are more likely to take responsibility for their work and may be more motivated to produce a high-quality product or service. This ultimately helps in improving productivity and reduce costs.

The Miller Beer facility in Trenton, Ohio, is an example of an organization built on team principles. This "brewery of the future" uses cross-functional and self-directed teams of 6 to 19 people to manage every aspect of the brewing, packaging, and distribution process. Team responsibilities include administration, personnel, safety, quality, productivity, and maintenance. Employees have access to information of every aspect of the competitive brewery business. The team approach has yielded a 30 percent increase in productivity in comparison to Miller's other plants, turnover is less than seven percent and absenteeism is less than two percent. The Trenton facility has received several awards as an innovative union operation. Managers attribute its success to the team design, as the plant's physical operating features are identical to its other plants.

The potential advantages of this program are realized on its effective implementation. However, self-managed teams are difficult to implement, and they can be a dismal failure when used in inappropriate situations or without competent leadership and adequate top management support. When used in an appropriate way, self-managed teams can increase member commitment and improve quality and productivity.

Self-managed teams are most appropriate for complex, self-contained projects that require a high level of initiative, skill, and motivation, and where individual efforts cannot help in accomplishing tasks. These teams, however, are not appropriate for independent tasks that are performed individually by employees rather than by a team. Other facilitating conditions for the effectiveness of self-managed teams include : (1) clearly defined objectives, (2) a complex and meaningful task, (3) a small team size and stable membership, (4) substantial team discretion over work processes, (5) access to relevant information, (6) appropriate recognition and rewards, (7) strong support by top management, (8) members who have strong interpersonal skills, and (9) a competent external leader who serves as a liaison with formal management and other teams.

### Democratic Decision Processes

Employees generally prefer democratic style of leadership and as such organizations prefer increasing empowerment by allowing members to elect and remove leaders and/or to have representatives on key decision making bodies. For example, many American universities often have a faculty senate with elected representatives who share authority for some types of decisions. In addition, the academic departments often have a chairperson with a defined term of office who is elected (or nominated) by department faculty. Voluntary organizations and local governments often have elected officers who are required to hold open hearings on major decisions, disclose budgets and financial transactions, and obtain member approval for increased assessments.

More extreme examples of industrial democracy can be found but are rare. The Glacier Metal company in London presents a unique case of employee democracy that survived for three decades (Heller, 2003). Glacier conducted monthly consultative meetings with employees from all levels of the company in issues involving individual employee and group problems. The elected employee representatives had complete veto power over any decision.

Germany, for example, a legal concept known as codetermination gives unions 50 percent membership on supervisory boards; the regulation has been in effect in the coal, iron, and steel industry since 1951. In some European countries, the board of directors for a company is required by law to include members representing employees, and some organizations have an employee council with elected representatives from different subunits, thus paving way for democratic style of leadership. In some employee-owned companies, the employees select top management and can vote to replace them if their performance is not satisfactory (Heller, 2000).

The Brazilian company Semco has diverse products and services, unique market niches, rising profits, highly motivated employees, and low turnover. There is no fixed CEO and board membership is open to any employee, with seats filled on a first-come-first-served basis. Workers choose their own training and can select jobs or projects that fit their interests. The company culture values democracy, open communications, constructive dissent, innovation, and the development of employees. The company believes in the theory of employees' job satisfaction for accomplishment of company's goals.

## Effectiveness of Empowerment Programs

In many cases, empowerment programs are often abandoned after an initial period when they do not produce the expected benefits. In some cases, companies terminated programs even after they increased employee satisfaction and performance. The following quote reveals the dilemmas posed by many empowerment programs.

*Many companies are attracted by a fantasy version of empowerment and simultaneously repelled by the reality. How lovely to have energetic, dedicated workers who always seize the initiative (but only when "appropriate"), who enjoy taking risks (but never risky ones), who volunteer their ideas (but only brilliant ones), who solve problems on their own (but make no mistakes), who aren't afraid to speak their minds (but never ruffle any feathers), who always give their very best to the company (but ask no unpleasant questions about what the company is giving them back). How nice it would be, in short, to empower workers without giving them any power.*

## Reasons for Failure

There are a variety of possible reasons for the lack of greater empowerment in companies and the relatively low level of success.

1. **Empowerment represents change.** Empowerment calls for change. True empowerment requires that managers relinquish some of their control to employees. Managers may have some apprehensions and may be afraid to delegate responsibility and power. Some managers are threatened by programs that would reduce their power and exalted status as heroic leaders. Managers need organizational support and training in empowering leadership behaviors in order to make empowerment efforts succeed.
2. **Empowerment takes time.** Transition is a long term process. Shifting from a command and control culture to employee empowerment requires a commitment to long-term change. Too often, management fads and quick fixes in the name of empowerment that have been implemented rather than relevant changes in management systems, structures, and cultural values. To be successful, empowerment must be seen as a long-term program of employee participation and involvement.
3. **Employees may resist empowerment.** There is a general tendency for employees to resist change. Employees may have been conditioned over the years to follow orders, not collaborate with management. Being given greater responsibility may induce fear of the unknown and insecurity in some employees. For empowerment efforts to succeed, employee development and training must include an overall plan with small steps toward empowerment.

A recent effort to implement self-managed teams provides an example of the difficulties (Becker & Mathieu, 2003). A Fortune 100 company opened a consumer products facility with the vision of incorporating state-of-the-art technology and a culture of empowered work teams. Employees were carefully selected and trained in team skills. But installation of the new equipment created unanticipated and lengthy delays. By the time the technology was up and running, it was too late; managers who supported the team culture were gone and corporate support for the team vision had eroded.

In summary, employee empowerment as a part of management program has been popular for at least 50 years, and there are many different empowerment programs and procedures. Despite all the rhetoric surrounding empowerment programs, however, they seldom achieve the potential benefits expected for them (Argyris, 1998). Any substantial increase in psychological empowerment requires top management support for major changes in the organization.

## PART 3
## THE FUTURE: WHAT NEEDS TO BE STUDIED

This section looks to the future and highlight areas that need to be further examined in research on psychological empowerment.

### Definition: The Many Faces of Empowerment

Inconsistencies remain in the conceptualization of empowerment. For example, we still lack clarity in the number of factors that comprise empowerment. Psychological empowerment has most typically been described in the literature as the compilation of four factors (meaningfulness, competence, choice, and impact), but issues of construct specification remain. Levels of analysis issues are also apparent. It is not clear whether the dimensions of empowerment are the same for individual employees, for groups, and for organizations. We need greater precision in the description of the construct of psychological empowerment, in order to provide clarity for management implementation and practice. Much of the lack of clarity is related to the wide diversity of uses of the term. Empowerment runs the gamut from worker perceptions of how they are treated to how teams, organizations, and even governments are run. The distinction between formal, normative structures and informal, face-to-face empowerment is not trivial (Wilpert, 1984). It is unrealistic to think that the same issues operate the same way at all of these levels of analysis. Empowerment is a broad concept and more precision is needed in its definition and measurement. We must move beyond narrowly focused, cross-sectional research toward more multilevel and systems approaches.

### Facilitating Conditions for Empowerment

More clarity is also needed about the conditions that determine whether empowerment will be effective. Results from empirical studies are too inconsistent to provide strong conclusions about the likely consequences. While much of the literature on the guidelines and facilitating conditions for effective empowerment is based on common sense and practitioners' insights, there is little systematic research to support them. Thus, results are quite inadequate.

Self-managed teams as a source of psychological empowerment can be quite successful. While teams are more difficult to implement and operate successfully, in comparison to other practices, they also offer greater rewards.

### Compatibility between Different Types of Empowerment

Organizations need greater understanding of the compatibility and 'fit' between different types of empowerment. This remains an important research issue for all types of empowerment at all levels of the organization. For example, research is needed on the effectiveness of leader empowering behaviors at the individual, team, and organizational level. In addition, research is needed to evaluate how these behaviors contribute to the overall effectiveness of the organization.

We remain hopeful because there are representative organizations in many industries that embrace principles of employee empowerment. Genentech prides itself on its low-key, nonhierarchical culture as a competitive advantage in the biotech industry. Genentech scientists are encouraged to take chances and pursue their research passions, even if they are long-term and high-risk. Ninety-five percent of Genentech employees are stockholders and it was recently ranked the best company to work for (Fortune, 2006). Southwest Airlines, Nucor, W.L. Gore and Associates, Xilinx, Harley-Davidson, UPS, Costco, and Alcoa all lead their industries as high-involvement, high-wage, high-profit companies (O'Toole & Lawler, 2006). The common denominator is that these companies share a business model that involves employees in decision making, rewards employees fairly, and provides training and career opportunities. As a result, these companies demonstrate higher productivity than workers in comparable low-wage companies. When workers have the opportunity to participate in decision making, training, profit-sharing, and stock ownership, they are more productive and this productivity offsets costs for higher salaries and benefits

## PART 4
## ACTIONS :
## HOW MANAGERS CAN BE MORE EMPOWERING

Despite mixed reviews of empowerment efforts at the organization level, there is real evidence that suggests that organizations can achieve benefits from empowering their employees.

### Guidelines for Managers

Research on participation and the normative decision process model suggests several tentative guidelines.

(1) Managers must study the type of employees, i.e. they should accurately diagnose whether participation of employees in the decision process is feasible. Identifying appropriate situations primarily involves as assessment of the importance

and intensity of the decision, the relevant participants in the decision, the likelihood of cooperation and acceptance of the decision, and whether it is practical to gather the participants together in a meeting to make the decision.

(2) Active support of managers to employees in the decision-making process is inevitable. One strategy is to describe initial proposals as tentative, and to solicit opinions on ideas as they are formulated. Managers must learn how to elicit ideas from everyone, even members who are hesitant to speak up. Managers must use good listening skills and avoid becoming defensive when participants express legitimate concerns. The ability to model leader behaviors, such as building on others' ideas, will help all to participate in the discussion.

(3) Managers must never miss to express sincere appreciation for the efforts of others, in order to build an environment of participation.

(4) Above all, training to develop different skills should be imparted at regular intervals.

(5) In order to determine what to delegate, managers should consider the task itself and the actor. Tasks that can be better performed by the subordinate should be delegated. Tasks related to the person's career should be delegated. Tasks not central to the manager 's role should be delegated. Both pleasant and unpleasant tasks, as well as tasks of the appropriate difficulty, should be delegated. But care should be taken to see that delegated responsibilities must be clear to the subordinate, with adequate authority and limits imposed. Progress toward goals should be monitored, as appropriate, such that the delegated activity becomes a positive learning experience for the subordinate. Others in the organization must be informed and reporting relationships must be specified in advance.

(6) Managers must learn from their mistakes. Research in psychological empowerment makes it evident that participative leadership and delegation are not the only types of leadership behavior that can make people feel empowered. Other types of leadership behaviors can directly affect psychological empowerment, and these behaviors may also enhance the effects of participative leadership and delegation.

(7) Managers must involve people in the decisions that will ultimately affect them, as people will have more interest in getting involved in matters of importance to them personally. Managers need to take into consideration the individual differences in the people in their workgroup, as variability in ability and motivation will impact involvement. Providing access to relevant information and resources will contribute to the likelihood of successful empowerment. Removing unnecessary bureaucratic controls and constraints will ease successful completion of tasks.

## CONCLUSION

As we disentangle 50 years of research on empowerment, it is apparent that there is much we have yet to learn. Empowerment remains an elusive concept. Part of the problem is definitional; all too often management initiatives evoke the name of empowerment when the initiatives are not truly empowering. The most common definition of psychological empowerment in the research literature includes the four factors of meaningfulness, competence, choice, and impact.

This is a good start, but we need greater precision and we need to have more clarity while putting it into practice.

It has been useful to differentiate between behaviors or programs to enhance empowerment and actual perception of empowerment by employees. Consistency between programs and perception is the need of the hour.

Managers need to use multiple sources of information and frequent checkups to be sure that their empowerment initiatives truly result in employees feeling empowered. The complexity of the construct of empowerment confounds many organizational attempts to increase it. In order to be sustained, empowerment needs to be part of the long-term strategy of the organization. Empowerment initiatives should be guided by the dual objectives of improving organizational effectiveness and improving the quality of work life for employees. Too often empowerment programs have been viewed as a simple way to motivate employees to do more. Ethical issues and long-term effects on employees must become part of the landscape for our empowerment efforts in the future.

# 12 Team Working and Team Building Strategies

## INTRODUCTION TO TEAM

The most obvious aspects of partnerships is that individual members bring different skills, interests, and perspectives to the shared vision. Though it is true that every member of the collaboration may not work on every aspect of the community policing initiative, but it is critical that all partners are informed, feel included, and have a sense of ownership of the entire effort. It is important to recognize that merely involving a group of individuals in an effort does not make that group a team. Decision making authority, power, responsibility, and credit should be shared in a team effort to make teams effective. This may also help the partners to build commitment and a sense of accomplishment. Based on the expertise inventory of the partners, roles and responsibilities should be designated.

Having efficient team building strategies is one of the surest and more successful ways to grow and achieve the goals of your company. the diet solution program in today's corporate world. Many businesses and corporations that understand the worth of team working invests in bringing all members of the team closer together so that they are able to function as a single unit for the same, mutual purpose. However, the strategies of work team building are often tough to frame and to implement. Here the head of training department would want to come up with unique Work Team Building ideas that are easy to implement in the organization.

One thing that has to be kept in mind is that all work team-building efforts always do not pay off the way you expect them to and it becomes necessary for managers to analyze all the reasons for it. First, members of team need to understand exactly why they are a part of the work team building and what role they are expected to play. Then right resources and motivation tools are to be provided. For instance, many firms employ professional Work Team Building experts and trainers for this purpose. The work team building activities and exercises that members will be made to do should be relevant and work towards creating values like team spirit, cooperation, patience and sportsman spirit in the exercises as well as in the workplace. As a part of motivation interesting activities like sports that all members of the team are genuinely interested in, should be provided.

In all of the work team building exercises, it is very important to simulate the office atmosphere by assigning responsibilities and allowing team members to devise strategies to achieve their goal which should be made clear to them as well. One more aspect of Work Team Building activities is having communication between all team members. This will directly reflect the relationship of the members in the office. It is essential that members are open, welcoming and patient towards the input and feedback of all members on the team.

Flexibility and ability of employees to adapt to cultural and organizational changes is highly essential for Work team building activities. This can help to bring out the creative side of employees, apart from having a certain drive and motivation that would help them to work towards the objectives of the company.

## TEAM BUILDING TRAINING

Teamwork may take the organization towards progress or it may completely ruin it. Having an effective team is the base of success, being able to work together as a team to achieve organizational goals while maintaining positive energy and trust. Nothing is more important than to share such features when you work together as a group. It is essential that each member in the team shares a culture of positivity and trust.

Getting people together and making them do specific tasks is not what teamwork is all about. Actually, the core element of such a structure is bringing people together and getting them to work towards a common objective. Different types of exercises and team building activities are required here. Team building training can thus be introduced. Team building training here is something that helps to train everyone individually as well as collectively to work in a team. This ensures that your work is going to be smooth and issue-free.

The teams can function successfully only when members put aside their differences for the sake of combined success. There should not be anyone trying to overshadow others and neither should there be any jealousy afloat in the team. This a manager has to teach while training. Team building training can be performed by many activities involving games. Games are a good way to have fun with your team as well as to improve aspects like communication, motivation and coordination amongst one another.

Now we shall discuss some different games that teams can play to improve their performance as a team. One of these games is **minefield**. Minefield makes you spread out different items across a room or any outdoor location that you like. Pairs will be made from the team members, so if one person is left out, s/he can be assigned as the coach of the game. Therefore, now that everyone is in pairs, one partner will be blindfolded and the other will guide the blinded partner verbally around the "minefield" to a specific finish point. The other technique requires the team members to think a little more than usual. The challenge here is to create the most inspirational and encouraging quote, and helps for better results at the end for real life problems.

## TEAM BUILDING GAMES

Team building games that fosters trust are highly effective. It is important that every member trusts one another and they are on the same level once it comes to getting the job done. This obviously paves way for encouragement. Encouragement is being and having the support of your peers to get the job done, effectively and efficiently. Encouragement is brought by your team members pushing you and persuading you to complete any given task. This brings a boost of confidence as well as shoots the level of your morale up. Motivating one another will get you all to work even harder than you previously were. Team building games are a way to create cohesiveness. Though Team building is a time consuming process, but the results you get in the end will be exactly what you want and worth all the effort. Building cohesiveness in your team will help to tackle any barriers of communication, encourage the team to indulge in discussions, induce commitment of members and increase their potential productivity. Team building games can do all of these. Team building games aid the members to improve their motivation and are simply fun. Thus, it is 'learn and fun' as such.

The **relay lock race** is a fun game. In this game, each person will select a partner and your team will have an even number of members otherwise one of you will be left alone. Each partner has to stand back-to- back and lock their arms from their elbows. Moreover, while this is done, they hold their own stomach using their hands. The coach, who can be played by the odd-numbered group member, has to give directions to get from one side of the playing area to the other. A specific set of orders should not be given because then they will not be able to improvise. This game not only helps to create laughter, but it also enhances creativity.

Another useful game is that of **"Truths and a Lie"**. In this game, each member of the group writes two facts about himself as well as one lie on a card and submits it to a coach. The coach then collects the card and reads it aloud to everyone. The rest of the team will try and guess who is being mentioned in the card.

## TEAM WORK CHALLENGES

Working in a team is an challenging task. There are so many different things that you need to keep in mind in order to prevent any problems or complications amongst the team members. Being capable and having the ability to be able to work in a team is considered a marketable skill that is highly valued. However, there are times when group work can get tedious. The members are recommended here to stay determined throughout and maintain the objective of overcoming any challenge that may come in the achievement of prime objective. Further care is taken to ensure a sound working environment amongst other team members.

Here it is necessary that members of the group meet regularly and discuss the issues in detail. Each member should be made to realize his individual as well as collective role. Problems are inevitable in the organizations.

In the end, it will not matter whether there were any difficulties in the group or not, the only thing that will matter is whether the issues were managed properly and whether the tasks were accomplished or not. Again, flexibility is of utmost important. Everyone in the group needs to be able to work according to the group rather than being stubborn and continuing to do the work the way they want. There is no "I" in team; everyone should be given importance and no one should be given priority over others, they should only get appreciation for doing a good job.

Once you start working in a team, members need to become one. There should be no differences or disputes. Each and every member of the team should be confident. None should be hesitant. Environment should be such that each one feels free to express his thoughts because useful ideas and suggestions can click to anyone at any time. No body should hesitate to seek help when required. Effective teams are something that companies worldwide strive. People should be willing and able to work together to achieve a unified goal. It is important that a team is optimistic and full of positive energy rather than jealousy, hatred and negligence as negativity like this usually brings a fall.

## TEAM BUILDING

Team building is a combination of strategies designed to build strong interpersonal relationships develop understanding of, and commitment to, team goals.

Common characteristics of team building experiences include unified efforts on tasks that:

- are unfamiliar;
- need a high level of cooperation to complete;
- need team members to rely on each other in ways that are not normally required in the everyday working environment, generating trust, mutual respect, rapport and support beyond what is commonly found in the workplace.

### Why Team Building?

The most important advantage of team is the increased productivity in a workplace. Teams that function well ensure the wellbeing of an organization. Differences and diversity of the members are accepted and employed in such a way that they become mutually supportive of each other's strengths and help building synergy in the organization.

Team members need to support each other at times when some or any of them experience any sort of disability or health condition, including mental illness.

### Team Building Process

The team building has to pass through the processes discussed below:

#### *(1) Problem Sensing*

(i) Often team itself defines which aspect of team building it wishes to work on.

(ii) The problem can be better identified in terms of what is hindering the general effectiveness.

(iii) Discussion among the members with different arguments as to what the real problem is may creep at this stage. It could be related to the organisation or person, etc.

(iv) The emphasis should be on consensus.

#### *(2) Examining Perceptual Differences*

Effective communication is required at this stage because it will help in classifying the actual problems to the members.

### *(3) Giving and Receiving Feedback*

Feedback helps members in evaluating and understanding themselves.

### *(4) Developing Interaction Skills*

Working in teams invariably calls for increasing the ability among the members to interact with one another and engage in constructive behaviour. Examples of constructive behaviour could be : Developing the ideas of others, encouraging others, understanding them etc. Examples of negative behaviour could be: Interrupting, criticising, undermining people. Regular discussion on developing interactive skills will encourage people to indulge in constructive behaviour and leave negative behaviour.

### *(5) Follow up Action*

(i) At this stage the total team is convened to review what has been learned and to identity the next step.

(ii) It involves overcoming any drawbacks.

(iii) It also involves deciding the role and responsibilities of members.

## TEAM EFFECTIVENESS

An effective team is one which contributes to the achievement of organizational objectives by performing the task assigned to it and providing satisfaction to its members.

### Factors Affecting Team Effectiveness

1. **Skills and role clarity**: Roles of each and every member of the team should be clear and specific. Skills are relevant for job performance.
2. **Supportive environment**: The environment in which members are supported to work needs to be conginial and supportive.
3. **Superordinate goals**: These are those goals which are above the goals of a single team or an individual. These goals serve to focus attention, in efforts and stimulate more cohesive team efforts.
4. **Team rewards**: Financial and Non-financial incentives help in motivating team members, thus positively influencing the performance and efficiency of team members.

### Difference between Teams and Work Groups

(a) The work group has a strong, clearly focused leader. The team has shared leadership roles.

(b) The work group has individual accountability. The team has individual as well as collective accountability.
(c) The goals of work groups are same as that of the organization, while teams may have their independent goals.
(d) The work group has individual work products. Team has collective work products.
(e) The work group measures effectiveness indirectly e.g. Financial performance of overall business. Team measures performance directly by assessing collective products.
(f) The work group runs efficient meetings. The team encourages open ended problem solving meetings.

## TEAM FUNCTIONS

Many organizations, now-a-days, have started resorting to team building just because this concept has become quite popular in the corporate world.. This is obviously a wrong reason. This practice should be introduced to get the positive benefits that can result from a team based environment, which may result in enhanced performance, employee benefits, reduced costs, organisational enhancements etc. Teams are associated with the following functions.

### (1) Orientation

The team socializes the members in the organization by making them aware of the work norms, work climate, social and formal relations, status and roles. Besides, this method infuses a sense of belongingness.

### (2) Cost Reduction

Empowered teams reduce scrap, make fewer errors, file fewer worker's compensation claims, and reduce absenteeism and turnover. Hence organizations based on teams show significant cost reductions. Team members feel that they have a stake in the outcomes so they are more committed to the team and its functioning thereby reducing cost.

### (3) Increased Motivation

Teams encourage employee involvement, thereby making the job more interesting for the members. Individuals are likely to perform better when they are working in a teams because they feel that their contribution is being valued. There is, in effect, enhanced ownership for the job.

### (4) Synergy

Diversity of the members in teams have the potential to create higher levels of productivity due to positive synergy created by them.

The output or the performance of the team is normally better than the sum of the outputs of individuals comprising the teams.

### (5) Creation of Social Life

Members of the team need to work collectively in both formal as well as informal groups. In the absence of informal groups, the organisational climate would be miserable and boring.

### (6) Increased Innovation and Flexibility

An important improvement in the organisation that results from moving from a hierarchically based, directive culture to a team based culture, includes increased innovation, creativity and flexibility. This system discards bureaucracy and flattens the hierarchy thereby bringing employees closer to the top management. Cross training is imparted to the members of the team. The feeling of importance and empowerment make teams more flexible and responsive to changing events than in case of traditional set ups. Teams have the capability to quickly assemble, deploy, refocus and disband. All this can happen because teams focus on processes rather than functions.

### (7) Teaching

The team teaches to its members how to perform their tasks, how to behave and conduct themselves, and how to get things done. Such learning obviously has a positive effect on the job performance.

### (8) Improved Quality of Work Life

Organizations as well as employees, both, tend to benefit in a team environment. Teams can provide a sense of self worth and self fulfilment that current and future workers seem to strive for. Rather than relying on the traditional, hierarchical manager based system, teams give employees freedom to grow and gain respect and dignity by managing themselves, making decisions about their work and really making a difference in the world around them. As a result employees have a better work life, faceless stress at work, and make less use of employee assistance programs.

### (9) Improved Organisational Communication

Teams encourage interpersonal dependencies with respect to communication. The individual members are required to interact considerably more than when they work alone. Cross functional teams create interfunctional or interdepartmental dependencies and improve organizational communication.

### (10) Improved Quality and Productivity

Working in teams enables workers to learn from other members of the team, avoid wasted effort, reduce errors and react better to customers, resulting in more output for each unit of employee input. Such enhancement results from pooling of individual efforts in new ways and from striving to continuously improve for the benefit of the team.

### (11) Benefits of Expanded Job Training

Through its training, the team members can develop their technical, decision making and interpersonal skills.

### (12) Commitment to Team Goals

Teams generally work with a common goal and purpose. There is a visible commitment to that purpose and agreement about the specific goal. Such agreement coupled with social pressures exerted by the team results in an usually high degree of commitment to the team goals. The rule is individual goals should subordinate common goals.

### (13) Collective Thinking

A team encourages discussion, interaction and exchange of ideas and views among members. It helps them in collective thinking and group discussions. Diversities are resolved and consensus is achieved before arriving at a decision.

## CLASSIFICATION OF TEAM

*Institutional and Operations Team.* Teams may be classified as institutional and operation teams. A team of the persons working in an organisation may be called *institutional team.* A small group of persons supporting institutional teams may be *operation team. Keith Davis* has defined the operation team "*as coordinated action by a cooperative small group in regular contact wherein members contribute responsibly and enthusiastically to task achievement*". The difference between the two is only of size. Operation team is thus a part of institutional team. The *operation team* may further be divided in *traditionally hierarchy team* and the *work team.*

These two teams reflect the behavioural difference. The *hierarchy team* follows chain of command and control. A team consisting of manager, superintendent, supervisor and workers may be called a hierarchy operation team.

A *work-team* has multidirectional interaction in terms of the needs of the situation, and studies the abilities of each member to contribute to those needs. In practice one arrangement overlays the other to reflect both, the way the group is organised and the way its member work together.

A group can work together as a team only when each one knows the role of the other persons with whom he has to interact in the group and each one must be qualified in performing his job effectively. It will promote cooperation among the members of the team, and will not necessarily wait for the orders from the top. In other words team members works voluntarily to the job situation and take necessary actions to further the team goals.

## Teams v. Groups

Groups and teams are not the same thing. A *group* is the interaction and interdependence of two or more individuals who have come together to achieve particular objectives. *A work group*, on the other hand, is a group that interacts primarily to share information and to make decisions to help each member perform within his or her area of responsibility. Work groups does not collective work or joint effort. So their performance is merely the summation of each group member's individual contribution. There is no positive synergy that would create an overall level of performance that is greater than the sum of the inputs. A *work team* generates positive synergy through coordinated effort. Their individual efforts results in better performance necessary for achievement of overall organizational goals.

These definitions help clarify why so many organisations have recently restructured work processes around teams. Management is looking for that positive synergy that will allow their organisations to increase performance. The extensive use of teams creates the *potential* for an organisation to generate greater outputs with no increase in inputs. Notice, however, we said "potential". There is nothing inherently magical in the creation of teams that ensures the achievement of this positive synergy. Merely calling a *group* a *team* does not automatically increase its performance. Successful or high-performing teams have certain common characteristics. If management hopes to gain increases in organisational performance through the use of teams, it will need to ensure that its teams possess these characteristics.

## Team and Teamwork

A fundamental belief in organizational development is that work teams are the building blocks of organizations. A second fundamental belief is that teams must manage their culture, processes, systems, and relationships in a manner so as to be positive and effective. Theory, research, and practice attest to the central role that teams play in organizational success. Teams and teamwork are part of the foundation of organization development.

Teams and teamwork are among the "hottest" things happening in, organizations today—gurus extol the virtues of teams; the noun *team* has become a verb, *teaming;* and team-related acronyms abound—SDTs (self-directed teams), QCs (quality circles), HPOs (high-performance organisations), HPWSs (high-performance work systems), STS (sociotechnical systems), to name just a few. Teams at Motorola produced its best-selling cellular phones; Team Taurus developed Ford's best-selling automobile; team Saturn produced the Saturn automobile; teams at 3M generate the hundreds of innovations that keep 3M ahead of its competition; cross-functional "design-build" teams developed the Boeing 777. Teams and teamwork are "in." The evidence is abundantly clear: Effective teams produce results far beyond the performance of unrelated individuals.

## Importance of Team

Teams are important for a number of reasons mentioned below:

1. Much individual behavior is rooted in the sociocultural norms and values of the work team. If the team, as a team, changes those norms and values, the effects on individual behavior are immediate and lasting.
2. Individual employees in the organizations have their limitations—both physical, as well as mental. Many tasks are so complex that they cannot be performed by individuals; people must work together to accomplish them.
3. In today's competitive times, organizations need to have the advantage of teams. Teams create synergy, that is, the sum of the efforts of team members is far greater than the sum of the individual efforts of people working alone. Synergy is a principal reason teams are so important.
4. Teams satisfy people's needs for social interaction, status, recognition, and respect- teams nurture human nature.

A number of OD interventions are specifically designed to improve team performance. Examples are team building, intergroup team building, process consultation, quality circles, parallel learning structures, sociotechnical systems programs, Grid OD, and techniques such as role analysis technique, role negotiation technique, and responsibility charting. These interventions apply to formal work teams as well as startup teams, cross-functional teams, temporary teams, and the like.

Team-building activities have thus become inevitable for organizations today. Teams periodically hold team-building meetings, people are trained in group dynamics and group problem-solving skills, and individuals are trained as group leaders and group facilitators. Organisations using autonomous work groups or self-directed teams devote considerable time and effort to ensure that team members possess the skills to be effective in groups. The net effect is that teams perform at increasingly higher levels, that they achieve synergy, and that teamwork becomes more satisfying for team members.

Investigators are discovering why some teams are successful while others are not. Larson and LaFasto studied a number of high-performance teams, and found eight characteristics always present:

(1) A clear, elevating goal;
(2) A results-driven structure;
(3) Competent team members;
(4) Unified commitment;
(5) A collaborative climate;
(6) Standards of excellence;
(7) External support and recognition; and
(8) Principled leaderships.

All these characteristics are required for superior team performance; when any one feature is lost, team performance declines. High-performance teams regulate the behavior of team members, help each other, find innovative ways around barriers, and set ever-higher goals. Larson and LaFasto also discovered that the most frequent cause of team failure was letting personal or political agendas take precedence over the clear and elevating team goal.

Another excellent source of information about teams is *The Wisdom of Teams: Creating the High-Performance Organisation,* by Jon Katzenback and Douglas Smith. They, too, studied a number of teams in a wide variety of settings. For them, a group of individuals becomes a team only when committed to achieving high-performance goals. Without demanding performance goals, groups never jell into teams. A key characteristic of high-performance teams is *discipline.* "Groups become teams *through disciplined action. They shape* a common purpose, *agree* on performance goals, *define* a common working approach, *develop* high levels of complementary skills, and hold themselves mutually accountable for results. And, as with any effective discipline, they never stop doing any of these things." It is hard work for groups to become teams, but hard work is required to create high-performance organisations.

Katzenbach and Smith believe that teams will become even more important in the future. They write: "In fact, most models of the 'organisation of the future' that we have heard about— 'networked', 'clustered', 'nonhierarchical', 'horizontal,' and so forth—are premised on *teams surpassing individuals as the primary performance unit in the company.*"

# 13 Changing Role of SHRM in Management

## INTRODUCTION

Traditionally HR department was viewed as playing passive role and not going beyond the administrative tasks like payroll processing. With the changes in business scenario and its growing expectations, the role of HR have changed drastically. Liberalization and industrialisation have paved an increasing pressure on organizations in India to change from indigenous, costly, sub-optimal levels of technology to performance based, competitive and higher technology provisions. HR now acts as a strategic partner and helps the company to achieve its goals.

Strategic Human Resource Management (SHRM) has received a great deal of attention in recent years, most notably in the fields of Human Resource Management (HRM), Organizational Behavior, and Industrial Relations. SHRM is not just the function of HR department, but is the responsibility of all the managers and the executives of the entire organization. Research shows that successful organization have several things in common, such as selective hiring, paying well , being decentralized, and training employees and sharing information. When organizations enable, develop, and motivate human capital, they improve accounting profits in the process.

HR should be prepared to answer the following questions:

- Does our company have required competence?
- Does our company have right rewards, measures, rewards and incentives to align people's efforts with the company strategy?

- Does our company have right structures, and policies to create a high performing organization?
- Can our company respond to uncertainty and learn to adapt to changes quickly?

## WHAT ARE STRATEGIES?

Strategy is a multi-dimensional concept going well beyond traditional competitive strategy concepts. Strategies are a specific, measurable, obtainable set of plans carefully developed with involvement by an institution's stakeholders. Strategies are broad statements that set a direction. These action statements are linked to an individual or individuals who are accountable and empowered to achieve the stated result in a specific desired timeframe. They are patterns of action, policies and decisions that guide a group toward a vision or goals.

## MEANING OF STRATEGIC HUMAN RESOURCE MANAGEMENT (SHRM)

In order to meet with the rapidly changing times, companies, today, need to focus either on low cost strategies or differentiating strategies to avail themselves of competitive advantage. Besides, a committed workforce along with developing core competencies is highly essential. Companies need to adapt themselves to the rapidly changing environment in order to grab business opportunities. Strategic human resource management is designed to help companies best meet the needs of their employees while promoting company goals. Human resource management deals with any aspect of a business that affects employees, benefits, training, and administration, hiring and firing of work force, pay systems and policies etc. Human resources may also provide work incentives, sick or vacation days and safety procedure information.

Strategic human resource management is proactive in the sense that it requires thinking ahead, planning in advance the needs of the employees in order to meet with the needs of the company. This may call for drastic change in the way human resources are being handled in the organizations. Companies who work hard to meet the needs of their employees can cultivate a work atmosphere conducive to productivity. The employees may also be willing to stay in such organizations. Improving the employee retention rate can reduce the money companies spend on finding and training new employees.

Strategic human resource management necessitates finding out what employees want or expect and what companies can reasonably supply. An important aspect of strategic human resource management is training and employee development. This process begins when a company is recruiting and interviewing prospective employees. Improved interviewing techniques can help to weed out applicants that may not be a good match for the company. To help employees perform at their best, a company can follow up with continual training programs, coaching, and regular assessment. Investing in the development of its employees can allow a company to turn out more consistent products.

Strategic human resource management is essential in both large and small companies. In small companies, it is less complicated as the owner or manager takes a little time every day to observe, assist, and assess employees, and provide regular reviews. Larger companies may have a whole department in charge of human resources and development. It is possible to improve the quality of staff members by meeting the needs of the employees in a way that also benefits the company,

### Definition of SHRM

Perhaps the most drastic change in HR's role today is its growing involvement in developing and implementing the company's strategy.

In order to understand the modern aspect of HR i.e. SHRM, lets discuss the terms which would help us in understanding the concept:

- **Core Competency:** Core competency can be defined as — a unique capability in the organization that creates high value and that differentiates the organization from its competition.
- **Mission:** A mission is a statement that explains purpose and reason for existence of a business; it is usually very broad, but not more than a couple of sentences and it serves as foundation for everything organization does.
- **Strategy:** Strategy is the company's plan of how it will balance its internal strengths and weaknesses with external opportunities and threats in order to maintain a competitive advantage. Earlier this role was performed by the line managers but now it is carried by the HR manager.

Strategies increasingly depend on strengthening organizational competitiveness and on building committed work teams, and these put HR in a central role. In the fast changing, globally competitive & quality oriented industrial environment, it is often the firm's employees—its human resources—who provide the competitive key. And so now it is a demand of the time to involve HR in the earlier stages of development and implementing the firm's strategic plan, rather than to let HR react to it. That means now the role of HR is not just to implement the things out but also to plan out in such a manner that the employees can be strategically used to get edge over the competitors, keeping in mind the fact that this is the only resource (HUMANS), which cannot be duplicated by the competitors.

"Strategic human resource management can be defined as the linking of human resources with strategic goals and objectives in order to improve business performance and develop organizational culture that foster innovation, flexibility and competitive advantage. In an organisation SHRM means accepting and involving the HR function as a strategic partner in the formulation and implementation of the company's strategies through HR activities such as recruiting, selecting, training and rewarding personnel." Rana Sinha

Strategic human resource management has been defined as 'the linking of human resources with strategic goals and objectives in order to improve business performance and develop organizational culture that foster innovation and flexibility'. Strategic HR means accepting the HR function as a strategic partner in the formulation of the company's strategies as well as in the implementation of those strategies through HR activities such as recruiting, selecting, training and rewarding personnel. Whereas strategic HR recognizes HR's partnership role in the strategizing process, the term HR Strategies refers to specific HR courses of action the company plans to pursue to achieve it's aims.

## THE IMPORTANCE OF HUMAN CAPITAL

The society of Human Resource Management's Research defines an organization's human capital as follows: "A company's human capital asset is the collective sum of attributes; life experience, knowledge, inventiveness, energy and enthusiasm that its people choose to invest in their work." Thus, the human capital is the skills acquired through training and experience that increases value of human resource in the market place. In the past HR professionals focused on compliance to rules and they tracked simple metrics like the number of employees hired or the number of hours of training delivered. Unfortunately, many HR professionals focused more on technical or operational aspects and less on strategic aspects. However, a new era emerged which requires a focus on outcomes and results and not numbers and compliance. HR professionals must track how employees are using the skills they've learned to attain goals, not just many hours they've spent in training. John Murabito, executive vice president and head of HR and Services at Cigna says, "anything that is administrative or transactional is going to get outsourced. For e.g. Bank of America outsourced its HR administration to Arinso where the latter will provide timekeeping, payroll processing and payroll services for 10,000 Bank of America employees outside the U.S. To keep a check on outsourcing, HR needs to stay accountable for its business results.

## KEY ELEMENTS OF HR

The four key elements of HR are summarized in the following figure. Each element of the HR system reflects best practice and maximizes employee performance.

*Figure : Key HR Elements*

Selection and placement

Diversity Management

KEY HR ELEMENTS

Jon design

Compensation and rewards

## SELECTION AND PLACEMENT

New hires should be well acquainted with the technical as well as behavioral competencies needed for performing a particular job. Behavioral competencies may have a customer focus; ability to understand customer's feelings and their view point or work management focus; i.e. ability to complete tasks efficiently or to know when to seek guidance.

Make the vision of the company clear to the new hires. In addition, make the organization's culture clear by discussing the values that underpin the organization—describe your organization's "heroes." For example, are the heroes of your company the people who go the extra mile to get customers to smile? Are they the people who toil through the night to develop new code? Are they the ones who can network and reach a company president to make the sale? By sharing such stories of company heroes with your potential hires, you'll help reinforce what makes your company unique. This, in turn, will help the job candidates determine whether they'll fit into your organization's culture.

## Job Design

Job design refers to the process of putting together various elements to form a job, organizational and individual worker requirements as well as health, safety and ergonomics considerations. Training helps the employees to perform all parts of these jobs and give them the authority and accountability to do so.

Job enrichment helps the organization to retain the employees. Motorola, being a global company operates in many countries and the management imparts appropriate training to its employees. But operating in China presents a challenge in terms of finding and hiring skilled employees. In a survey conducted by American Chamber of Commerce in Shanghai, 37% of US owned enterprises operating in China said that recruiting skilled employees was their biggest operational problem. The reason behind this failure is the fact that Chinese Universities do not turn out the candidates with the skill set as expected by the business corporate. Motorola has created its own training and development programs to bridge the gap. For e.g. Motorola's China Accelerated Management Program is designed for local managers, where as Motorola's Management Foundation program is designed to help managers in areas like communication and problem solving. Also it offers high tech MBA program in partnership with Arizona State University and Tsinghua University. Such programs are made to train the low skilled but highly motivated Chinese employees.

## Compensation

Compensation includes incentives, gainsharing, profit sharing and skill based pay reward for those employees who learn new skills and put those skills to work in the organization. Employees who have acquired more skills through training are more likely to grow on the job. Such training enables them to make more valuable contribution to the company. Rewards need to be linked with performance, so that employees are naturally inclined to contribute in such a way that will gain rewards and in return will further the organization's success.

## DIVERSITY MANAGEMENT

Unity in diversity is a punch line for all successful business organizations. Teams whose members have complementary skills are often more successful because members can gain diversified skills and can learn from one another's blind spots. Diversity helps company teams to come up with more creative solutions. Diversity management involves actively appreciating and using the differing perspectives that individuals bring to the work place.

As James Surowiecki shows in The Wisdom of Crowds, the more diverse the group in terms of expertise, gender, age, and background, the more ability the group has to avoid the problems of groupthink. Diversity helps company teams to come up with more creative and effective solutions. Teams whose members have complementary skills are often more successful because members can see one another 's blind spots. Members will be more inclined to make different kinds of mistakes, which means that they'll be able to catch and correct those mistakes.

## INTRODUCTION TO TALENT MANAGEMENT

Talent management is a term emerged in the 1990s to incorporate developments in HRM which placed more emphasis on the management of human resources or talent. It goes hand in hand with succession planning, which ensures that employees are recruited and developed to fill each key role within the company. However, most companies do not plan ahead for the talent they need by which they face shortage of critical skills at some times and surpluses at other times. It is expensive to develop all talent internally; rather than developing everyone internally, companies can hire from outside. Thus, the solution is to either make or buy; that is to train some people and to hire the experienced skills from the external market. "Making" an employee means hiring a person who doesn't have all the needed skills but who can be trained to develop them. The "buy" decision means hiring an employee required to perform a job who has necessary skills and experience. Major aspects of talent management include: performance management, leadership development, workforce planning and recruiting. Besides, make or buy decision, another important principle that works well in talent management is to run smaller batch size. Thus, rather than sending employees for long training programs, they can be sent to short programs more frequently. With this approach managers don't have to make training decision far in advance, thus ensuring that employees are trained on the skills they'll actually use.

The most important aspect in talent management is attracting right workers—the one who feel enthusiastic about their work and whose goals and aspirations match with those of the company. Thus, the organizations need to be very clear about the kind of talent it wants to capture.

## ATTRACTING THE RIGHT WORKERS TO THE ORGANIZATION

It is challenging to attract right workers—the ones who are enthusiastic about their work. Enthusiasm for the job requires more than having a good attitude about receiving good pay and benefits. It means that an employee's goals and aspirations also matches with those of the company. Therefore, it is important to identify employees' preferences and mutually assess how well they align with the company's strategy. To do this, the organization must first be clear about the type of employee it wants. Companies need to develop a profile of the type of workers they want to attract i.e whether they need entrepreneurial types of employees who seek autonomy and believe in continual learning, or do you want team players who enjoy collaboration, stability, and structure? Neither employee type is inherently "better" than another, but an employee who craves autonomy may feel constrained within the very same structure in which a team player would thrive.

Earlier, we said that it was important to "mutually assess" how well employees' preferences aligned with the company's strategy. One-half of "mutual" refers to the company, but the other half refers to the job candidates. They also need to know whether they'll fit well into the company. One way to help prospective hires make this determination is to describe to them the "signature experience" that sets your company apart. As Tamara Erickson and Lynda Gratton define it, your company's signature experience is the distinctive practice that shows what it is really like to work at your company.

For example, here are the signature experiences of two companies, Whole Foods and Goldman Sachs: At Whole Foods, team-based hiring is a signature experience—employees in each department vote on whether a new employee will be retained after a four-week trial period. This demonstrates to potential hires that Whole Foods is all about collaboration. In contrast, Goldman Sachs's signature experience is multiple one-on-one interviews. The story often told to prospective hires is of the MBA student who went through 60 interviews before being hired. This story signals to new hires that they need to be comfortable meeting endless new people and building networks across the company. Those who enjoy meeting and being interviewed by so many diverse people are exactly the ones who will fit into Goldman's culture.

The added benefit of hiring workers who match your organizational culture and are engaged in their work is that they will be less likely to leave your company just to get a higher salary.

## KEEPING STAR EMPLOYEES

The war for talent stems from the approaching shortage of workers. As we mentioned earlier in this chapter, the millions of baby boomers reaching retirement age are leaving a gaping hole in the U.S. workforce. What's more, workers are job-hopping more frequently than in the past. According to the U.S. Bureau of Labor Statistics, the average job tenure has dropped from 15 years in 1980 to 4 years in 2007. As a manager, therefore, you need to give your employees reasons to stay with your company. One way to do that is to spend time talking with employees about their career goals. Listen to their likes and dislikes so that you can help them use the skills they like using or develop new ones they wish to acquire.

Don't be afraid to "grow" your employees. Some managers want to keep their employees in their department. They fear that helping employees grow on the job will mean that employees will outgrow their job and leave it. But, keeping your employees down is a sure way to lose them. What's more, if you help your employees advance, it'll be easier for you to move up because your employees will be better able to take on the role you leave behind.

In some cases, your employees may not be sure what career path they want. As a manager, you can help them identify their goals by asking questions such as:

- What assignments have you found most engaging?

- Which of your accomplishments in the last six months made you proudest?
- What makes for a great day at work?
- What Employees Want?

Employees want to grow and develop, stretching their capabilities. They want projects that engage their heads as well as their hearts, and they want to connect with the people and things that will help them achieve their professional goals. Here are two ways to provide this to your employees: First, connect people with mentors and help them build their networks. Research suggests that successful managers dedicate 70% more time to networking activities and 10% more time to communication than their less successful counterparts. What makes networks special? Through networks, people energize one another, learn, create, and find new opportunities for growth. Second, help connect people with a sense of purpose. Focusing on the need for purpose is especially important for younger workers, who rank meaningful work and challenging experiences at the top of their job search lists.

## BENEFITS OF GOOD TALENT MANAGEMENT

Global consulting firm McKinsey and Company conducted a study to identify a possible link between a company's financial performance and its success in managing talent. The survey results, reported in May 2008, showed that there was indeed a relationship between a firm's financial performance and its global talent management practices. Three talent management practices in particular correlated highly with exceptional financial performance:

- Creating globally consistent talent evaluation processes.
- Achieving cultural diversity in a global setting.
- Developing and managing global leaders.

The McKinsey survey found that companies achieving scores in the top third in any of these three areas had a 70% chance of achieving financial performance in the top third of all companies.

Let's take a closer look at what each of these three best practices entail. First, having consistent talent evaluation means that employees around the world are evaluated on the same standards. This is important because it means that if an employee from one country transfers to another, his or her manager can be assured that the employee has been held to the same level of skills and standards. Second, having cultural diversity means having employees who learn something about the culture of different countries, not just acquire language skills. This helps bring about open-mindedness across cultures. Finally, developing global leaders means rotating employees across different cultures and giving them international experience. Companies who do this best also have policies of giving managers incentives to share their employees with other units.

## EFFECTIVE SELECTION AND PLACEMENT STRATEGIES

Selecting the right employees and placing them in the right positions within the company is a key HR function and is vital to a company's success. Companies should devote as much care and attention to this "soft" issue as they do to financial planning because errors will have financial impact and adverse effects on a company's strategy.

## JOB-DESCRIPTION—BEST PRACTICES

Walt has a problem. He works as a manager in a medium-sized company and considers himself fortunate that the organizational chart allows him a full-time administrative assistant (AA). However, in the two years Walt has been in his job, five people have held this AA job. The most recent AA, who resigned after four weeks, told Walt that she had not known what the job would involve. "I don't do numbers, I'm not an accountant," she said. "If you want someone to add up figures and do calculations all day, you should say so in the job description.

Besides, I didn't realize how long and stressful my commute would be—the traffic between here and my house is murder!"

Taken aback, Walt contacted the company's HR department to clarify the job description for the AA position. What he learned was that the description made available to applicants was, indeed, inadequate in a number of ways. Chances are that frequent turnover in this AA position is draining Walt's company of resources that could be used for much more constructive purposes.

An accurate and complete job description is a powerful SHRM tool that costs little to produce and can save a bundle in reduced turnover. While the realistic description may discourage some applicants (for example, those who lack an affinity for calculations might not bother to apply for Walt's AA position), those who follow through with the application process are much more likely to be satisfied with the job once hired. In addition to summarizing what the worker will actually be doing all day, here are some additional suggestions for writing an effective job description:

- List the job requirements in bullet form so that job seekers can scan the posting quickly.
- Use common industry terms, which speak to knowledgeable job seekers.
- Avoid organization-specific terms and acronyms, which would confuse job seekers.
- Use meaningful job titles (not the internal job codes of the organization).
- Use key words taken from the list of common search terms (to maximize the chance that a job posting appears on a job seeker's search).
- Include information about the organization, such as a short summary and links to more detailed information.
- Highlight special intangibles and unusual benefits of the job and workplace (e.g., flextime, travel, etc.).
- Specify the job's location (and nearest large city) and provide links to local community pages (to entice job seekers with quality-of-life information).

## TAILORING RECRUITMENT TO MATCH COMPANY CULTURE

Managers who hire well don't just hire for skills or academic background; they ask about the potential employee's philosophy on life or how the candidate likes to spend free time. These questions help the manager assess whether the cultural fit is right. A company in which all work is done in teams need team players, not just individual employees. Here, the manager ask questions like, "Do you have a personal mission statement? If not, what would it be if you wrote one today?" to identify potential hires' preferences.

At Google, for example, job candidates are asked questions like, "If you could change the world using Google's resources, what would you build?" Google want employees to think and act on a grand scale, employees who will take on the challenges of their jobs, whatever their job may be. Take Josef DeSimone, who's Google's executive chief. DeSimone, who has worked everywhere from family-style restaurants to Michelin-caliber ones, was amazed to learn that Google had 17 cafes for its employees. "Nobody changes the menu daily on this scale," he says. "It's unheard of." When he was hired, DeSimone realized, "Wow, you hire a guy who's an expert in food and let him run with it! You don't get in his way or micromanage." Google applies this approach to all positions and lets employees run with the challenge.

Traditionally, companies have built a competitive advantage by focusing on what they have—structural advantages such as economies of scale, a well-established brand, or dominance in certain market segments. Companies such as Southwest Airlines, by contrast, see its people as their advantage: "Our fares can be matched; our airplanes and routes can be copied. But we pride ourselves on our customer service," said Sherry Phelps, director of corporate employment. That's why Southwest looks for candidates who generate enthusiasm and leans toward extraverted personalities. Southwest hires for attitude. Flight attendants have been known to sing the safety instructions, and pilots tell jokes over the public address system.

Southwest Airlines makes clear right from the start the kind of people it wants to hire. For example, recruitment ads showed Southwest founder Herb Kelleher dressed as Elvis and read: "Work in a Place Where Elvis Has Been Spotted...The qualifications? It helps to be outgoing. Maybe even a bit off- center. And be prepared to stay awhile. After all, we have the lowest employee turnover rate in the industry." People may scoff or question why Southwest indulges in such showy activities or wonder how an airline can treat its jobs so lightly. Phelps answers, "We do take our work seriously. It's ourselves that we don't." People who don't have a humane, can-do attitude are fired. Southwest has a probationary period during which it determines the compatibility of new hires with the culture. People may be excellent performers, but if they don't match the culture, they are let go. As Southwest's founder Kelleher once said, "People will write me and complain, 'Hey, I got terminated or put on probation for purely subjective reasons.' And I'll say, 'Right! Those are the important reasons.'"

In many states, employees are covered under what is known as the at-will employment doctrine. At-will employment is a doctrine of American law that defines an employment relationship in which either party can break the relationship with no liability, provided there was no express contract for a definite term governing the employment relationship and that the employer does not belong to a collective bargaining unit (i.e., a union). However, there are legal restrictions on how purely subjective the reasons for firing can be. For instance, if the organization has written hiring and firing procedures and does not follow them in selective cases, then those cases might give rise to claims of wrongful termination. Similarly, in situations where termination is clearly systematic, for example, based on age, race, religion, and so on, wrongful termination can be claimed.

## TOOLS AND METHODS : INTERVIEWING AND TESTING

To make good selection and placement decisions, you need information about the job candidate. Two time-tested methods to get that information are testing and interviewing.

A detailed interview begins by asking the candidate to describe his work history and then getting as much background on his most recent position (or the position most similar the open position). Ask about the candidate's responsibilities and major accomplishments. Then, ask in-depth questions about specific job situations. Called situational interviews, these types of interviews can focus on past experience or future situations. For example, experienced-based questions are "Tell me about a major initiative you developed and the steps you used to get it adopted." Or, "Describe a problem you had with someone and how you handled it." In contrast, future-oriented situation interview questions can be asked candidates to describe how they would handle a future hypothetical situation, such as: "Suppose you came up with a faster way to do a task, but your team was reluctant to make the change. What would you do in that situation?"

In addition to what is asked, it is also important that interviewers understand what they should not ask, largely because certain questions lead to answers that may be used to discriminate. There are five particularly sensitive areas. First, the only times you can ask about age are when it is a requirement of a job duty or you need to determine whether a work permit is required. Second, it is rarely appropriate or legal to ask questions regarding race, color, national origin, or gender. Third, although candidates may volunteer religious or sexually-orientated information in an interview, you still need to be careful not to discriminate. Ask questions that are relevant to work experience or qualifications. Fourth, firms cannot discriminate for health or disabilities; you may not ask about smoking, health-related questions, or disabilities in an interview. Finally, you may not ask questions about marital status, children, personal life, pregnancy, or arrest record. These kinds of questions could be tempting to ask if you are interviewing for a position requiring travel; however, you can only explain the travel requirements and confirm that the requirements are acceptable.

In addition to interviews, many employers use testing to select and place job applicants. Any tests given to candidates must be job related and follow guidelines set forth by the Equal Opportunity Employment Commission to be legal. For the tests to be effective, they should be developed by reputable psychologists and administered by professionally qualified personnel who have had training in occupations testing in an industrial setting. The rationale behind testing is to give the employer more information before making the selection and placement decision—information vital to assessing how well a candidate is suited to a particular job. Most preemployment assessment tests measure thinking styles, behavioral traits, and occupational interests. The results are available almost immediately after a candidate completes the roughly hour-long questionnaire. Thinking styles tests can tell the potential employer how fast someone can learn new things or how well he or she can verbally communicate. Behavioral traits assessments measure energy level, assertiveness, sociability, manageability, and attitude. For example, a high sociability score would be a desirable trait for salespeople.

## INTERNATIONAL STAFFING AND PLACEMENT

In our increasingly global economy, managers need to decide between using expatriates or hiring locals when staffing international locations. On the surface, this seems a simple choice between the firm-specific expertise of the expatriate and the cultural knowledge of the local hire. In reality, companies often fail to consider the high probability and high cost of expatriates failing to adapt and perform in their international assignments.

For example, cultural issues can easily create misunderstandings between expatriate managers and employees, suppliers, customers, and local government officials. At an estimated cost of $200,000 per failed expatriate, international assignment decisions are often made too lightly in many companies. The challenge is to overcome the natural tendency to hire a well-known, corporate insider over an unknown local at the international site. Here are some indications to use to determine whether an expatriate or a local hire would be best.

Managers may want to choose an expatriate when:

- Company-specific technology or knowledge is important.
- Confidentiality in the staff position is an issue.

There is a need for speed (assigning an expatriate is usually faster than hiring a local).

- Work rules regarding local workers are restrictive.
- The corporate strategy is focused on global integration.

Managers may want to staff the position with a local hire when:

- The need to interact with local customers, suppliers, employees, or officials is paramount.

- The corporate strategy is focused on multidomestic/market-oriented operations.
- Cost is an issue (expatriates often bring high relocation/travel costs).
- Immigration rules regarding foreign workers are restrictive.

There are large cultural distances between the host country and candidate expatriates.

## THE ROLES OF PAY STRUCTURE AND PAY FOR PERFORMANCE

Pay can be thought of in terms of the "total reward" that includes an individual's base salary, variable pay, share ownership, and other benefits. A bonus, for example, is a form of variable play. A bonus is a one-time cash payment, often awarded for exceptional performance. Providing employees with an annual statement of all these benefits they receive can help them understand the full value of what they are getting.

## PAY SYSTEM ELEMENTS

As summarized in the following table, pay can take the form of direct or indirect compensation. Non-monetary pay can include any

TABLE I

**Elements of a Pay System**

| | |
|---|---|
| Non-monetary pay | Includes benefits that do not involve tangible value. |
| Direct pay | Employee's base wage. |
| Indirect pay | Everything from legally required programs to health insurance, retirement, housing, etc. |
| Basic pay | Cash wage paid to the employee. Because paying a wage is a standard practice, the competitive advantage can only come by paying a higher amount. |
| Incentive pay | A bonus paid when specified performance objectives are met. May inspire employees to set and achieve a higher performance level and is an excellent motivator to accomplish goals. |
| Stock options | A right to buy a piece of the business that may be given to an employee to reward excellent service. An employee who owns a share of the business is far more likely to go the extra mile for the operation. |
| Bonuses | A gift given occasionally to reward exceptional performance or for special occasions. Bonuses can show an employer appreciates his or her employees and ensures that good performance or special events are rewarded. |

benefit an employee receives from an employer or job that does not involve tangible value. This includes career and social rewards, such as job security, flexible hours and opportunity for growth, praise and recognition, task enjoyment, and friendships. Direct pay is an employee's base wage. It can be an annual salary, hourly wage, or any performance-based pay that an employee receives, such as profit-sharing bonuses.

Indirect compensation is far more varied, including everything from legally required public protection programs such as social security to health insurance, retirement programs, paid leave, child care, or housing. Some indirect compensation elements are required by law such as social security, unemployment, and disability payments. Other indirect elements are up to the employer and can offer excellent ways to provide benefits to the employees and the employer as well. For example, a working parent may take a lower-paying job with flexible hours that will allow him or her to be at home when the children get home from school. A recent graduate may be looking for stable work and an affordable place to live. Both of these individuals have different needs and, therefore, would appreciate different compensation elements.

## SETTING PAY LEVELS

When setting pay levels for positions, managers should make sure that the pay level is fair relative to what other employees in the position are being paid. Part of the pay level is determined by the pay level at other companies. If your company pays substantially less than others, it is going to be the last choice of employment unless it offers something overwhelmingly positive to offset the low pay, such as flexible hours or a fun, congenial work atmosphere. Besides these external factors, companies conduct a job evaluation to determine the internal value of the job—the more vital the job to the company's success, the higher the pay level. Jobs are often ranked alphabetically—"A" positions are those on which the company's value depends, "B" positions are somewhat less important in that they don't deliver as much upside to the company, and "C" positions are those of least importance—in some cases, these are outsourced.

The most vital jobs to one company's success may not be the same as in other companies. For example, information technology companies may put top priority on their software developers and programmers, whereas for retailers such as Nordstrom, the "A" positions are those frontline employees who provide personalized service. For an airline, pilots would be a "B" job because, although they need to be well trained, investing further in their training is unlikely to increase the airline's profits. "C" positions for a retailer might include back office bill processing, while an information technology company might classify customer service as a "C" job.

When setting reward systems, it is important to pay for what the company actually hopes to achieve. Steve Kerr, vice-president of corporate management at General Electric, talks about the common mistakes that companies make with their reward systems, such as saying they value teamwork but only rewarding individual effort. Similarly, companies say they want innovative thinking or risk taking, but they reward people who "make the numbers." If companies truly want to achieve what they hope for, they need payment systems aligned with their goals. For example, if retention of star employees is important to your company, reward managers who retain top talent. At Pepsico, for instance, one-third of a manager's bonus is tied directly to how well the manager did at developing and retaining employees. Tying compensation to retention makes managers accountable.

## PAY FOR PERFORMANCE

As its name implies, pay for performance ties pay directly to an individual's performance in meeting specific business goals or objectives. Managers (often together with the employees themselves) design performance targets to which the employee will be held accountable. The targets have accompanying metrics that enable employees and managers to track performance. The metrics can be financial indicators, or they can be indirect indicators such as customer satisfaction or speed of development. Pay-for-performance schemes often combine a fixed base salary with a variable pay component (such as bonuses or stock options) that vary with the individual's performance.

## INNOVATIVE EMPLOYEE RECOGNITION PROGRAMS

In addition to regular pay structures and systems, companies often create special programs that reward exceptional employee performance. For example, the financial software company Intuit, Inc., instituted a program called Spotlight. The purpose of Spotlight is to "spotlight performance, innovation and service dedication." Unlike regular salaries or year-end bonuses, spotlight awards can be given on the spot for specific behavior that meets the reward criteria, such as filing a patent, inventing a new product, or meeting a milestone for years of service. Rewards can be cash awards of $ 500 to $ 3,000 and can be made by managers without high-level approval. In addition to cash and noncash awards, two Intuit awards feature a trip with $ 500 in spending money.

## PAY STRUCTURES FOR GROUPS AND TEAMS

So far, we have discussed pay in terms of individual compensation, but many employers also use compensation systems that reward all of the organization's employees as a group or various groups and teams within the organization. Let us examine some of these less traditional pay structures.

### GAINSHARING

Sometimes called profit-sharing, gainsharing is a form of pay for performance. In gainsharing, the organization shares the financial gains with employees. Employees receive a portion of the profit achieved from their efforts. How much they receive is determined by their performance against the plan. Here's how gainsharing works: First, the organization must measure the historical (baseline) performance. Then, if employees help improve the organization's performance on those measures, they share in the financial rewards achieved. This sharing is typically determined by a formula.

The effectiveness of a gainsharing plan depends on employees seeing a relationship between what they do and how well the organization performs. The larger the size of the organization, the harder it is for employees to see the effect of their work. Therefore, gainsharing plans are more effective in companies with fewer than 1,000 people. Gainsharing success also requires the company tô have good performance metrics in place so that employees can track their process. The gainsharing plan can only be successful if employees believe and see that if they perform better, they will be paid more. The pay should be given as soon as possible after the performance so that the tie between the two is established.

When designing systems to measure performance, realize that performance appraisals need to focus on quantifiable measures. Designing these measures with input from the employees help make the measures clear and understandable to employees and increase their motivation if measures are reasonable.

### TEAM-BASED PAY

Many managers seek to build teams, but face the question of how to motivate all the members to achieve the team's goals. As a result, team-based pay is becoming increasingly accepted. In 1992, only 3% of companies had team-based pay. By 1996, 9% did, and another 39% were planning such systems.

With increasing acceptance and adoption come different choices and options of how to structure team-based pay. One way to structure the pay is to first identify the type of team you have—parallel, work, project, or partnership—and then choose the pay option that is most appropriate to that team type. Let's look at each team type in turn and the pay structures best suited for each. Parallel teams are teams that exist alongside (parallel to) an individual's daily job. For example, a person may be working in the accounting department but also be asked to join a team on productivity. Parallel teams are often interdepartmental, meet part time, and are formed to deal with a specific issue. The reward for performance on this team would typically be a merit increase or a recognition award (cash or non-cash) for performance on the team.

A project team is likewise a temporary team, but it meets full time for the life of the project. For example, a team may be formed to develop a new project and then disband when the new product is completed. The pay schemes appropriate for this type of team include profit sharing, recognition rewards, and stock options. Team members evaluate each other's performance.

A partnership team is formed around a joint venture or strategic alliance. Here, profit sharing in the venture is the most common pay structure. Finally, with the work team, all individuals work together daily to accomplish their jobs. Here, skill-based pay and gainsharing are the payment schemes of choice, with team members evaluating one another's performance.

## PAY SYSTEMS THAT REWARD BOTH TEAM AND INDIVIDUAL PERFORMANCE

There are two main theories of how to reward employees. Nancy Katz characterized the theories as two opposing camps. The first camp advocates rewarding individual performance through plans such as commissions-sales schemes and merit-based-pay. The claim is that this will increase employees' energy, drive, risk taking, and task identification. The disadvantages of rewarding individual performance are that employees will cooperate less, that high performers may be resented by others in the corporation, and that low performers may try to undermine top performers.

The second camp believes that organizations should reward team performance, without regard for individual accomplishment. This reward system is thought to bring the advantages of increased helping and cooperation, sharing of information and resources, and mutual-respect among employees. The disadvantages of team-based reward schemes are that they create a lack of drive, that low performers are "free riders," and that high performers may withdraw or become tough cops.

Katz sought to identify reward schemes that achieve the best of both worlds.

These hybrid pay systems would reward individual and team performance, promoting excellence at both levels. Katz suggested two possible hybrid reward systems. The first system features a base rate of pay for individual performance that increases when the group reaches a target level of performance. In this reward system, individuals have a clear pay-for-performance incentive, and their rate of pay increases when the group as a whole does well. In the second hybrid, the pay-for-performance rate also increases when a target is reached. Under this reward system, however, every team member must reach a target level of performance before the higher pay rate kicks in. In contrast with the first hybrid, this reward system clearly incentivizes the better performers to aid poorer performers. Only when the poorest performer reaches the target does the higher pay rate kick in.

## DESIGNING A HIGH-PERFORMANCE WORK SYSTEM

Now it is your turn to design a high-performance work system (HPWS). HPWS is a set of management practice that attempts to create an environment within an organization where the employee has greater involvement and responsibility. Designing a HPWS involves putting all the HR pieces together. A HPWS is all about determining what jobs a company needs to be done, designing the jobs, identifying and attracting the type of employee needed to fill the job, and then evaluating employees' performance and compensating them appropriately so that they stay with the company.

## E-HRM

At the same time, technology is changing the way HR is done. The electronic human resource management (e-HRM) business solution is based on the idea that information technologies, including the Web, can be designed for human resources professionals and executive managers who need support to manage the workforce, monitor changes, and gather the information needed in decision making. At the same time, e-HRM can enable all employees to participate in the process and keep track of relevant information. For instance, your place of work provides you with a Web site where you can login; get past and current pay information, including tax forms (i.e., 1099, W-2, and so on); manage investments related to your 401(k); or opt for certain medical record-keeping services.

More generally, for example, many administrative tasks are being done online, including:

- providing and describing insurance and other benefit options;
- enrolling employees for those benefits;
- enrolling employees in training programs; and
- administering employee surveys to gauge their satisfaction.

Many of these tasks are being done by employees themselves, which is referred to as employee self-service. With all the information available online, employees can access it themselves when they need it.

Part of an effective HR strategy is using technology to reduce the manual work performance by HR employees. Simple or repetitive tasks can be performed self-service through e-HRM systems that provide employees with information and let them perform their own updates. Typical HR services that can be formed in an e-HRM system include:

- Answer basic compensation questions.
- Look up employee benefits information.
- Process candidate recruitment expenses.
- Receive and scan resumes into recruiting software.
- Enroll employees in training programs.
- Maintain training catalog.
- Administer tuition reimbursement.
- Update personnel files.

Organizations that have invested in e-HRM systems have found that they free up HR professionals to spend more time on the strategic aspects of their job. These strategic roles include employee development, training, and succession planning.

## THE VALUE OF HIGH-PERFORMANCE WORK SYSTEMS

Employees who are highly involved in conceiving, designing, and implementing workplace processes are more engaged and perform better. For example, a study analyzing 132 U.S. manufacturing firms found that companies using HPWSs had significantly higher labor productivity than their competitors. The key finding was that when employees have the power to make decisions related to their performance, can access information about company costs and revenues, and have the necessary knowledge, training, and development to do their jobs—and are rewarded for their efforts—they are more productive.

For example, Mark Youndt and his colleagues demonstrated that productivity rates were significantly higher in manufacturing plants where the HRM strategy focused on enhancing human capital. Delery and Doty found a positive relationship between firm's financial performance and a system of HRM practices. Huselid, Jackson, and

Schuler found that increased HRM effectiveness corresponded to an increase in sales per employee, cash flow, and company market value.

HPWS can be used globally to good result. For example, Fey and colleagues studied 101 foreign-based firms operating in Russia and found significant linkages between HRM practices, such as incentive-based compensation, job security, employee training, decentralized decision-making, and subjective measures of firm performance.

## IMPROVING ORGANIZATIONAL PERFORMANCE

Organizations that want to improve their performance can use a combination of HR systems to get these improvements. For example, performance measurement systems help underperforming companies improve performance. The utility company Arizona Public Service used a performance measurement system to rebound from dismal financial results. The company developed 17 "critical success indicators," which it measures regularly and benchmarks against the best companies in each category. Of the 17, nine were identified as "major critical success indicators." They are:

- cost to produce kilowatt hour;
- customer satisfaction;
- fossil plants availability;
- operations and maintenance expenditures;
- construction expenditures;
- ranking as corporate citizen in Arizona;
- safety all-injury incident rate;
- nuclear performance; and
- shareholder value return on assets.

Each department sets measurable goals in line with these indicators and a gainsharing plan rewards employees for meeting the indicators.

In addition, companies use reward schemes to improve performance. Better-performing firms tend to invest in more sophisticated HRM practices, which further enhances organizational performance. Currently, about 20% of firms link employee compensation to the firm's earnings. They use reward schemes such as employee stock ownership plans, gainsharing, and profit-sharing. This trend is increasing.

Researcher Michel Magnan wanted to find out: Is the performance of an organization with a profit-sharing plan better than other firms? And, does adoption of a profit-sharing plan lead to improvement in an organization's performance?

The reasons profit-sharing plans would improve organizational performance go back to employee motivation theory. A profit-sharing plan will likely encourage employees to monitor one another 's behavior because "loafers" would erode the rewards for everyone. Moreover, profit sharing should lead to greater information sharing, which increases the productivity and flexibility of the firm.

Magnan studied 294 Canadian credit unions in the same region (controlling for regional and sector-specific economic effects). Of the firms studied, 83 had profit sharing plans that paid the bonus in full at the end of the year. This meant that employees felt the effect of the organizational performance reward immediately, so it had a stronger motivational effect than a plan that put profits into a retirement account, where the benefit would be delayed (and essentially hidden) until retirement.

Magnan's results showed that firms with profit-sharing plans had better performance on most facets of organizational performance. They had better performance on asset growth, market capitalization, operating costs, losses on loans, and return on assets than firms without profit-sharing plans. The improved performance was especially driven by activities where employee involvement had a quick, predictable effect on firm performance, such as giving loans or controlling costs.

Another interesting finding was that when firms adopted a profit-sharing plan, their organizational performance went up. Profit-sharing plans appear to be a good turnaround tool because the firms that showed the greatest improvement were those that had not been performing well before the profit-sharing plan. Even firms that had good performance before adopting a profit-sharing plan had better performance after the profit-sharing plan.

## SUCCESSION PLANNING

Succession planning is a process whereby an organization ensures that employees are recruited and developed to fill each key role within the company. In a recent survey, HR executives and non HR executives were asked to name their top human capital challenge. Nearly one-third of both executive groups cited succession planning, but less than 20% of companies with a succession plan addressed nonmanagement positions. Slightly more than 40% of firms didn't have a plan in place.

Looking across organizations succession planning takes a number of forms (including no form at all). An absence of succession planning should be a red flag, since the competitive advantage of a growing percentage of firms is predicated on their stock of human capital and ability to manage such capital in the future. One of the overarching themes of becoming better at succession is that effective organizations become much better at developing and promoting talent from within.

## Levels of Succession Planning

Level 1: No planning at all.

Level 2: Simple replacement plan. Typically the organization has only considered what it will do if key individuals leave or become debilitated.

Level 3: The company extends the replacement plan approach to consider lower-level positions, even including middle managers.

Level 4: The company goes beyond the replacement plan approach to identify the competencies it will need in the future. Most often, this approach is managed along with a promote-from-within initiative.

Level 5: In addition to promoting from within, the organization develops the capability to identify and recruit top talent externally. However, the primary source of successors should be from within, unless there are key gaps where the organization does not have key capabilities.

Dow Chemical exemplifies some best practices for succession planning:

- Dow has a comprehensive plan that addresses all levels within the organization, not just executive levels.
- CEO reviews the plan, signaling its importance.
- Managers regularly identify critical roles in the company and the competencies needed for success in those roles.
- Dow uses a nine-box grid for succession planning, plotting employees along the two dimensions of potential and performance.
- High potential employees are recommended for training and development, such as Dow Academy or an MBA.

Interpublic Group, a communications and advertising agency, established a formal review process in 2005 in which the CEOs of each Interpublic business would talk with the CEO about the leaders in their organization. The discussions span the globe because half of the company's employees work outside the United States. A key part of the discussions was to meet with the individual employees to tell them about the opportunities available to them. "In the past, what I saw happen was that an employee would want to leave and then all of a sudden they hear about all of the career opportunities available to them," he says. "Now I want to make sure those discussions are happening before anyone talks about leaving," said Timothy Sompolski, executive vice president and chief human resources officer at Interpublic Group.

The principles of strategic human resource management and high-performance work systems apply to nonprofit enterprises as well as for-profit companies, and the benefits of good HR practices are just as rewarding. When it comes to succession planning, nonprofits face a particularly difficult challenge of attracting workers to a field known for low pay and long hours. Often, the people attracted to the enterprise are drawn by the cause rather than by their own aspirations for promotion. Thus, identifying and training employees for leadership positions is even more important. What's more, the talent shortage for nonprofits will be even more acute: A study by the Meyer Foundation and CompassPoint Nonprofit Service found that 75% of nonprofit executive directors plan to leave their jobs by 2011.

# 14 Human Resource Environment

## INTRODUCTION

This chapter examines the numerous factors that make up the environment of human resources as well as emerging trends. Human resource environment is currently more turbulent especially after World War II. During the last decade of the twentieth century, many political developments, both at home and abroad, had massive impacts on human resources. Eastern European countries were freed from occupation by the Soviet Union, civil wars broke out and East and West Germany were united. The economic sphere of the European community as well as North American Free Trade Agreement (NAFTA) became a reality.

Technology also had massive impacts, as many Dot companies were created resulting in thousands of e-business and ecommerce operations. Companies providing infrastructure for the Internet, Oracle, Sun Microsystem and Microsoft became some of the largest companies in the world. Such developments affect business and human resources. During such times of rapid change, the difficult processes of formulating viable competitive strategies and planning for their implementation became more difficult and essential. The framework for scanning is composed of the following categories: technology and organizational structure, worker values and attitudinal trends, managerial trends, demographic trends and international developments.

## TECHNOLOGY AND ORGANIZATIONAL STRUCTURE

Technology has a major impact on the structure of organizations and on the nature of managerial work. Information systems such as

Oracle, SAP and Peoplesoft have eliminated the need for many middle management positions as much of middle management functions involve coordination and dissemination of information. HR strategists will need to consider changes in the nature of managerial work that will result from the accumulation of knowledge power in non managerial, technical positions. Managers require new skills to become effective in such environments.

Thus, in information based, lean and flat organizations, alternative job assignments are needed for the development of high level managers. Another impact of technology is the increase in the skill and managerial educational requirements. Although managers in advanced technological environments cannot have detailed knowledge of all aspects of technology, they must have a conceptual understanding in order to provide effective support and direction.

New product development approaches like parallel learning avoid the delays of sequential developmental processes. Information system like HRIS (Human Resource Information System) provides immediate information to decision-makers about the organization's human resource capability. Executives can now include more human resource information in the equation when making strategic or operational decisions. For e.g. Managers and employees can now use personal computers or kiosks to complete many HR transactions and to effect changes in their personal information like home address, without going through any sign-off loops. Line managers can complete routine tasks such as appraisals and salary changes.

## REDEPLOYMENT OF HUMAN RESOURCE STAFF TO OPERATING UNITS

Human resource generalists have been redeployed from human resource departments to individual operating units. Such decentralization provides better service to the units because the staff member is on site Staff management reports to the line management while retaining functional reporting relationship to human resource department. But because of the redundancies and costs associated with the deployment of human resource generalists to operating units, some experts have questions such arrangements.

## NEW ORGANIZATIONAL STRUCTURES

The distinctions between management and labor have become blurred. There is a shift from individual to joint accountability because more group members have the same information for decision-making. More work is being performed in task force team and project-oriented work groups. Organizations are becoming more flexible, adaptive and porous. New forms of superior-subordinate relations and rotating leadership roles require different managerial skills.

There are four new forms of interest: 1. Unbundled corporations 2. Network organizations 3. Cellular organizations, 4. Respondent organizations.

### Unbundled Corporations

Unbundled corporations employ a portfolio or a conglomerate approach towards their peripheral business units. Units are retained or divested as per their profitability and risk criteria. An example is Johnson & Johnson which has 190 autonomous operating companies in 51 countries and has had over 100 consecutive years of profitability. In unbundled organizations, many of the traditional support services of bureaucracies are outsourced to consultants and vendors. Some of the HR functions like training, compensation and payroll can be outsourced to vendors in order to redeploy resources to more profitable alternatives.

### Network Organizations

One of the driving forces for network organizations is the need to outsource the activities that other companies, consultants, or joint ventures partners can perform better or more quickly. The term *virtual* organizations are used to describe similar types of organizations in which there is heavy reliance on outsourcing and a critical need for speed. Membership in network organizations may include companies from throughout the world. The managerial requirements in network organizations include: 1. referral skills, 2. partnering skills, and 3. relationship management.

### Cellular Organizations

A form organization consisting of a collection of self managing firms or cells held together by mutual interest is a cellular organization. A cellular organization works on the principle of self-organization, member ownership and entrepreneurship. Each cell within the organization not only shares common features and purposes with its sister cells but also function independently.

Cellular organizations are characterized by small, autonomous groups that largely self govern and can grow, reproduce and form relations with other units. The cellular organization has an inward focus for knowledge exchange within teams or units coupled with boundary spanning across cells and in to the market place in order to gain access to external sources of knowledge while at the same time harboring inside knowledge for creative and competitive benefits. It has more knowledge exchange within subunits. This form is most suited for research forms where more varied approaches to knowledge development and access are needed across the sub units.

## Respondent Organizations

The respondent organization is essentially an entrepreneurial corporation that exists by filling niches to supply customized services to unbundled corporations. In such corporations, decision-making is retained at the level of the central entrepreneurial figure. However these corporations have high failure rates. Some of the today's Internet players are respondent corporations.

## Management Trends

Trends discussed in this section are: management of diversity, total quality management and reengineering.

## Management of Diversity

Because of the increased heterogeneity of the work force, managers must be prepared to deal with the challenges associated with such demographic changes. It has been demonstrated that ethnic heterogeneity in small groups is associated with increased quality of ideas generated for solving problems. It may also bring another benefit of prevention of "group think" that occurs in cohesive groups. However, these benefits will be obtained only if diversity is managed well. Organizations that do a good job of managing diversity tend to be more flexible because they have broadened their policies, have developed skills in dealing with resistance to change. For minorities and females, obtaining jobs with companies is less a problem than it was in the past. Groups should pay careful attention on how much to increase diversity. Too much diversity can lead to communication problems and unavoidable conflict.

## Work Teams

Companies such as Procter and Gamble and Motorola have developed substantial expertise in the utilization of teams. John R. Katzenback and Douglas K. Smith define work teams as "a small number of people with complementary skills who are committed to common purpose, performance goals and approach for which they hold themselves mutually accountable." A number of benefits have been attributed to the use of work teams who work for the organization. They are improved decision making, improved flexibility and improved quality of work. It may also lead to reduced labor costs, lower employee turnover, and shorter product development cycles. There are also disadvantages with the use of work teams like group think and norms of production restriction.

In design and production, cross functional work teams have been found to be effective. Such teams which typically include both design and production engineering personnel are ideally housed in the same area. Virtual teams have members who work closely together even though they are based at different locations. Advances in telecommunications, such as internet, e-mail and video-conferencing made virtual teams a possibility. A team at a Johnson & Johnson unit provides a good example of a virtual team. The team consists of members from Arlington, Texas and Juarez, Mexico where production facilities are located.

### Human Resource Outsourcing

Human Resource outsourcing is understood as contracting out permanently activities previously performed in house. Recent surveys found as many as 91 to 93 percent of responding companies engaging in outsourcing. From the strategic perspective, major companies have attempted to shift their focus and resources to a more strategic role through the use of outsourcing. To accomplish this, companies do outsource those HR functions which are low value-added and of routine nature.

### Integrated Manufacturing

Integrated Manufacturing Systems provide a new approach for manufacturing. Such systems include Advanced Manufacturing Technology (AMT), TQM and JIT (Just in time) inventory control methods. AMT is a manufacturing approach based on advanced computerized technologies such as computer-aided manufacturing (CAM). TQM have already been discussed in the previous section. JIT is a method for delivering manufacturing components to the production line at the shortest practical time before they are needed. Integrated manufacturing systems have the potential to provide greater dissemination of information and remove barriers associated with functional specialization.

### Reengineering

Reengineering has been practiced since the late 1980s, often by companies facing intense competitive pressures. Reengineering is directed at achieving large cost savings by eliminating unneeded components and consolidating work. **Business process re-engineering** is the analysis and design of workflows and processes within an organization. According to Davenport (1990), a business process is a set of logically related tasks performed to achieve a defined business outcome. An example of it is provided by its application at Texas Instruments. The driving force was the desire to reduce time required for making customized semiconductor chips for the customers. However, reengineering require cross functional coordination and the crossing of organizational boundaries. It many disrupt existing power relationships and eliminate organizational jobs and so it has high potential for conflict. Considering this point, organizations should not engage in reengineering unless they perceive a serious need. Some high level executives are not convinced of the ultimate value of reengineering as elimination of jobs increase the workload of remaining employees. Because of such reactions, the use of reengineering may diminish somewhat in the future. Re-engineering is the basis for many recent developments in management. The cross-functional team, for example, has become popular because of the desire to re-engineer separate functional tasks into complete cross-functional process.

### Demographic Trends

Many of the major demographic trends have important implications for human resource management. Many changes include an aging workforce, the baby boom, baby bust labor shortage, increased racial diversity and greater feminization of the workforce.

### An Aging Workforce

Some of the implications of aging workforce are that workforce will be more experienced, stable and reliable. An older workforce may lead to less flexibility as such workforce may not adapt to a dynamic economy. Greater costs will also result from pension contributions that are likely to be associated with an aging workforce. Another implication of this is as workforce ages there should be correspondingly greater health care cost. Noticeably, during postwar period in which Japan's remarkable economic growth occurred, it had relatively smaller proportion of retired people.

### Labor Shortages

At the beginning of twenty-first century, firms faced the tightest U.S. labor markets in 30 years to the extent that in some states the unemployment rates for adults fell below three percent. Employers were expected to respond to the shortages of workforce by hiring retired workers and even mentally challenged workers. A number of companies have achieved excellent results by hiring disabled employees. For e.g. at Carolina Fine Snacks, 50 percent of the employees have various impairments. Nonetheless after hiring these employees, company's productivity climbed from 50 to 60 percent of capacity to over 90 percent. Du Pont also has a long history of hiring disabled employees. Hewlett-Packard are using innovative approaches in staffing with older workers, frequently hiring their own retirees.

The most admired companies like General Electric, Microsoft and Dell Computer have high ratios of applicants to jobs. The advent of internet has created many jobs for highly skilled workers and helped the labor market work more efficiently by providing information about jobs. Internet recruiting has become so important that trade journals publish ratings of the top job sites such as Monster.com or Jobs.com.

### Greater Racial Diversity

Both domestically and internationally, organizations find themselves leading workforces that have variety of cultures and consist of a largely diverse population of women, men, young and old people, blacks, whites, Latins, Asians, Arabs and many others. Diversity may cause lack of cohesion that result in unit's inability to take concerted action. As mentioned earlier in this discussion of management of diversity, organizations will need to plan to take the advantage of diversity instead of forcing conformity.

### Changing Occupational Distribution for Women

In order to attract talented women, many employers have work arrangements that better accommodate child birth, as well as care of young children. Such approaches include, flextime, flexi-scheduling and allowing workers part time work at home. The trend towards flexi work is increasing which is evident from the examples of General Motors and Citibank. Between 1991 and 1997, the proportion of the civilian labor force working on flextime increased from 15 percent to 27 percent.

### Dual Career Couples

The number of couples having two wage earners has increased rapidly. In order to accommodate such families many employers offer support services such as "sick child" care programs and day care. Such services can positively influence productivity as they are believed to produce reductions in absenteeism and lower turnover. For e.g. referral services for child care is provided by IBM.

## TRENDS IN THE UTILIZATION OF HUMAN RESOURCE

### Telecommuting

The most important dimension of the technological environment in international management is telecommunications. It is no longer necessary to hardwire a city to provide residents with telephone service. With the advent of cellular phones, pagers and other telecommunications service, this can be done wirelessly. Technology is merging the telephone and the computer. As a result, in Europe and Asia growing number of people are using Web through their cell phones, while this development has not attracted a large market in the U.S.A. A form of technologic leapfrogging is occurring in which regions of the world are moving from a situation where phones are unavailable to one where cellular is available everywhere, including rural areas, because the infrastructure needed to support this can be set-up both quickly and relatively inexpensively.

One reason for rapid increase in telecommunications services in many countries is the belief that without an efficient communication system, their economic growth may stall. Most telecommunications operations which were state owned in Asia Pacific region a decade ago, are now run by the private enterprises as governments are accepting that the only way to attract foreign investment is to give up the control to private industry.

Telecommuting has brought many benefits including individual time savings from the avoidance of commuting as well as home child care, ease of working for multiple employers, access to jobs by disabled workers and lifestyle advantages. Also, it has positive impact on environment, when there are fewer employees on the highways. From the organization point of view, it helps in recruiting advantages, lower costs in using part time workers, reduced likelihood of unionization, productivity improvements and employee retention. Nonetheless, there are some problems with such arrangements, which include, control difficulties, social isolation, less sense of belonging and career limitations related to lack of visibility.

## Relocation of Work

Telecommunications advances have allowed information workers to migrate from cities to rural areas and small towns. Companies also relocate their operations. Automobile rental companies and hotels locate their reservation operations in areas of the country where they can get wage advantages. In Information Systems, relocation takes place where there are favourable cost advantages. Reservations operations for Hyatt Hotels are located in Carrolton, Texas as these areas offer wage advantages over many areas in the United States and location is irrelevant to the nature of work being performed.

## Growing Use of Temporary and Contingent Workers

Another important human resource issue is the increasing use of temporary workforce. They are often used to provide a buffer of protection for the jobs of the core permanent employees and there is likely to be additional unbundling in the future. Contingent employees have short term affiliations with employers. Examples include subcontracted workers, consultants, temporaries and leased employees.

Nature of temporary jobs is changing as there is shift towards the higher skill levels. Temporary employees include accountants, computer specialists, engineering personnel and financial executives. In information systems, employees providing temporary management services during project management or during installation of new system, belong to this category.

Because of economic uncertainty, many employers are reluctant to hire permanent employees and have increased their use of contingent employees. Fluctuating work load is the main reason for this. Companies also can avoid paying overtime pay by using temporary workers especially during peak demand periods. The use of temporaries who can be dismissed on short notice allows these companies to protect the core of permanent employees. In tight labor markets, it may be difficult to obtain qualified temporary employees. Other factors prompting the use of temporary workers include avoidance of recruiting, hiring and training expenses for workers who are to be used for short time. In addition to the benefits to the organization, there are some benefits for the workers, which include the flexibility to match lifestyle and family obligations with work and the ease of finding an elite job.

### Factors Limiting the Use of Temporary Employees

There are some disadvantages in hiring temporary employees. One is the increased likelihood of missing affirmative goals. With temporary workforce, disadvantage includes inordinate emphasis on short-term financial performance and absence of company loyalty. Disadvantage for temporary workers include lower opportunities to receive health insurance benefits, lower pay and fewer training opportunities.

## INTERNATIONAL DEVELOPMENTS

### Global Competition

Companies competing on a global basis will need to use world-class labor to obtain the quality needed for some product markets. Moving foreign nationals across international boundaries is another approach for using highly skilled individuals. In some U.S. companies with large overseas holdings, the number of U.S. expats is relatively small.

### Global Sourcing of Labour

Several Asian countries such as Korea, Singapore, Malaysia and Indonesia are major U.S. trading outsourcing partners. Nonetheless, the dramatic changes in Eastern Europe also have implications for labor supplies.

## SHRM ISSUES AND CHALLENGES IN GLOBAL MARAKETS

The coming of the 21st century globalization poses distinctive SHRM challenges to businesses especially those operating across national boundaries as multinationals or global enterprises. Global business is characterized by the free flow of human and financial resources especially in the developed economies of European Union (EU), the North American Free Trade Agreement (NAFTA), other regional groupings such as the Association of South East Asian Nations (ASEAN), the Economic Community of West African States (ECOWAS), the Southern African Development Community, etc. These developments are opening up new markets in a way that has never been seen before. This accentuates the need to manage human resources effectively to gain competitive advantage in the global market place. To achieve this, organizations require an understanding of the factors that can determine the effectiveness of various HR practices and approaches. This is because countries differ along a number of dimensions that influence the attractiveness of Direct Foreign Investments in each country. These differences determine the economic viability of building an operation in a foreign country and they have a particularly strong impact on SHRM in that operation. A number of factors that affect SHRM in global markets are identified: (1) Culture (2) Economic System (3) Political System—the legal framework and (4) Human capital. Human capital means the skills, capabilities or competencies of the workforce. This is in consonance with the believe that competency-based human resource plans provide a source for gaining competitive advantage and for countries profoundly affect a foreign country's desire to locate or enter that country's market. This partly explains why Japan and US locate and enter the local markets in South-East Asia and Mexico respectively.

In the case of developing countries, globalization poses distinct challenges to governments, the private sector and organized labour. These challenges, Strategic human resources management is largely about integration and adaptation. Its concern is to ensure that: (1) human resources (HR) management is fully integrated with the strategy and the strategic needs of the firm; (2) HR policies cohere both across policy areas and across hierarchies; and (3) HR practices are adjusted, accepted, and used by line managers and employees as part of their everyday work.

## STRATEGIC HRM AND ORGANIZATIONAL PERFORMANCE

Researchers in SHRM strongly insist on the fact that greater use of such practices help in improving and enhancing organizational performance. They firmly believe that organizations with stronger pay-for-performance norms achieve better long-term financial performance than did organizations with weaker pay-for-performance norms.

Instead of focusing on a single practice (e.g., staffing), they insists that simultaneous use of multiple sophisticated HR practices have positive co-relation with organizational productivity and financial performance. Such practices control absenteeism and turnover in the organizations.

HR personnel need to have both, professional as well as business-related skills and competencies to meet global challenges. A study of Singaporean companies found that when HR managers lack the necessary skills to perform their duties competently, line managers and executives take over some of the functions of HR managers (Nee & Khatri, 1999).

Experts believe that the internal dynamism of the HR function serves as the most critical mechanism to keep the integration process going after it has been started under favorable organizational and strategic circumstances.

There exist a significant relationship between SHRM practices and firm's performance. It has been found out that (1) HR-related competencies and, to a lesser extent, business-related competencies increase the extent of effective implementation of SHRM practices and (2) investments in human resources are a potential source of competitive advantage.

Many others believe that larger organizations should adopt more sophisticated and socially responsive SHRM practices because they are more visible and are under more pressure to gain legitimacy.

There are emerging evidences that HR practices may differ in organizations depending on the level of technological sophistication in terms of training, performance appraisal and reward systems.

The following are the main observations :

1. Human resource managers may have achieved higher levels of HR professional competencies and lower levels of business related competencies.
2. The incidence of implementing strategic HR practices is lower in organizations especially in the developing countries.
3. Both HR professional competence and knowledge of the business (business-related competence) significantly contribute to the extent of implementing SHRM Practices
4. Managerial competencies are significantly related to organizational performance.
5. The extent of implementing SHRM practices contribute significantly to firm level outcomes.
6. The relationship between SHRM and organizational performance is affected by organizational context variables (firm size, level of technology and union coverage).

It may be pertinent to point out here that the six propositions derived from the framework are particularly relevant for giving insights into the HRM challenges facing organizations in the new era globalization. In other words, these propositions will help us organize thought on the level of readiness (and otherwise) of organizations in response to the challenges of the global business environment. For example, if HR personnel especially in developing countries demonstrates higher levels of HR professional competence relative to the business-related competence. As stated earlier, it would be important to set right this wrong as a stepping stone for succeeding in global business. This is because to succeed in the new era of globalization, the human factor is central. That is why it is necessary for HR personnel to prove themselves beyond reasonable doubt that they are capable of playing key roles in enhancing the status of the HR department, possess a thorough understanding of business and also capable of acting as important influences in the level of integration between HR management and organizational strategy.

As governments and corporate bodies brace up for the new millennium characterized by an ever-increasing global challenge, developing countries have no choice but to develop and continuously, upgrade the human resource and business competencies of their workforce. In the case of developing countries, distinct competencies are important to deal not only with the HR issues but also with others including partnerships in economic recovery. In South-East Asia, for example, dealing with the "big boys", the fund managers, concerns over possibility of fraud in E-commerce with fast spread of Information Technology. Similarly, implementing prescriptions for recovery and growth taking into consideration the development agenda and unique circumstances of individual countries is an important issue. Addressing these issues is a necessary step towards facing the challenges of globalization into the next millennium.

# 15 The Role of SHRM in Risk Management

## INTRODUCTION

Human resources have two roles in risk management. On one hand, people are an important source of risk, e.g. an organization runs a risk of shortage of people, some people doing sloppy work, an employee leaving an organization after the completion of one year training program or an employee refusing to take additional responsibility. On the other hand, employees are most important source in handling risk, for, e.g. an employee showing their loyalty towards the organization, an employee redesigning his/her job to avoid unnecessary working for long hours or going an extra mile for the good of the organization. Human resources include full time and part time people, seasonal and year around employees. Risk specialists have focused more attention on factors like natural calamities such as weather or disease and have prescribed ways to deal with it. However, they have paid little attention to the more serious human resource calamities such as divorce, chronic illness, accidental death or the impact of interpersonal relations on business.

It is through people that managers can accomplish what they have planned. In case of smaller businesses, over dependence on family members for management and labor negatively affects family business as a family may have highly talented people in one area but may fall short in another area concerning management and labor. Thus, including human resource in risk management reflects that people are fundamental to accomplishing goals. Human resource affects most production, financial and marketing decisions.

## HR PARADIGMS

A manager's paradigms are the mind sets reflecting the knowledge, beliefs, perceptions and assumptions about the world in which he or she functions. Thus, they are the eyeglasses through which manager's view how people contribute to the business. There are 2 contrasting sets of paradigms, first set says that :

- people are unavoidable and unfortunate obstacles;
- the Role of SHRM in Risk Management is crucial; and
- hired labor doesn't care about the business.

Contrastingly the other set says:

- people are the most important key to the success of organization; and
- motivated human resource shows high level of dedication and loyalty.

Each firm's culture reflects its uniqueness in terms of values, norms and tradition. In order to change the paradigm, management team should change the culture and environment within which its people are functioning.

Managers incorporate their paradigms in to the firm's culture. To illustrate, a paradigm that view employees as not caring about the business will cause management to be hesitant to the employees to delegate responsibility to them. This leads to a culture in which employees are distrusted and it creates a gap between the employees and management. A paradigm that views workers as caring and dedicated to the business will lead managers to trust their workers. Thus, paradigms about people and the firm's culture together determine the environment within which people do their jobs.

## THE HUMAN RESOURCE MANAGEMENT/ RISK MANAGEMENT INTERFACE

Human resources are pervasive in the business. Human resource management when integrated with decision making is most effective. The choice that is made, the decision that is carried out, monitoring and follow-up all depends on people. To understand how HRM is inter-related with risk management, it is necessary to understand the concept of HRM. It is staffing, training and development, motivation and maintenance of employees. Each production, financial and marketing decision has a human component or influence. Thus, isolating employee issues from production, financial and marketing frustrates people and creates unnecessary risk in a business enterprise.

More specifically, HRM can be broken down into various activities like job analysis, writing job descriptions, hiring, conducting orientation, arranging training, conducting performance appraisals, compensation and discipline. Failure to successfully carry out these activities may not allow organization to take the advantage of what its people could be contributing.

This can be listed most effectively in the following manner:

- Conducting job analysis.
- Hiring appropriate human resources.
- Conducting orientation and training.
- Maintaining discipline.

The first activity of HRM is job analysis. It is the combination of job description and job specification. Job analysis is determining the duties and skill requirements of a job and the kind of person to fill it.

Job descriptions summarize for both employees and employers just what a job entails: job title, duties, compensation and skills, knowledge and abilities to do the job.

Hiring is the next human resource management activity. The objective of hiring is to staff each job with a person who can succeed in the position. In today's exceptionally tight labor market, hiring is one of the most difficult human resource activities. The position must be described carefully and creatively to potential applicants. From among the pool of applicants, people must be carefully chosen if they and the employer are to have a successful relationship.

The next activity after hiring is orientation and training.

Orientation is introducing the new hires to the firm's mission, culture and history. Training gives the employees the required skills and abilities to succeed in the job. Performance appraisal is the continuous assessment of how he or she is doing relative to the standards laid out in job description. Performance appraisal also includes identifying whatever corrective action be necessary by which the employee can advance in his/her career.

Discipline includes stating clearly the rules, regulations, policies and procedures and then working with the employee to get behavior consistent with employer expectations.

HR activities have four important implications for risk management. First, it is necessary to keep HR activities in line with the risk management tools adopted by the management team. As risk management decisions are carried out by people, it is important to have a right person at the right place that can be trained, motivated and rewarded in a proper way. Second, many HR calamities like divorce, chronic illness or accidental death can hamper carefully made risk management decisions. Though most of them are difficult to predict, risk management should anticipate the likelihood of the calamities. Third, considering the fact that no management team stays together, management succession is a significant source of risk. Fourth, HR performance evaluation should be tied to risk management. As risk management strategies are carried out through people, failure in any of the HR process can cause the best planned risk management strategies to fail.

The effective integration of HR with risk management requires managers to have following qualities :

- powerful skills of leadership,
- communication, training,
- motivation,
- conflict management, and
- evaluation.

Leadership is one of the most important qualities required by the manager. It is through effective leadership, that group comes close to its potential. The other management functions like planning, organizing, staffing and controlling can substitute to some extent for leadership. However, delegation of authority and responsibility to employees and empowering them can reduce the need for leadership. Still as it is the fact that each ship requires a captain, the importance of leadership cannot be underestimated.

Another most important skill required by the managers is communication. For the smooth functioning of the organization, it is extremely necessary for the managers to build the rapport with the team members. Besides, the management processes like recruitment, selection, orientation, performance appraisal, interviews and conflict management all require effective communication. Mediocre communication skills tremendously complicate these activities. Training is imparting skills and knowledge to the employees. It requires patience on the part of managers and an understanding of how the adults prefer to learn as well as its effective evaluation.

Motivating employees puts a real challenge in front of managers. There is no fix recipe as to how managers can motivate their employees. Some managers are more effective than the others in motivating employees. They use combination of free flow of communication, empowering and encouraging employees, compensating them fairly, creating an environment where employees can work with minimum frustration and treating them equitably. The skills to motivate the employees are nebulous yet real.

Conflict is inevitable. It can occur among employees, between employees and management team and among management team members. Avoiding conflict simply postpones the pain and agony that occurs due to personnel blowups. Conflict management strategies provide positive steps for addressing the conflict. Effectiveness with the strategies is an essential skill. Both supervisors and employees need training in evaluation for it to be useful and pleasant for both parties.

Evaluation is one of the most critical functions of management. Sometimes, supervisors find it difficult to share performance evaluation in an honest manner. Resultant effect of it is vague communication and inflated evaluations.

## CONCLUSION

Managing risk is the most critical function of management. Understanding of HRM and HR skills determine the success an organization will have with people. Management can make HRM one of their strengths by carefully planning all the HR process, thus reducing the risk of failure associated with HRM. The result will be better risk management and greater satisfaction of people and management.

# 16 Characteristics of Organisation Learning and Learning Organization

## INTRODUCTION TO ORGANIZATIONAL LEARNING

It has been found that as organizations grow, they lose their natural capacity to learn as company structures become rigid. To remain competitive, many organizations have restructured which means those who remain need to work more effectively. To create a competitive advantage, companies need to develop a customer responsive culture. Modern organizations need to update their knowledge about new products and processes, understand what is happening in the external environment and produce creative solutions using the knowledge and skills of all employed within the organization.

Organizational learning is a term introduced in the 1970s by Chris Argyris and Donald Schon. Argyris (1977) defines organizational learning as the process of detection and correction of errors. Organizational learning as described in the past "the process within the organization by which knowledge about action-outcome relationships and the effect of the environment on these relationships is developed. The learning organization includes a wide range of practical approaches advocated by consultants and practitioners. Senge (1990) defines learning organization as " a group of people continually enhancing their capacity to create what they want to create." In yet another view, Weick (1991) notes: "Perhaps organizations are not built to learn. Instead, they are pattern of means-ends relations deliberately designed to make the same routine response to different stimuli, a pattern which is antithetical to learning in the traditional sense." Thus, we have contrasting views on organizational learning.

## INTRODUCTION TO LEARNING ORGANIZATION

The Learning Organisation is a term that derives in part from OL, and includes a wide range of practical approaches advocated by consultants and practitioners, drawing on the fields of socio-technical systems; organisational strategy; production; economic development; systems dynamics; human resources; and organisational culture. These approaches do not have the same rigour of research associated with them as do the core concepts of OL.

Senge (1990) defines the Learning Organization as the organization "in which you cannot learn because learning is so insinuated into the fabric of life." Also, he defines Learning Organization as "a group of people continually enhancing their capacity to create what they want to create." I would define Learning Organization as an "Organization with an ingrained philosophy for anticipating, reacting and responding to change, complexity and uncertainty." The concept of Learning Organization is increasingly relevant given the increasing complexity and uncertainty of the organizational environment. As Senge (1990) remarks: "The rate at which organizations learn may become the only sustainable source of competitive advantage."

McGill *et al.* (1992) define the Learning Organization as "a company that can respond to new information by altering the very "programming" by which information is processed and evaluated."

## DISCIPLINES OF LEARNING ORGANIZATION

A learning organization exhibits five main characteristics: systems thinking, personal mastery, mental models, a shared vision and team learning.

### System Thinking

This is a conceptual framework that allows people to study businesses as bounded objects. This concept is very important and learning organization employs this method of thinking by developing information system that views the performance of the organization as a whole and of its various components. All characteristics listed must be apparent at once in an organization for it to be a learning organization. However, O'Keeffee believes that the characteristics of a learning organization are factors that are developed gradually rather than developed simultaneously. Thus, the essence of systems thinking lies in seeing interrelationships rather than linear cause-effect chains and seeing processes of change rather than snapshots.

## Personal Mastery

Learning cannot be forced upon an individual if he/she is not receptive to learning. Research shows that most learning in the workplace is incidental, rather than product of formal training. People with a high sense of personal mastery, feel connected to others, have a clear sense of purpose and never arrive on their learning-in- progress journey. They do not see failure as a sign of unworthiness; rather they see failure as an opportunity. Thus, personal mastery is the commitment by an individual to the process of learning. People with high sense of personal mastery have a commitment to truth and reality. Learning organizations have been defined as sum of individual learning, but it is important that there are mechanisms by which individual learning can be transferred into organizational learning.

## Mental Models

Mental models are the terms given to ingrained assumptions held by individuals. To become a learning organization, these assumptions have to be challenged. Individuals tend to espouse theoretical concepts, which they intend to follow, and theories in use, which is what they actually practice. Organizations also tend to have 'memories' which preserve certain behaviors and values. In the creation of a learning environment confrontational attitudes have to be replaced with an open culture that promotes inquiry and trust. Thus, if there are unwanted values held by the organization, these need to be discarded in a process called 'unlearning'.

## Shared Vision

The concept of shared vision creates a common identity that can provide focus and energy for learning. Visions of the people at the top usually may not be shared except at the top. Senge argues that there must be a shared appreciation of the current reality, and of the gap between the vision and the reality and the work needed to reduce the gap. However, creation of shared vision is likely to be hindered by traditional structures where a company vision is imposed from above. As a result, organizations tend to have flat, decentralized organizational structures.

## Team Learning

Learning organizations have structures that facilitate team learning. Team learning is the accumulation of individual learning; it is a process of aligning the individual within the team and developing the capacity of the team to achieve the results it is seeking. Open communication, shared meaning, and understanding are the prerequisites of team learning. Team learning requires individuals to engage in dialogue and discussion. Discussion is presenting of views and defending them in a search for the best argument. Dialogue always needs the involvement of a facilitator of some sort.

## ORGANIZATIONAL LEARNING V. LEARNING ORGANIZATION

Ang & Joseph (1996) contrast Organizational Learning and Learning Organization in terms of process versus structure.

McGill (1992) do not distinguish between Learning Organization and Organizational Learning. He defines Organizational Learning as the ability of an organization to gain insight and understanding from experience through experimentation, observation, analysis, and a willingness to examine both successes and failures.

## ADAPTIVE LEARNING V. GENERATIVE LEARNING

The current view of organizations is based on adaptive learning, which is about coping. Senge (1990) notes that increasing adaptiveness is only the first stage; companies need to focus on Generative Learning or "double-loop learning." In Senge's (1990) view, Generative Learning is about creating—it requires "systemic thinking," "shared vision," "personal mastery," "team learning," and "creative tension" (between the vision and the current reality.)

Adaptive learning or single loop learning focuses on solving problems in the present examining the appropriateness of current learning behaviors. The current organization is based on adaptive learning, i.e. about coping. Increasing adaptiveness is only the first stage or single loop learning. Generative learning or double loop learning emphasizes continuous experimentation and feedback in the ongoing processes of the organization. Adaptive learning focus on incremental improvements, wherein fundamental assumptions underlying the existing ways of doing work are not challenged. But to maintain adaptability, organizations should maintain themselves in a state of frequent, nearly-continuous change in structures, processes and goals. Generative learning is about creating, it requires—system thinking, shared vision, personal mastery, team learning and creative tension. Generative learning requires new ways of looking at the world.

## BARRIERS IN THE LEARNING ORGANIZATION

Most of the problems arise from an organization not fully embracing all the facets outlined above that are necessary in a learning organization. If these problems are traced out, they can be worked out.

### Organizational Barriers to Learning

If individuals do not engage with shared vision, personal mastery could be used to advance their own vision. The concept of personal mastery is intangible, the benefits of which cannot be quantified. Rather it can be seen as a threat to the organization. Lack of pro-learning culture can be seen as a barrier to learning. A learning organization need to remove traditional hierarchies so that there will be free flow of knowledge sharing process.

### Individual Barriers to Learning

Resistance to learning can occur within a learning organization by people who feel threatened by change or believe that they have the most to lose. Learning can be viewed as elitist and restricted to more senior levels of the organization. In this case, learning will not be viewed as a shared vision. If training and development is compulsory, it can be viewed as a form of control, rather than a form of personal development.

Argyris (1977) asserts that the problem of using IT is in its reinforcement of the prevailing rigid structure.

## MANAGER'S ROLE IN THE LEARNING ORGANIZATION

Leader's role in the Learning Organization is that of a designer and of a teacher, who can build shared vision, and challenge prevailing mental models. Thus, ultimately, leaders are responsible for learning, under whose guidance people are continually expanding their capabilities.

The key ingredient of the Learning Organization is in how organizations process their managerial experiences. Learning Organizations learn from their experiences being bound by past experiences. Generative learning is not measured by what an organization knows (the product of learning), but rather by how it learns (the process of learning). Management practices encourage, recognize and reward openness, efficacy and creativity.

# 17 Competency Mapping

## INTRODUCTION TO COMPETENCY MAPPING

Competency mapping is a way of assessing the strengths and weaknesses of a worker or organization. It is about identifying a person's job skills and strengths in areas like teamwork, leadership and decision making. Thus, it is about identifying a person's job skills and strengths in the areas like teamwork, leadership and decision-making.

Many competency mapping models break down strengths in to two major areas: functional and behavioral. Functional skills include practical knowledge that a person needs to perform a job. For e.g. functional requirements for a secretary might include familiarity with computer systems and office machinery as well as bookkeeping knowledge. These skills are generally easy to measure through skill tests and can define whether a worker is capable of carrying out his or her responsibilities.

Behavioral assessment is more difficult to quantify and is the focus of most competency studies. It examines personal skills such as leadership, active listening, teamwork and morale. This type of testing is important for getting a complete picture of an individual's skill set.

The use of Competencies can include: assessment during recruitment through specific work-based exercises and relevant, validated, psychometric tests; assessment of further development; as a profile during assessment to guide future development needs; succession planning and promotion; organisational development analysis.

Techniques used to map Competencies include Critical Incident Analysis and Repertory Grid.

Competency mapping is an approach that has the objective of helping an organization align individual development with the strategic objectives of the company. The following is the step-by-step process for competency mapping.

### Step 1. Development of Core Competencies

In this step, the leadership of the organization meets to brainstorm which core competencies the organization requires in order to achieve its objectives, goals, and vision. Examples of core competencies that are usually essential in organizations are problem-solving, team-building, decision-making, and communication skills.

### Step 2. Assessing Competency Levels Required Across Positions

After the leadership decides which competencies are essential, it is necessary to determine the degree to which, and manner in which, these competencies are required in each type of position (i.e., Sales Manager, Receptionist, and CEO). This assessment can be made through interviews with incumbents of sample positions, using a Position Information Questionnaire (PIQ).

### Step 3. Developing Competency-based Job Descriptions

Following the interview process, job descriptions can be developed that include not only duties and reporting relationships but the core competency descriptions that are tailored to each position. The same competencies are included in each employee's performance appraisal instrument so that he/she is evaluated on the same criteria that are specified in the job description.

### Step 4. Competency-Based Matrix

For career development purposes, new employees (or potential employees) will be interested in career progression options available once they master different competency levels. As career options become more complex and sophisticated, the core competencies are elevated in terms of sophistication as well.

### Step 5. Individual Development Planning

Using the job descriptions and the performance appraisal process as a foundation, Human Resources can provide coaching for individuals based on their unique developmental needs. For example, if a sales representative is interested in a position as Sales Manager, Human Resources professional can counsel this person about current strengths and areas for improvement and point out the competency levels required for the higher level position.

Then the employee and the HR person can jointly map out a plan for the employee's development (courses, workshops, mentoring, etc.)

## CORE COMPETENCIES EXPLAINED

Major competencies for which employers look, along with some of the behaviors associated with each. The following is a summarized list of the 31 competencies listed by "cluster" (similar competencies related to a common skill set). Each competency includes a definition and the observable behaviors that may indicate the existence of a competency in a person.

### I. Competencies Dealing with People

#### *The Leading Others Cluster*

1. *Establishing Focus*: This competency is the ability to develop and communicate goals in support of the business mission. The leader here—
   - Acts to align own unit's goals with the strategic direction of the business.
   - Ensures that people in the unit understand how their work relates to the business' mission.
   - Ensures that everyone understands and identifies with the unit's mission.
   - Ensures that the unit develops goals and a plan to help fulfill the business' mission.
2. *Providing Motivational Support*: The ability to enhance others' commitment to their work is covered under this competency.
   - Recognizes and rewards people for their achievements.
   - Acknowledges and thanks people for their contributions.
   - Expresses pride in the group and encourages people to feel good about their accomplishments.
   - Finds creative ways to make people's work rewarding.
   - Signals own commitment to a process by being personally present and involved at key events.
   - Identifies and promptly tackles morale problems.
   - Gives talks or presentations that energize groups.
3. *Fostering Teamwork*: As a team member, the ability and desire to work cooperatively with others on a team; as a team leader, the ability to demonstrate interest, skill, and success in getting groups to learn to work together is a part of this competency—

***Behaviors for Team Members—Here each Member of the Team***

- Listens and responds constructively to other team members' ideas.
- Offers support for others' ideas and proposals.
- Is open with other team members about his/her concerns.
- Expresses disagreement constructively (e.g., by emphasizing points of agreement, suggesting alternatives that may be acceptable to the group).
- Reinforces team members for their contributions.
- Gives honest and constructive feedback to other team members.
- Provides assistance to others when they need it.
- Works for solutions that all team members can support.
- Shares his/her expertise with others.
- Seeks opportunities to work on teams as a means to develop experience, and knowledge.
- Provides assistance, information, or other support to others, to build or maintain relationships with them.

***Behaviors for Team Leaders—The Team Leader, under this Competency***

- Provides opportunities for people to learn to work together as a team.
- Enlists the active participation of everyone.
- Promotes cooperation with other work units.
- Ensures that all team members are treated fairly.
- Recognizes and encourages the behaviors that contribute to teamwork.

4. *Empowering Others*: The ability to convey confidence in employees' ability to be successful, especially at challenging new tasks; delegating significant responsibility and authority; allowing employees freedom to decide how they will accomplish their goals and resolve issues are covered under this competency.

This competency—

- Gives people latitude to make decisions in their own sphere of work.
- Is able to let others make decisions and take charge.
- Encourages individuals and groups to set their own goals, consistent with business goals.

- Expresses confidence in the ability of others to be successful.
- Encourages groups to resolve problems on their own; avoids prescribing a solution.

5. *Managing Change*: This competency encourages the ability to demonstrate support for innovation and for organizational changes needed to improve the organization's effectiveness; initiating, sponsoring, and implementing organizational change; helping others to successfully manage organizational change.

***Employee Behaviors—Here the Employee***

- Personally develops a new method or approach.
- Proposes new approaches, methods, or technologies.
- Develops better, faster, or less expensive ways to do things.

***Manager/Leader Behaviors—In this Competency, the Manager***

- Works cooperatively with others to produce innovative solutions.
- Takes the lead in setting new business directions, partnerships, policies or procedures.
- Seizes opportunities to influence the future direction of an organizational unit or the overall business.
- Helps employees to develop a clear understanding of what they will need to do differently, as a result of changes in the organization.
- Implements or supports various change management activities (e.g., communications, education, team development, coaching).
- Establishes structures and processes to plan and manage the orderly implementation of change.
- Helps individuals and groups manage the anxiety associated with significant change.
- Facilitates groups or teams through the problem-solving and creative-thinking processes leading to the development and implementation of new approaches, systems, structures, and methods.

6. *Developing Others*: The ability to delegate responsibility and to work with others and coach them to develop their capabilities is a part of this competency—
   - Provides helpful, behaviorally specific feedback to others.
   - Shares information, advice, and suggestions to help

others to be more successful; provides effective coaching.

- Gives people assignments that will help develop their abilities.
- Regularly meets with employees to review their development progress.
- Recognizes and reinforces people's developmental efforts and improvements.
- Expresses confidence in others' ability to be successful.

7. *Managing Performance*: This competency includes the ability to take responsibility for one's own or one's employees' performance, by setting clear goals and expectations, tracking progress against the goals, ensuring feedback, and addressing performance problems and issues promptly.

### *Behaviors for Employees—The Employee Here*

- With his/her manager, sets specific, measurable goals that are realistic but challenging, with dates for accomplishment.
- With his/her manager, clarifies expectations about what will be done and how.
- Enlists his/her manager's support in obtaining the information, resources, and training needed to accomplish his/her work effectively.
- Promptly notifies his/her manager about any problems that affect his/her ability to accomplish planned goals.
- Seeks performance feedback from his/her manager and from others with whom he/she interacts on the job.
- Prepares a personal development plan with specific goals and a timeline for their accomplishment.
- Takes significant action to develop skills needed for effectiveness in current or future job. Behaviors for managers.
- Ensures that employees have clear goals and responsibilities.
- Works with employees to set and communicate performance standards that are specific and measurable.
- Supports employees in their efforts to achieve job goals (e.g., by providing resources, removing obstacles, acting as a buffer).
- Stays informed about employees' progress and performance through both formal methods (e.g., status

reports) and informal methods (e.g., management by walking around).

- Provides specific performance feedback, both positive and corrective, as soon as possible after an event.
- Deals firmly and promptly with performance problems; lets people know what is expected of them and when.

***Communication and Influencing Cluster***

8. *Attention to Communication*: The ability to ensure that information is passed on to others who should be kept informed in the main aspect of this competency—The manager:
   - Ensures that others involved in a project or effort are kept informed about developments and plans.
   - Ensures that important information from his/her management is shared with his/her employees and others as appropriate.
   - Shares ideas and information with others who might find them useful.
   - Uses multiple channels or means to communicate important messages (e.g., memos, newsletters, meetings, electronic mail).
   - Keeps his/her manager informed about progress and problems; avoids surprises.
   - Ensures that regular, consistent communication takes place.
9. *Oral Communication*: This includes the ability to express oneself clearly in conversations and interactions with others. The communicator:
   - Speaks clearly that can be easily understood.
   - Tailors the content of speech to the level and experience of the audience.
   - Uses appropriate grammar and choice of words in oral speech.
   - Organizes ideas clearly in oral speech.
   - Expresses ideas concisely in oral speech.
   - Maintains eye contact when speaking with others.
   - Summarizes or paraphrases his/her understanding of what others have said to verify understanding and prevent miscommunication.
10. *Written Communication*: The ability to express oneself clearly in business writing in developed here. The communicator:

- Expresses ideas clearly and concisely in writing.
- Organizes written ideas clearly and signals the organization to the reader (e.g., through an introductory paragraph or through use of headings).
- Tailors written communications to effectively reach an audience.
- Uses graphics and other aids to clarify complex or technical information.
- Spells correctly.
- Writes using concrete, specific language.
- Uses punctuation correctly.
- Writes grammatically.
- Uses an appropriate business writing style.

11. *Persuasive Communication*: The ability to plan and deliver oral and written communications that make an impact and persuade their intended audiences is the essence of this skill. The communicator:
    - Identifies and presents information or data that will have a strong effect on others.
    - Selects language and examples tailored to the level and experience of the audience.
    - Selects stories, analogies, or examples to illustrate a point.
    - Creates graphics, overheads, or slides that display information clearly and with high impact.
    - Presents several different arguments in support of a position.
12. *Interpersonal Awareness*: This competency includes the ability to notice, interpret, and anticipate others' concerns and feelings, and to communicate this awareness empathetically to others. Here the employees—
    - Understands the interests and important concerns of others.
    - Notices and accurately interprets what others are feeling, based on their choice of words, tone of voice, expressions, and other non-verbal behavior.
    - Anticipates how others will react to a situation.
    - Listens attentively to people's ideas and concerns.
    - Understands both the strengths and weaknesses of others.
    - Understands the unspoken meaning in a situation.
    - Says or does things to address others' concerns.

- Finds non-threatening ways to approach others about sensitive issues.
- Makes others feel comfortable by responding in ways that convey interest in what they have to say.

13. *Influencing Others*: The ability to gain others' support for ideas, proposals, projects, and solutions is the heart of this competency. The manager, here:
    - Presents arguments that address others' most important concerns and issues and looks for win-win solutions.
    - Involves others in a process or decision to ensure their support.
    - Offers trade-offs or exchanges to gain commitment.
    - Identifies and proposes solutions that benefit all parties involved in a situation.
    - Enlists experts or third parties to influence others.
    - Develops other indirect strategies to influence others.
    - Knows when to escalate critical issues to own or others' management, if own efforts to enlist support have not succeeded.
    - Structures situations (e.g., the setting, persons present, sequence of events) to create a desired impact and to maximize the chances of a favorable outcome.
    - Works to make a particular impression on others.
    - Identifies and targets influence efforts at the real decision makers and those who can influence them.
    - Seeks out and builds relationships with others who can provide information, intelligence, career support, potential business, and other forms of help.
    - Takes a personal interest in others (e.g., by asking about their concerns, interests, family, friends, hobbies) to develop relationships.
    - Accurately anticipates the implications of events or decisions for various stakeholders in the organization and plans strategy accordingly.

14. *Building Collaborative Relationships*: The ability to develop, maintain, and strengthen partnerships with others inside or outside the organization who can provide information, assistance and support is the core of this competency. Here the manager:
    - Asks about the other person's personal experiences, interests, and family.

- Asks questions to identify shared interest, experiences, or other common ground.
- Shows an interest in what others have to say; acknowledges their perspectives and ideas.
- Recognizes the business concerns and perspectives of others.
- Expresses gratitude and appreciation to others who have provided information, assistance, or support.
- Takes time to get to know coworkers, to build rapport and establish a common bond.
- Tries to build relationships with people whose assistance, cooperation, and support may be needed.
- Provides assistance, information, and support to others to build a basis for future reciprocity.

15. *Customer Orientation*: This competency focuses on developing the ability to demonstrate concern for satisfying one's external and/or internal customers. The leaders:
    - Quickly and effectively solves customer problems.
    - Talks to customers (internal or external) to find out what they want and how satisfied they are with what they are getting.
    - Lets customers know he/she is willing to work with them to meet their needs.
    - Finds ways to measure and track customer satisfaction.
    - Presents a cheerful, positive manner with customers.

## II. Compentencies Dealing with Business

### *The Preventing and Solving Problems Cluster*

16. *Diagnostic Information Gathering*: This competency means the ability to identify the information needed to clarify a situation, seek that information from appropriate sources, and use skillful questioning to draw out the information, when others are reluctant to disclose it. Here, the leader—
    - Identifies the specific information needed to clarify a situation or to make a decision.
    - Gets more complete and accurate information by checking multiple sources.
    - Probes skillfully to get at the facts, when others are reluctant to provide full, detailed information.
    - Routinely walks around to see how people are doing and to hear about any problems they are encountering.
    - Questions others to assess whether they have thought through a plan of action.

- Questions others to assess their confidence in solving a problem or tackling a situation.
- Asks questions to clarify a situation.
- Seeks the perspective of everyone involved in a situation.
- Seeks out knowledgeable people to obtain information or clarify a problem.

17. *Analytical Thinking*: The ability to tackle a problem by using a logical, systematic, sequential approach is the essence of this competency. The manager–
    - Makes a systematic comparison of two or more alternatives.
    - Notices discrepancies and inconsistencies in available information.
    - Identifies a set of features, parameters, or considerations to take into account, in analyzing a situation or making a decision.
    - Approaches a complex task or problem by breaking it down into its component parts and considering each part in detail.
    - Weighs the costs, benefits, risks, and chances for success, in making a decision.
    - Identifies many possible causes for a problem.
    - Carefully weighs the priority of things to be done.
18. *Forward Thinking*: This competency is the ability to anticipate the implications and consequences of situations and take appropriate action to be prepared for possible contingencies. The leader–
    - Anticipates possible problems and develops contingency plans in advance.
    - Notices trends in the industry or marketplace and develops plans to prepare for opportunities or problems.
    - Anticipates the consequences of situations and plans accordingly.
    - Anticipates how individuals and groups will react to situations and information and plans accordingly.
19. *Conceptual Thinking*: This competency lays emphasize on developing the ability to find effective solutions by taking a holistic, abstract, or theoretical perspective. The leader here–
    - Notices similarities between different and apparently unrelated situations.

- Quickly identifies the central or underlying issues in a complex situation.
- Creates a graphic diagram showing a systems view of a situation.
- Develops analogies or metaphors to explain a situation.
- Applies a theoretical framework to understand a specific situation.

20. *Strategic Thinking*: This competency is the ability to analyze the organization's competitive position by considering market and industry trends, existing and potential customers (internal and external), and strengths and weaknesses as compared to competitors. Here, the managers—
    - Understands the organization's strengths and weaknesses as compared to competitors.
    - Understands industry and market trends affecting the organization's competitiveness.
    - Has an in-depth understanding of competitive products and services within the marketplace.
    - Develops and proposes a long-term (3-5 year) strategy for the organization based on an analysis of the industry and marketplace and the organization's current and potential capabilities as compared to competitors.
21. *Technical Expertise*: The ability to demonstrate depth of knowledge and skill in a technical area is developed in this competency. The Manager—
    - Effectively applies technical knowledge to solve a range of problems.
    - Possesses an in-depth knowledge and skill in a technical area.
    - Develops technical solutions to new or highly complex problems that cannot be solved using existing methods or approaches.
    - Is sought out as an expert to provide advice or solutions in his/her technical area.
    - Keeps informed about cutting-edge technology in his/her technical area.

### The Achieving Results Cluster

22. *Initiative*: This competency is the ability to identify is the ability to what needs to be done and doing it before being asked or before the situation requires it. The person here—
    - Does more than what is normally required in a situation.

- Seeks out others involved in a situation to learn their perspectives.
- Takes independent action to change the direction of events.

23. *Entrepreneurial Orientation*: The ability to look for and seize profitable business opportunities; willingness to take calculated risks to achieve business goals are the core of this competency. The entrepreneur—
    - Notices and seizes profitable business opportunities.
    - Stays abreast of business, industry, and market information that may reveal business opportunities.
    - Demonstrates willingness to take calculated risks to achieve business goals.
    - Proposes innovative business deals to potential customers, suppliers, and business partners.
    - Encourages and supports entrepreneurial behavior in others.
24. *Fostering Innovation*: This competency believes in developing the ability to develop, sponsor, or support the introduction of new and improved method, products, procedures, or technologies. The innovator—
    - Personally develops a new product or service.
    - Personally develops a new method or approach.
    - Sponsors the development of new products, services, methods, or procedures.
    - Proposes new approaches, methods, or technologies.
    - Develops better, faster, or less expensive ways to do things.
    - Works cooperatively with others to produce innovative solutions.
25. *Results Orientation*: The ability to focus on the desired results of one's own or one's unit's work, setting challenging goals, focusing effort on the goals, and meeting or exceeding them is the essence of this competency. The manager—
    - Develops challenging but achievable goals.
    - Develops clear goals for meetings and projects.
    - Maintains commitment to goals in the face of obstacles and frustrations.
    - Finds or creates ways to measure performance against goals.
    - Exerts unusual effort over time to achieve a goal.
    - Has a strong sense of urgency about solving problems and getting work done.

26. *Thoroughness*: This is the ability of ensuring that one's own and others' work and information are complete and accurate; carefully preparing for meetings and presentations; following up with others to ensure that agreements and commitments have been fulfilled. The manager, here—
    - Sets up procedures to ensure high quality of work (e.g., review meetings).
    - Monitors the quality of work.
    - Verifies information.
    - Checks the accuracy of own and others' work.
    - Develops and uses systems to organize and keep track of information or work progress.
    - Carefully prepares for meetings and presentations.
    - Organizes information or materials for others.
    - Carefully reviews and checks the accuracy of information in work reports (e.g., production, sales, financial performance) provided by management, management information systems, or other individuals and groups.
27. *Decisiveness*: The ability to make difficult decisions in a timely manner is the base of this competency. Here, the manager—
    - Is willing to make decisions in difficult or ambiguous situations, when time is critical.
    - Takes charge of a group when it is necessary to facilitate change, overcome an impasse, face issues, or ensure that decisions are made.
    - Makes tough decisions (e.g., closing a facility, reducing staff, accepting or rejecting a high-stakes deal).

## III. Self-management Compentencies

28. *Self-Confidence*: This competency develops the faith in one's own ideas and capability to be successful; willingness to take an independent position in the face of opposition. An individual—
    - Is confident of own ability to accomplish goals.
    - Presents self crisply and impressively.
    - Is willing to speak up to the right person or group at the right time, when he/she disagrees with a decision or strategy.
    - Approaches challenging tasks with a "can-do" attitude.
29. *Stress Management*: This competency develops the ability to

keep functioning effectively when under pressure and maintain self control in the face of hostility or provocation. An individual, here—

- Remains calm under stress.
- Can effectively handle several problems or tasks at once.
- Controls his/her response when criticized, attacked or provoked.
- Maintains a sense of humor under difficult circumstances.
- Manages own behavior to prevent or reduce feelings of stress.

30. *Personal Credibility*: Demonstrated concern that one be perceived as responsible, reliable, and trustworthy. Here, an individual—
    - Does what he/she commits to doing.
    - Respects the confidentiality of information or concerns shared by others.
    - Is honest and forthright with people.
    - Carries his/her fair share of the workload.
    - Takes responsibility for own mistakes; does not blame others.
    - Conveys a command of the relevant facts and information.
31. *Flexibility*: This competency develops openness to different and new ways of doing things; willingness to modify one's preferred way of doing things. An individual—
    - Is able to see the merits of perspectives other than his/her own.
    - Demonstrates openness to new organizational structures, procedures, and technology.
    - Switches to a different strategy when an initially selected one is unsuccessful.
    - Demonstrates willingness to modify a strongly held position in the face of contrary evidence.

# 18 Multiskilling

## DEFINITION

A formal approach to train individuals to undertake a variety of work tasks within the same organization is known as multiskilling. Another definition regards labour unions and their structure, which promotes workers who have a range of skills for working on several different projects, which may or may not be included in the worker's technical job content. Multiskilling enables management to increase the capacity without increasing headcount, i.e. being able to do more with the same resources.

Multiskilling is one redesign strategy being used or considered in some service delivery settings in an attempt to enhance cost-effectiveness, increase efficiency, improve quality, and ensures coordination of services. The concept is not a new one.

Increasing capacity without increasing headcount means being able to do more with the same resources, or doing the same with fewer resources. It also means increasing the speed at which business is conducted.

There are a number of approaches to reducing the time it takes to do business :

- Improving the speed at which staff works—this can be done with the good old industrial engineering methods such as stopwatches and time and motion study and the new methods of six sigma;
- Eliminating work that adds no value to the customer, i.e. eliminating waste; and

- Doing the value-adding work in a different way so as to avoid monotony of work.

One such extremely rich source of ideas on different ways of doing things in financial services comes from Lean Manufacturing methods that were developed to eliminate waste was incorporated by Toyota to achieve extraordinary productivity gains year-in and year-out.

It uses Lean Manufacturing methods to increase productivity by 3-4% each quarter. Consequently, it has been able to tap lower-cost location and is now the only plant controlled by one of the major multinational electronics makers that continues to produce personal computers in Europe.

Most service businesses then copied the same industrial systems in their design, as these were successful systems that had demonstrated ability to achieve economies of scale, and consequently, to reduce costs. However, although Lean Manufacturing has become the benchmark in industry, it is in the inception stage in most of the organizations and its lessons have only just begun to be applied in service businesses. The JSK Solutions is at the forefront of this movement.

## CLASSIFICATION OF MULTISKILLING

"We consider multiskilling to fall into the following categories as defined by Cordery (1995).

### 1. Vertical Multiskilling

Here the employee takes on supervisory tasks such as overseeing or leading a self-management team. It can be considered as a form of empowerment. Thus, it is the extent to which supervisory or administrative support tasks are learned. For e.g. a worker learns some element of management, e.g. production scheduling, quality control, etc.

### 2. Horizontal Multiskilling

This is learning skills from another discipline or function within an organisation. For example an electrician learning some mechanical tasks or a process operator learning some maintenance skills. Horizontal Multiskilling can again be divided into two main types:

- *Skill broadening*—Here minor elements and tasks are learned on top of the predominant activity (major task). So expertise is maintained and efficiency is enhanced. For example, a mechanical engineer may learn how to isolate and disconnect a motor to avoid the use of an electrician.

- *Cross skilling/dual skilling*–Here another major activity is learned in addition to his main task and a person is considered competent to carry out any activity in these two main disciplines. For example, multiskilled craftsmen considered competent to carry out both mechanical and electrical tasks.

### 3. Depth Multiskilling

This is acquisition of more complex skills within the same job in order to offer a better overall service to the customers. For e.g. a pest control worker who empties and clean rat alarms, might be trained to repair the defects of alarms onsite, which would be adding value for the customer. Depth multiskilling may be used in companies where operators are multiskilled to carry out simple maintenance tasks. This frees time for maintenance craftsmen to carry out more complex activities.

### 4. Multiskilled Teams

A multiskilled team is a group of individuals who collectively have a range of skills. There are two main types of multiskilled team, those composed of traditional single skilled individuals collected into one team and managed by one supervisor, or a team of multiskilled individuals. The intent is to have a team where the strengths and specialisation are combined, which increases the range of skills available to tackle certain issues.

### 5. Typical Examples of Multiskilling

Cross-skilling is yet another type of multiskilling. Cross-skilling would be where, an individual is trained in the main discipline, and would be competent in skills of other disciplines as well. Traditionally craftsmen learnt just one trade. Some of the examples of multiskilling found in organizations are listed below:

An electrician would learn mechanical skills such as:

- pipework skills;
- basic manual handling;
- check monitoring;
- bearings and seals;
- basic access.

Some organisations also multiskill to ensure that incident management is adequate and appropriate. In these situations individuals are equipped with adequate skills and knowledge to enable them to handle an abnormal or emergency situation. Multiskilling becomes imperative in oraganizations where an incident or event has to be managed at all times. This means that there has to be flexibility within the team to ensure competent cover for lunch and other breaks, as well as for training and holidays.

In case of emergency management, multiskilling staff shares elements of vertical and horizontal multiskilling, where the members may have to assume a more senior role than their status traditionally allows because of the incident scenario.

## LEAN MANUFACTURING METHODS TO INCREASE CAPACITY AND IMPROVE SERVICE

Increasing capacity without increasing headcount means increasing the speed at which business is conducted. If one analyse the total time used to complete a transaction from getting the order from the customer to satisfying the customer's needs, one will identify that only a small portion of the total elapsed time is spent actually working on the transaction. JSK's experience is that in most service processes, the amount of time spent adding value to a transaction relative to the total time taken by the transaction from start to finish (the lead time) is well below 10%. The astonishing fact is that if one tries to make employees more efficient when they are processing the transaction, then one is only attacking 5% of the time. And even significant improvements are only a large percentage of 5%. The emphasis must therefore be on reducing the 80% waste.

## ELIMINATION OF ERRORS

Corrections and rework to fix errors cause a lot of time wastage. It means that errors have to be eliminated at source and a 'right first time' mentality has to be inculcated into the business.

Organizations have now started considerable steps to eliminate errors in their processes. However, the challenge that often remains is to eliminate errors flowing from their customers. The cost of fixing these errors can result in avoiding elimination of customers. The amount of the benefit implies the amount of investment that is worthwhile making to work with customers to eliminate errors on their side. For example, poor reference data in the capital markets industry cause failed trades that have been estimated to cost the industry $12 bn a year to fix. The cost can be used to determine a price to charge customers for the work that they create. Somewhat surprisingly, the experience has been that customers often elect to pay these penalties without complaint rather than fix their systems and processes to eliminate the charge.

There are many techniques for error-proofing processes. A three pin electric plug is a classic example of error-proofing. This is technique in which it is impossible to put it into the socket the wrong way round. In clerical environments, techniques include drop-down lists of valid names or codes, designing input screens to follow the flow of the manual forms, pre-filling data on forms and screens with what is already known.

Despite necessary precautions errors cannot be eliminated absolutely. There are still huge productivity gains to be derived from attacking the remaining causes of waste, the 80% noted in the discussion above, by changing the way business is done. Below we review half a dozen systemic issues that the managers often encounter in financial service processes.

## A ONE-SIZE-FITS-ALL APPROACH

This is a method in which the design of standardized systems are so framed that all transactions of the same type are handled in the same way. For example, all motor claims or current account applications are dealt with in the same way.

The impact on productivity is like a hidden tax as a single control system is exercised for the entire process. But as we know some transactions are more complex than others and some customers are more important to the business than others, yet they are all handled the same way. Simple transactions go through the same routines as the complex ones. In other words, far more effort than is necessary is applied to the simple transactions and they take far longer to process than necessary. The cost of this hidden tax can be easily computed, but our estimates show that it is often of the order of 30% of transaction processing costs. This cost is then compounded by poor service to key customers. The total cost is thus calculated.

## HAND-OFFS

Hand-offs (where the transaction is passed from one person or department to another) are a key source of delay and error. Delays occur because the transaction goes into a queue or in sequence. Errors and unnecessary effort occur during the start-up of processing a transaction when the new person has to learn his part of work.

The more that existing information about a transaction is required to continue processing, the greater the start-up effort and the higher the risk of error. Hence, hand-offs should be avoided. When they are essential, the timing of the hand-off to minimize the carry-forward information is critical.

## EXCESSIVE CONTROL

As all transactions have to go through the same process, even the simple transactions go through the same control procedures as the complex transaction (for which the controls were designed) which causes excessive control in the processes. In addition, many times additional controls are applied to cater for specific circumstances, but as we know, such circumstances do not occur regularly but the controls often remain. Similarly, controls are often demanded by internal auditors or compliance people. This then becomes the part of company culture as a 'safety first interpretation', or as a policy or on regulation grounds.

The most befitting example here is of 'gold-plating' of know your customer procedures that has even caused the FSA to comment on their excessiveness. A less obvious example of a pretty useless/ineffective control is the typical supervisory review. The supervisor is required to use their experience to determine what, if anything is wrong with a transaction. In most of the cases, it is not at all obvious what might go wrong, how it might go wrong, what the risk is or how significant the consequences could be, or even how to establish these. Now-a-days, it is easy to provide documents to prove validity of the occurrence of an error. An effective review is one where a risk analysis has identified the potential for error and the likely cause of the error. Effective supervisory review specifies what to check and how to identify an error.

## PENDING WORK

In-trays or queues of work waiting for a person or team in a workflow environment is also becoming a major drawback of many organizations today. In industry, the approach to allocating work pieces in advance of the work is known as a 'push' approach. The limitation of method is that a person or team may hit a complex transaction or other delays, while other items would still be in their queue as other people have no work to do. Thus, there is an imbalance in the workload. The other option is a 'pull' approach where each person pulls a transaction from the pool of transactions as they complete the previous one. A pull approach also enables key customer transactions to be inserted at the top of the queue to be dealt with by the next available processor, with the obvious benefits for customer service.

## PEAK WORKLOADS

How to handle peaks in demand is always a challenge. Here, Lean Manufacturing could be used a strategy to cope without increasing headcount. Another method is to use the 'pull' approach to ensure that critical transactions are handled during the peak, whilst others are held back for later processing. This approach works well in the fund management arena where there is a daily processing window. High value purchases and sales are handled during the peak whilst low value transactions are processed later.

Another such method is multiskilling. As we know multiskilling is combining the two skill sets in the teams to enable to control the situation during peak workloads. Multi-skilled teams also have the benefit of being able to minimize the disruption of the hand-off from call-handler to correspondence person because the hand-off is within the team. The correspondence person can look across the work area to ask more questions of the person who took the call.

## CO-LOCATION

Co-locating provides a real step-change in customer service and lead-time reduction. For example, it has become a regular practice in insurance companies for underwriters to take full responsibility for satisfying the customer's request. The ability to put a client on hold or promise a call-back and then be able to discuss additional information requirements, terms and even premium amounts with an underwriter there and then and get straight back to the client has a stunning impact. This increases staff morale immensely, dramatically improves customer service and delivers a major increase in conversion rates and sales.

## LEAN MANUFACTURING AND PEOPLE AND ORGANIZATION STRUCTURES

For the real success of Lean manufacturing in organizations, the staff has to be managed, motivated and rewarded and the organizations have to be structured in a more effective manner.

In planning a move to Lean Manufacturing, there are 4 key factors that have to be addressed from a People/Organizational Perspective:

### Rewards and Recognition

Rewards in the organizations are more quantity-oriented than quality oriented i.e. rewards are based on transaction numbers rather than service quality. In many organizations the staff is paid for turning up, clocking in and clocking out; that is, no change from the 'old' industrial model. In a Lean Manufacturing environment, the emphasis is put on increased efficiency and effectiveness is rewarded and this, in turn, leads to a continuous drive to become more efficient.

There is a considerable change in the approach to work now. In the' old model' it is about working harder, in the Lean model it is about working smarter. So a move to the Lean Manufacturing model requires a radical change in the reward system at all levels of the business (both financial and non-financial rewards), to that prople are driven to 'work smarter' environment.

### Management

The impact of Lean Manufacturing is not restricted to the 'workers'. Management has to change as well.

Usually it is observed in the organizations that most managers only concentrate on their small area. They very seldom have an organization wide perspective. They manage what is in front of them. For Lean Manufacturing to be successful, this silo mentality has to change.

In addition, managers need to 'think out of the box' to be able to accept some of the recommendations for improvement that are going to come from their staff.

### Organizational Design

The elimination of hand-offs changes organization boundaries. The elimination of errors at source often forces change in organizational design. This is a challenging task to sort cooperation across traditional organizational boundaries. Managers need to be open to input from colleagues—they need an agenda set by the CEO that clarifies the requirement for a 'team first, me second' stance, so that the business can be organized in the most efficient way possible for the ultimate goals.

### Multiskilling

As we discussed, multiskilling is a formal approach to train individuals to undertake a variety of work tasks within the same organization. Multiskilling enables management to increase the capacity without increasing headcount i.e. being able to do more with the same resources.

Multiskilling is a big part of Lean Manufacturing to ensure that capacity is not wasted by job specialization—having people on hand that can't do the work available. But there are certain questions that need serious deliberation. These few key questions are:

- Is the existing workforce capable of mutiskilling or not?
- If not—how can this be dealt with in the most supportive way possible?
- If yes—what combination of training, mentoring and coaching will be required to bring about the change in skill levels?
- What management and HR approaches need to be changed/ developed to support successful multiskilling?

- How will the multiskilling concept be 'sold' to the workforce for its effective implementation?

To conclude, we can say that both, people and process sides are of utmost importance to the organizations. Hence, unless the people side of Lean Manufacturing receives as much emphasis as the process side—any apparent capacity gains will not be realized even in medium-term. It is not simply increasing capacity without increasing headcounts. Lean Manufacturing provides a rich source of methods that can be adapted profitably by financial service businesses. These require continuous and combined efforts on the part of the staff as well as that of management. But successful implementation of these techniques is the need of the hour.

## ADVANTAGES OF MULTISKILLING BENEFITS FOR THE SERVICE PROVIDER

From the service provider's perspective, the main benefits are lower costs and increased flexibility. Overall personnel costs are reduced through (a) layoffs due to better utilisation of existing personnel, (b) lower temporary personnel recruitment costs, as employees will be better able to stand in for each other, and (c) increased flexibility and improved productivity.

(a) Increased profitability is also one major advantage of multi-skilling. One study of 131 US companies by the Texas Center for Productivity and Quality of Work Life showed that profits increased by up to 40% as a result of multiskilling and other innovative work practices.
(b) Flexibility increases because more employees are able to stand in for each other. This ultimately results in increased customer satisfaction and enhanced work quality. In several case studies, added flexibility is highlighted as the no. 1 benefit of multiskilling.

But, one thing that must be kept in mind is that training costs are likely to increase. However, tempting it may be to implement new job designs without investing in training, this is a mistake. Without proper training, quality will decrease, thus reducing customer satisfaction. The employees are also likely to experience reduced job satisfaction if they are asked to do jobs without having the requisite skills.

Another problem associated with multiskilling is that it may make 'jacks-of-all-trades' out of employees who formerly mastered one specialised job. Without careful consideration, a lack of specialised employees may impair service quality and also safety and effectiveness.

## BENEFITS FOR THE EMPLOYEE

From the employee's perspective the main benefits are better use of skills, increased job variety, higher pay and increased job motivation. Let us discuss them in detail.

(a) The employees may receive higher pay as a result of the company's increased productivity and higher profit on multiskill contracts. The surveys conducted so far reveals a fact that for some types of multiskilling, employees demand higher pay for the 'added' jobs or tasks.

(b) Employee promotion prospects often improve as the employee receives more training and more often supervisory and management training where vertical multiskilling is introduced.

(c) Interestingly, multiskilling may even be demanded by employees in the future. Today, work is central to employees' professional and personal identity and multiskilling is one way of improving the status of a job and, hence, quality of life. The current challenge is to make employees feel emotionally attached to the job as much as to the company. Multiskilling does just that.

But the issues that the employees are likely to face cannot be overlooked Many employees will undoubtedly worry about their ability to take on the new jobs and the people skills of the management team will have decisive influence on whether employees take a positive or a negative view of job variety. Also, there is full possibility of employees resisting to organizational change that are inevitable when multiskilling is introduced. Change management is a central but often neglected discipline in this context.

## BENEFITS FOR THE CUSTOMER

The ultimate benefit will pass over to customer by way of reduced price, better quality of service and faster response time. The fact that service employees can stand in for each other means that the client will experience significantly fewer disruptions to the overall service. If the customer organisation decides to introduce multiskilling itself (i.e. there is no service provider involved) all the benefits listed above accrue to the customer as well.

## JOB SATISFACTION

Job satisfaction is one of the most frequently used metrics in industrial psychology—and with good reason. It is stable over time, well documented and it correlates well with performance, employee turnover, customer service and absenteeism.

Job satisfaction is defined as "a measure of how employees feel about their work on the basis of a cognitive evaluation of the job". Various attributes constituting job satisfaction are often surveyed to arrive at a better and more complete understanding of the employee's job satisfaction. Common aspects are pay, promotion prospects, supervision, co-workers, security, communication, job conditions and the nature of the actual work.

## ANTECEDENTS OF JOB SATISFACTION

What makes employees satisfied with their jobs? The leading theory suggests that job satisfaction is a combination of the characteristics of the job itself and the employee's personal values.

The characteristics of the job-based on the Job Characteristics Model (JCM)—show that job satisfaction is predicated on five job characteristics:

- *Task identity*—the degree to which the job involves completing a whole, identifiable piece of work rather than simply a part.
- *Task significance*—the extent to which the job has an impact on other people, inside or outside the organisation.
- *Skill variety*—the degree to which the job requires different skills.
- *Autonomy*—the extent to which the job allows jobholders to exercise choice and discretion in their work.
- *Feedback*—extent to which the job itself (as opposed to other people) provides job-holders with information on their performance.

## IMPLEMENTATION OF MULTISKILLING

It is undoubtedly important for the service provider to approach multiskilling as a win/win potential for all stakeholders and not only as a way of reducing costs and improving profitability. Improving job satisfaction and motivation for the individual workers is equally important.

A best practice implementation process depends on two key factors:

## 1. Change Management

Our survey showed that employees are generally positive towards multiskilling but the people-management side of the process often lets them down. Change management issues such as communications, involvement and people management must be carefully considered.

Communication must be honest, simple and meaningful. Honest implies clarity regarding important matters such as headcount reductions, job change, pay and benefits. It must be comprehensive otherwise rumours, gossip and speculation will prevail.

Finally, the communication must be meaningful and related to the employees' situation. It is necessary to have involvement of employees throughout the entire process. Studies have demonstrated a negative link between the level of employee involvement and level of resistance to a change project. Employees are simply more likely to embrace and appreciate a change if they are actively involved. The employees also have valuable knowledge about the day-to-day work and insights into which jobs can be combined and how. Customers must also be involved to make the process more meaningful.

Finally, managers must display strong people management skills. This includes listening to issues of workers and dealing with them on a one-to-one basis as well as considering each individual's needs in the design process.

## 2. Project Management

This includes using a robust, well-tested project process comprising job planning, training, assessment and skills maintenance. The company will have to analyse the new job designs, the training to be provided and the skill to be improved, the selection process for employee assignments and the new jobs, as well as monitor any skills attrition.

Both change management and project management may be viewed as two distinct life cycles, and indeed both should be dealt with separately, according to two separate plans. But they should also be considered as one, since they both constitute the combined implementation of multiskilling.

## CONCLUSION

Multiskilling is a revolutionary approach. It is an effective and practical way of organising work in outsourcing. It has the potential to create a win/win situation among all internal and external stakeholders. The benefits include cost reduction, improved service levels, increased job satisfaction, improved pay and conditions for the worker and unlocking of talents in the workforce.

Thus, it can be concluded that multiskilling does indeed increase job satisfaction if—and only if—the process of introducing multiskilling is handled properly. The studies reveal a surprising fact that employees with multiple skills do not indicate higher job satisfaction than single-skilled employees and the main reason is the way in which the new job designs are introduced. People management skills are very important throughout the entire project.

Multiskilling should be approached as a win/win potential for all stakeholders and not only as a way of reducing costs and improving profitability. Improving job satisfaction and motivation for the individual workers is equally important. A best practice implementation process includes an equal focus on change management and project management.

# 19 Succession Planning

## INTRODUCTION

The workforce in the organization does not remain stagnant. Change in personnel positions is a natural phenomenon. Succession planning is an ongoing system of selecting competent employees ready to move into key jobs in the organization, should these become vacant. Job-person matches are made between existing employees and future jobs they are likely to assume.

These future jobs are usually higher level positions. But, succession planning may be for key jobs above, at the same level, or even below the job an employee now holds.

Increasingly, succession planning is for lateral job moves (e.g., to a different function, department, project team, or territory).

A successful succession planning system needs to fulfill following criteria:

1. One, preferably two, well-qualified internal candidates are identified as ready to assume any key job as and when it becomes vacant.
2. A record of successful promotions (or other job placements) is prepared and referred to as and when require.
3. Few superior performers leave the organization because of "lack of opportunity." Hence, a second line of defense has to kept ready.

Competency-based succession planning is little complicated. This system identifies the competency requirements for critical jobs, assess candidate competencies, and evaluate possible jobperson matches. Career path "progression maps" identify key "feeder" jobs for lateral or higher level "target" positions within a job family or across job families.

A competency-based succession planning system assesses how many employees in which feeder jobs have (or have the potential to develop) the competencies to perform well in key target jobs. There are two ways of doing this.

- The first is to compare the competencies of people in the feeder job with the competency requirements of the target job. Thus, the gaps are identified.
- The second is to compare the competency requirements of the feeder job and the target job.

## ORGANIZATIONAL ISSUES

The issues that indicate a need for competency-based succession planning systems are discussed here:

- Promotion or placement outcomes are poor; too many people promoted or irrational transfers to new responsibilities result into failure to discharge responsibilities successfully or to quit.
  Typical examples are promoting the best technical professional to supervisor or the best salesperson to sales manager and then noticing the lack of essential interpersonal understanding and skills.
- In downsizing organizations, the key placement question may be which managers have kept up with their technical and professional competencies so they are able to return to individual contributor roles. "Lean and mean" organizations offer fewer vertical promotional or career path opportunities, with the result that more succession planning is lateral.
- In the times of rapidly changing situations organizations require employees with different competencies. Globalizing firms need employees with the competencies to function in different parts of the world. Stagnant firms need employees with innovative and entrepreneurial competencies to survive in markets with shorter product life cycles and fast moving foreign competitors. Downsizing firms need to decide who stays and who is to let go, that is, which employees have the competencies to fill demanding "same amount of work with fewer people" jobs in the new, smaller organization.

- Mergers, acquisitions and reorganizations require the surviving firm to decide which existing employees are needed and who can adapt in the new structure. Mergers of similar firms often result in an organization with two marketing departments, two sales forces, duplicate staffs in many functions. Merger efficiencies come from elimination of the double headcount. As with downsizing organizations, the question of who stays and who goes is determined on the basis of capacity and capabilities of employees.

## STEPS IN DEVELOPING A COMPETENCY-BASED SYSTEM

### 1. Identify Key Jobs

Key jobs are the base on which the existence of organizations is decided. Identifying these jobs in the organization's structure or the structure it wants for the future usually includes identifying the firm's strategy, its critical value-added target jobs, and key feeder jobs to these target jobs. Most organizations will have some variant of the seven levels shown in Table 1 for line, technical/professional, or functional staff, and team/project manager job families.

TABLE 1

**Generic Organizational Structure: Feeder Jobs and Levels**

LINE

1. *Individual Contributor*: Seasoned professional new hire
2. *First Line Supervisor*: Homogenous work
3. *Department*: Manages several work units managed by subordinate supervisors
4. *Several Departments*: Manages plant, region, several departments, function managers
5. *Business Unit*: President or General Manager
6. *Division*: Manages many business units (e.g., Group VP of large firm)
7. *Major Corporation CEO*: Large complex multidivision organization.

STAFF

1. *Individual Contributor*: Seasoned professional New hire
2. *Lead professional*: Integrates other professional's work
3. *Function Manager*: (finance, human resources) for a small business unit
4. *Several Functions*: (e.g., finance and administration)

5. *Top Function Manager*: For a business: VP Finance, VP Marketing
6. *Corporate Executive VP*: Chief Financial Officer.

**TEAM PROJECT**

1. *Individual Contributor*: Seasoned professional New hire
2. *Team/Project Leader*: without permanent reports
3. *Project Manager*: Coordinates Project/Team Leaders from several work groups
4. *Large Project Manager*: Manages other Project managers
5. *Major Product Manager*: Coordinates all functions—R&D, marketing, manufacturing, HR
6. *Mega Project Manager*: $100+ million (e.g., NASA, military weapons acquisition). Vertical progression in a job family is:
   a. *Individual contributor, often divided into two subgroups*: new hire and seasoned professional,
   b. First-level functional supervisor, managing a homogeneous group of individual contributors (e.g., a move from engineer to chief engineer or programmer to software development team leader). For functional technical/professionals and project job families, this level may be a lead professional who acts as a temporary team leader, assists and integrates other professionals' work, and mentors junior employees, but does not have any permanent reports,
   c. Department, function or project managers, who manage supervisors or lead professionals of several work groups,
   d. Multiple departments or functions managers, who manage several other departments, function, or project managers (e.g., a plant or regional manager, or director of finance and administration),
   e. Business unit general manager, such as CEO of a small firm (less than $20 million in annual revenues); top functional manager, such as Marketing or Finance Vice President of a medium-size firm ($20-$200 million revenues); or manager of a major project,
   f. Division general manager, such as CEO of a medium-size firm ($200 million revenues); top functional executive in a large firm ($200+ million revenues), or mega-project manager, and
   g. CEO of a large, complex multidivision organization.

### 2. Develop Competency Models for Critical Target and Feeder Jobs

This step calls for development of competency models for each of several steps in a job family ladder. BEIs conducted with four superiors and two averages at each level are analyzed to identify competencies required for a superior performance at the level and also to highlight how the competencies change or grow as an employee advances up the ladder.

### 3. Assess Candidates (and Current Job Holders) Against Competencies for Target Jobs

As in competency-based selection programs, substeps are (a) identify cost-effective assessment methods, and (b) train assessors to evaluate candidates for (and incumbents in) target jobs. Assessment for succession planning can require considerable resources. Each level down an organization goes in assessing people in feeder jobs increases the population to be assessed. For example, if span of control is five employees in a feeder job to each higher level job, one level down requires 5 assessments, two levels: 5 × 5 = 25 assessments, and three levels: 5 × 5 × 5 = 125 assessments.

### 4. Make Decisions about Job Incumbents and Candidates

Job incumbents are evaluated on their competencies to do their jobs and potential to go higher in the future. People are usually classified as:

a. Promotable, either: (1) Ready now, or (2) Developable (i.e., could be ready in the future if they develop specific competencies to the level required by the future jobs for which they are candidates)

b. Not promotable:
   (1) Competent in their current job, and/or
   (2) Have potential to transfer laterally to some other job

c. Not competent in their current job and not a fit with other jobs in the organization as it will be in the future. These people are candidates for early retirement or outplacement. If the organization finds there is no one promotable or developable for key jobs, the only alternative is to recruit new hires with needed competencies.

### 5. Develop a Human Resource Management Information System

Computerized human resource information system has become inevitable now-a-days. Succession planning for more than a few positions also requires to keep track of the competency requirements of all jobs, competencies of these people assessed, and evaluation of possible job—person matches.

## 6. Develop a Development/Career Pathing System (Optional)

Succession planning systems create demand for competency-based development and career pathing systems. Once employees understand the competency requirements for higher jobs and the gaps between their competencies and those required by the jobs they want, they organize training or other developmental activities to fill the gap. Similarly, once an organization is aware of the competencies it needs to be successful and the gaps between these needs and the capabilities of its existing or projected staff, it seeks selection or developmental programs to fill these gaps.

# Cross-cultural Training

## MEANING OF CULTURAL TRAINING

Countries, now-a-days, operate across borders and hence, cross cultural training has now crept in Indian organizations. This is an aspect of training which helps an individual to understand the vivid cultural aspects and norms of other cultures across the globe. It is essential to know, understand and respect cultural differences so as to alleviate misunderstandings that occur due to cultural differences. It also entails learning foreign languages, foreign mannerism and styles. Cross-cultural training is especially important for anyone who has international relations with different cultures.

The business scenario of the country has changed in last few decades. International businesses are facing new challenges to their internal communication structures due to major reforms brought about through internationalization, downsizing, mergers, acquisitions and joint ventures.

## LACK OF COMMUNICATION

Lack of investment or inadequate investment in cross cultural training and language tuition often leads to deficient internal cohesion. The loss of clients/customers, poor working relations, misunderstandings, stress, poor productivity, poor staff retention, lack of competitive edge, internal conflicts/power struggles and lack of co-operation are all by-products of poor cross-cultural communication. To overcome these problems, cross cultural communications consultants are appointed in organizations and they make efforts to minimise the above consequences of poor cross-cultural awareness.

There are some common hurdles to effective cross cultural communication within companies. Here we outline a few examples of these obstacles to cross cultural co-operation:

> It may seem obvious to state that non-communication is probably the biggest contributor to poor communication. Yet it continues to prove itself as the major problem within most companies.

Communication with staff members to built formal as well as informal relations is inevitable. A management which does not and will not communicate and interact physically with staff demonstrates a lack of interest, trust and respect. Lack of communication with staff is not solely due to lack of spoken dialogue. Many times it is done deliberately to conceal some important information. For example, not giving feedback (negative or positive), informing staff of decisions and actions that will affect their roles or failure to properly communicate expectations are all ways in which information can be withheld from staff. This may have negative repercussion in long run.

If managers are too selective in providing information, this can cause suspicion and jealousy among staff and will eventually result in internal strife instead of cohesion.

In the West it is often the case that communication lines are vertical. Staff report up to managers and managers up to senior levels and so on. Ideally lines of communication should run both ways, and if necessary, in zigzag ways. Those with a subordinate place in the communication process tend to feel estranged, indifferent and possibly even belligerent. Lack of communication in all its forms is unhealthy. Companies and managers must be aware of how, what and to whom they are communicating.

## LANGUAGE

Communication difficulties through language come in two forms: Use of inappropriate language. Communication has to be supported by proper words and proper gestures. Language carries with it subliminal meanings and messages transmitted through vocabulary, stress and tone. The wrong use of words or emotions hidden behind phrases can send messages that affect staff self-perception, confidence and attitude. Critical language causes poor interpersonal relationships and low self-confidence whereas supportive language and tones has the opposite effect.

## FOREIGN LANGUAGES

These days, offices may have native speakers of over 50 languages all under one roof. Yet, it is important that the main language of the office is established, whether it be English, French or Spanish. Once this is constituted all employees should only converse in the main language. This avoids the feeling of being alien in the group. In addition, a company should ensure that all its employees are fully conversant with the main language. Language tuition should be seen as a necessity not a luxury.

## CULTURE

International businesses with a highly diverse workforce in terms of nationality and cultural background face challenges from the differences in language, values, belief systems, business ethics, business practices, behaviour, etiquette and expectations.

Cross-cultural differences can negatively impact a business in a variety of ways, whether in team cohesion or in staff productivity. Acceptance of cultural diversity of people working under single roof is very tough. Efforts should be made to develop unity in such diversity.

In such multicultural companies, objective help may be needed through a cross cultural consultant who will show teams and individuals how to manage cultural diversity and work together more cohesively and productively.

## COMPANY CULTURE

Each company has its own culture that is unique in its way. Company culture pertains to the internal culture of a company in terms of how it is managed. For example, does the company view its different departments such as sales, production, administration and HR as closed or open systems? A closed system is one in which there is a total lack of synergy between the sales and production department due to the structure and communication lines between the two. An open system claims for team efforts. It is vital that team work, team building and team spirit are encouraged in order to create open systems.

Such open systems are seen more in case of joint ventures and mergers whereby co-operation between two or more companies requires their total commitment to an open system.

To stand in today's competitive era, many companies are primarily focused on the financial and strategic side of company operations. International businesses are now realising that many of their business problems have roots in man-management and communication.

In summary, we can conclude that the biggest hurdle to effective cross cultural adaptation is a reluctance to invest in the expertise and resources needed to overcome the problems as outlined above. Cross-cultural hurdles are easily negotiable with some objective and well-qualified assistance.

## BENEFITS OF CROSS-CULTURAL TRAINING

Many educational institutions offer students a chance to be trained on different aspects of the various world cultures. Usually, larger institutions offer this cross-cultural courses and foreign languages to their students free of charge. A student who intends to be on the international front as a part of his career should therefore grab such opportunities. The benefits include are manifolds.

Cross-cultural training, widens the vision, breaks down barriers developed due to prejudiced perceptions and preconceptions towards other cultures. When such barriers are demystified, better relationships between people of different cultures can be formed.

Effective communication is attained when people learn foreign languages. This helps in eliminating many misunderstanding. It also ensures that important information can be passed to the targeted group without any hindrance. This is a big benefit to organisations which work with multicultural communities.

Cross-cultural training helps building mutual trust and confidence. Mutual understanding is driven by trust and for this co-operation between cultures is enhanced.

Career development is another area which benefits from cross-cultural training. An individual who has received cross-cultural training has a competitive career advantage as compared to those who are not exposed to multicultural interactions.

Cross-cultural training helps one to understand his own culture. You cannot learn another culture unless you have a good understanding of your own. It, therefore, helps an individual to explore his own cultural values and to study how they are perceived by other cultures.

As a result of cross-cultural training, learners are able to develop good tolerance, interpersonal and listening skills.

Intercultural training helps an individual to adjust to a new working or living environment fast, and thus helps broaden ones vision. It reduces culture shock as one is trained to think positively and to embrace new cultures. Hence, organizations do not consider spending on cross-cultural training as their costs but treat it as their investment that reaps a fruit after some time.

# 21 Case Studies

## 1. F.J. BENJAMIN : TRAINING TO SERVE

The name behind fashion and lifestyle brands like Banana Republic, Gap, La Senza, and RAOUL, and timepiece brands such as Guess Watches, Nautica and Victorinox, F.J. Benjamin Holdings Ltd. has a significant foothold in the service sector. While the industry has immense talent management challenges such as traditionally high attrition rates and other recruitment issues, F.J. Benjamin still looks to develop its people through training.

Being squarely in the service industry, the group invests heavily in upgrading the service quality of its retail staff with regular and consistent training. "Our multiple industry sector-topping performance in the Retail Industry Mystery Shopping (RIMS) is testament to the effectiveness of our training, and the dedication of our people at every level of the organisation," says Terence Lim, F.J. Benjamin's Divisional Manager—HR. "We recognise the true value of our people, and investing in them is a top priority."

For instance, when many smaller retailers hire new sales associates, only basic training in how to operate the cash register is provided. They start work immediately without knowing the finer points of service, or how to handle different situations that inevitably arise in-store. F.J. Benjamin believes that by the time new staff enter its boutiques, they should already possess the mind-set and skills needed to provide customers with an exceptional experience. "I think it's evident that without training, service suffers," says Lim.

## Clocking the Hours

Clocking over 22,000 hours in employee training since 2009 is no mean feat. The luxury and lifestyle retailer accomplished this through mandatory basic service training as well as advanced specialised programmes like foreign language courses and 'Styling for Success'—a course that equips retail staff with working knowledge of the fundamentals of fashion styling techniques.

The company adopts a practical approach when planning training schedules for personnel. As most of F.J. Benjamin's shops are already running a tight ship, the training department has its work cut out for it.

"Our training section works hand-in-hand with our retail operations to find suitable times for training," says Lim. "There is commitment on both sides to make it work, because we understand the importance of customer service."

For instance, HR works around major sale periods, as well as manpower requirements, even increasing the number of available training dates to accommodate lean store headcounts.

Operations managers also frequently adjust their rosters to ensure that everyone in their brand has the opportunity to be trained. Furthermore, a significant proportion of training is done on-the-job, within the work environment, which allows flexibility in terms of venue and timing.

This year, F.J. Benjamin hopes to develop new Singapore Workforce Skills Qualifications (WSQ) modules to enhance its training capability, as well as increase the number of staff trained through the WSQ framework. "In previous years, SPUR funding has been a great aid to our budget, and needless to say, we will miss its demise," says Lim. The Skills Programme for Upgrading and Resilience (SPUR) was a funding scheme developed to subsidise training programmes during the economic downturn and was made available until 30 November 2010.

## Training Leaders

However, that has not deterred F.J. Benjamin from partnering with Temasek Polytechnic to avail the WSQ Diploma in Retail Management certification to senior retail operations staff in late 2008, at the height of the recession. Its inaugural intake graduated in July last year. The second batch of promising staff is currently attending the diploma course.

The course includes modules that address such areas as merchandising, service excellence and retail operations to marketing strategies and finance. The holistic programme ensures that employees will acquire critical retail knowledge while applying a wide range of capabilities for decision making in a dynamic environment.

With course fees fully subsidised by the WDA and F.J. Benjamin, 10 promising senior level candidates are selected to undergo a rigorous 17-month course each year, graduating with a Diploma in Retail Management on completion.

Employees have to undergo a stringent selection process to qualify for enrolment. Besides positive performance appraisal ratings, they must display aptitude and potential to be groomed for management positions within their organisation.

"These are staff we have earmarked as potential future leaders," says Lim. "Of course, there are many factors that determine their future with the company, however, sponsoring their diplomas shows our commitment to providing professional academic opportunities for our employees' career progression."

This highly successful endeavour has highlighted the value of WSQ to the industry, and to F.J. Benjamin. Staff have had the double benefit of graduating with a nationally-recognised diploma, while at the same time applying what they have learnt on the sales floor. Many of those from the July graduation were promoted, and are now part of vibrant leadership teams in the company's numerous brands.

"The feedback so far has been fantastic, with our diploma students saying that the programme has helped them gain a bird'seye view of how the organisation works, and how various departments and processes integrate with each other," says Lim.

## Learning Principles

In any organisation, a vision is set from the top. The group's CEO has long held the belief that "employers have a responsibility to provide personnel with professional academic opportunities that will enable their career progression". The company has stood behind his words steadfastly.

"Our approach to talent management is to identify potential leaders and groom them for higher positions," says Lim.

For example, most of the individuals who were earmarked to attend the diploma programme have just recently been promoted to supervisory roles where their experience, leadership potential, and learning can come together, enabling them to lead more effectively.

"When someone is promoted in F.J. Benjamin, we also want to equip them with new skills that they will need for their new roles and responsibilities; promoting someone without equipping them adequately is counterproductive and can hinder more than help them," says Lim.

To stay ahead in the fast-paced service industry, F.J. Benjamin is also embarking on a landmark analysis throughout the organisation to determine if the training needs of staff at every level—from senior management right down to front-line staff in stores—can be met more effectively.

## 2. STANDARD CHARTERED : HERE FOR PEOPLE

### A Great Place to Work

This simple tagline neatly sums up Standard Chartered's philosophy towards its human capital. Engagement is a key driver of its performance culture and the bank has a variety of programmes and initiatives in place to ensure that employees develop the capabilities to reach their maximum potential.

Standard Chartered's HR focus is on providing the right employee experience, says David Thomas, the bank's Global Head of Country HR. "It is all about creating a motivated and highly engaged, diverse and inclusive work environment that attracts the right talent for the right roles."

The Bank has also been expanding rapidly, increasing its headcount from 35,000 to 85,000 in the past seven years. The market is getting tougher and there is a need to develop and retain good leadership talent, especially in emerging markets like India and China, Thomas adds.

### Taking Control

Employees who see a long-term future in their organisation are more likely to stay loyal and committed. However, staff development is not the sole responsibility of HR. At Standard Chartered, employees are encouraged to take charge of their own personal development.

Those working in the Consumer Banking division for example, have access to an online career planning tool called Excelerate, which features more than 140 career paths over 100 roles and 10 business functions. "It encourages staff to have a long-term view of their career within the bank, plan their development in line with their aspirations and have quality conversations with their line managers and regional HR managers," Thomas says. It helps employees prepare for the required capabilities to assume both their aspired roles and the intermediate roles leading to them, when the opportunity arises.

In addition, the tool also enables line managers to drive performance by helping employees build the relevant role capabilities through available learning opportunities and coaching, Thomas says. "We show employees that they can follow non-traditional paths, pursue their genuine interests and use individual strengths."

## Grooming Great Managers

Research has shown that a line manager's behaviour is often directly related to employee engagement, job satisfaction and performance. We are very aware that people leave managers, not organisations, Thomas says. "Therefore, it is important for us to ensure employee engagement is at the forefront of our minds and our focus is on helping them become the best leaders in the market." Standard Chartered's latest results on employee engagement have shown a consecutive increase for the past three years. "This is genuinely linked to the sponsorship and leadership of management teams across our markets, helping us to create a real competitive advantage," Thomas says.

Standard Chartered introduced its Great Manager Programme in 2007 to improve the way people managers engage their teams for higher performance. Its main aim is to encourage managers to have conversations with their teams about their development, performance and strengths. The programme is applicable to all people managers regardless of their years of experience.

The programme is delivered through podcasts, workshops and online learning. Some of the topics covered include Developing People and Careers, Engaging for Performance and Making Performance Conversations Count. Almost 10,000 managers at the bank have attended the programme to date.

The Development and Networking Alliance is another HR initiative at Standard Chartered that aims to help high potential employees increase their leadership capabilities, through group mentoring. Led by senior leaders, the programme encourages employees to learn from each other instead of merely through formal training or on-the-job training. "Both mentors and mentees benefit and develop their leadership capability through getting inspired and learning from other alliance members," Thomas says.

Lasting between six to nine months, this group mentoring programme also serves as a useful platform for development and networking across different business functions. "It widens an individual's exposure and stimulates their thinking about work and life experiences through a series of self-driven interactive meetings," Thomas explains.

## Bringing in New Blood

Attracting new talent into the organisation is another critical component of HR strategy and Standard Chartered is constantly on the lookout for the best and brightest in the market. Driving this effort is its International Graduate Programme (IGP) which seeks out candidates from a variety of degree disciplines for Business Functions across the organisation.

During the course of the programme, graduates receive the opportunity to work on diverse team projects, testing their ability to work with people from different backgrounds. They are placed on a series of rotations that exposes them to different areas within their chosen function.

During induction, graduates are also given the opportunity to tap into the experience of guest speakers from different geographies, industries and specialist fields to gain a better understanding of how the business works. "With any recruitment procedure, it's not just about us finding the right fit for the bank. Future employees have the opportunity to 'self-select' and decide if our culture is the right fit for them," says Thomas.

The IGP strongly encourages graduates to form international networks within the company. This can become useful, for example, when dealing with international clients at any level. Another example is the bank's "Action Learning Project" (ALP), where Senior leaders invite and sponsor teams of graduates to conduct their own research and give ideas regarding any area of strategic importance for the bank. The winning team is given an opportunity to personally present to Peter Sands, Standard Chartered's Group CEO and the bank's Group Management Committee.

## 3. McDONALD'S : DELIVERING VALUE

"We are looking to hire 5,000 people next year," says Judy Harman, managing director for McDonald's Singapore. This statement might seem a tad confident but given the fact that the franchise currently has 115 restaurants around the island and is still planning to open more in the next few years, it seems an accurate count.

However, she admits that in the food & beverages industry, it is challenging to attract talent. "The services sector in Singapore is a very challenging one. There are many players and more are coming in. Being able to find talented, qualified people to staff our restaurants is our greatest challenge," she says.

## Attracting the 'Mctalented'

McDonald's Singapore boasts a diverse restaurant crew from the ages of 14 to 80 which comprises of part-timers and full-timers. Harman, who is a McDonald's veteran of 26 years, states that she has found some fundamental qualities among McDonald's employees. "We call it 'ketchup in your blood'. Some of the characteristics are being people-oriented, like working with others, and being in a team environment," she explains.

It is not surprising that a majority of its 8,500 workforce work in the restaurants. The organisation specifically looks for an employee who is people-oriented, and recruiting techniques for this type of person range from word-of-mouth hiring to career fairs.

The majority of the service employees are hired through the 'Bring a Friend' referral programme and since it is word-of-mouth, applicants generally already have an idea about the job, states Harman. The organisation offers cash rewards to the employee who has introduced the friend and more cash when the new hire stays for more than 90 days. For Trainee Manager positions, the organisation looks to hire graduates at career fairs at tertiary institutions such as NUS, NTU, and Temasek Polytechnic.

Globally, the McDonald's brand has taken some criticism over recent years from several groups, chiefly health organisations. Moreover, Harman says that in some markets the reputation has not been good due to unattractive pay or insufficient career development opportunities. However, she assures the employer branding in Singapore is strong. In fact, McDonald's Singapore has won several accolades including the Aon Hewitt Best Employer Award three times, which has helped attract talent into the organisation, even in the competitive labour market.

It helps that at the crew level, employees can choose between full-time and part-time flexible working hours that make it appealing to many. Though the attrition rate is 50% for crew and under 20% for managers, Harman points out that "most of our crew are working part-time; they are students in their first job, earn some money, and then move on to the career for which they are studying." She candidly says that it is fine that the organisation is used as a stepping-stone for many, but it does retain some who go on to have careers in McDonald's Singapore.

## Developing 'Ketchup in the Blood'

Training plays a great part in developing and retaining employees in McDonald's Singapore and it starts on the first day of work with the help of a colleague. Harman calls it "shoulder training". Employees at the crew level get monthly feedback from their shift or restaurant managers, and every six months they get a detailed performance review, which HR tracks to ensure that it is carried out.

As in any company, McDonald's employees need a few years of learning and training to reach managerial level. They are offered the management development programme (MDP) that involves a total of 2,000 hours which takes four years to complete. The training is broken into four levels - trainee manager, second assistant manager, first assistant manager and restaurant manager. As an employee progresses through the training, he or she will learn various new skills such as how to put together a crew schedule and interview a crew person, explains Harman.

High-potential candidates go through the training at a quicker pace just two years. Harman states that these individuals have a dedicated coach who gives regular feedback and a "support system to move the person through the pace, as so much is learned by doing, and it is difficult to go through it quickly."

Employees are given the chance to further their education as well as their careers with the University Accredited Programme (UAP), under which graduates attain a diploma or a degree in hospitality. To date, 400 people have taken the Diploma in Hospitality while another 10 are going through the degree course.

There are other learning and development programmes spanning different departments, and not all of them are technical courses. The organisation will be introducing a core course, 'Winning with Diversity and Inclusion', next year for all employees. With an incredibly diverse workforce, it will prove to be helpful. The hour-long course will teach employees and managers about various groups of people working together and understanding each other.

### Communal Giving and Recognition

Harman is candid when she says: "Arguably, some of the jobs are not that fun, like standing in front of the fryer the whole day, but we try to bring fun into the restaurant. People talk about 'McFamily' and we try to encourage the idea that the co-worker is more than just a co-worker."

The McFamily culture is about recognising and celebrating successes and it comes in many forms—from simple acknowledgement to monetary rewards. The organisation also follows a quirky tradition of giving new hires a bottle of ketchup to indicate they are now part of the McDonald's Singapore family.

Employees who have spent some time in the organisation might find their stories published in the McDonald's website, under i-stories. "The stories have been a wonderful source of inspiration for people and they demonstrate that we provide opportunities for people to do things they never dreamed of," says Harman. She highlights that these stories are more common instead of being unique, and sharing them makes them real and shows that everyone can grow in the ranks.

Besides weekly and monthly updates to all employees, Harman regularly meets up with all restaurant managers and first assistants each quarter. The NABIT (Nuts and Bolts Integration Team) half-day get-together is a time to share updates and make plans for the next quarter, but also recognises those who gave done a good job. Harman recalls that in one NABIT session, "we recognised people who made a difference in the community". A couple of restaurants donated food to an orphanage, while employees from a few restaurants went to children's homes and painted the walls.

Monetary schemes are also offered to acknowledge as well as encourage McDonald's Singapore employees. There is an incentive or bonus programme for the office staff, while the restaurant staff have a quarterly incentive programme. Also, for the winner of the Service Speed Challenge there are several prizes offered to crew members, including a night's stay at a hotel or an iPad.

Globally, McDonald's gives out a significant amount in monetary awards. The top one per cent of employees from the entire McDonald's organisation across the globe receive the President's Awards as well as a cash prize of US$ 20,000. There is also the Ray Kroc (the founder of McDonald's) award for the top five per cent of restaurant managers from around the globe that comes with a cash prize.

It is not always about receiving but also about giving in the McFamily culture, as the organisation is very much involved with community work. Currently, restaurant managers can choose to spend money on incentives for their crew as well as the community. Harman says that McDonald's Singapore wants to do more and has introduced "McDonald's Cares". Under this programme, charity and community work can be done more regularly, and local schools and community centres can approach a McDonald's restaurant for help. The organisation's management has set aside funds from next year's budget to support this. Harman concluded that with 115 restaurants in the country, they can give back to the community. "We are a big brand and we should be making a difference."

## 4. THINK FUN, THINK YAHOO!

"We make it our business to have fun at work every day," says Jessie Lim, HR Director—Southeast Asia, Yahoo! In an organisation whose very name exudes fun, its corporate culture is no different. Fun and innovation are built into the fabric of every 'Yahoo's uniform'. Potential employees are even assessed for their ability to have fun when being considered for a role in the company, while fun in the workplace can also extend to pranks on colleagues. For instance, employees who go on leave for an extended period of time are prepared to come back to a totally different or unrecognisable desk!

### Life@yahoo!

Yahoo!'s core business is creating innovative products and content for consumers. Naturally, the company thrives on creativity and ingenuity. "We seek the innovations and ideas that can change the world," says Lim. "A fun and relaxed environment is the perfect breeding ground for these innovations and ideas."

Now that Yahoo! is seeing an increasingly diverse group of generation Y and Z coming onto the scene, maintaining a fun and innovative workplace culture becomes even more important in keeping staff engaged.

"These young people demand speed, creativity, flexibility, mobility and leadership opportunities. They know what they want, how and when to get it," says Lim. "Our job is to facilitate this development and harness their energy. We give our employees the space to grow, research and discover independently, and develop at their own schedule."

Yahoo! offers opportunities for cross-functional/departmental networking. One such program the Singapore office launched within Southeast Asia is 'SEA Innovation Day', modelled on the corporate office's 'Yahoo! Hack Days' whereby teams of cross-functional members take a Yahoo! product and 'hack' it—for the better. They have six months to work in teams of four on a specific Yahoo! product and at the end of six months, the winning team wins $5,000 plus resources internally to bring their idea to fruition.

In Singapore, Yahoo! has another internal program—Fun@SEA in which teams organise monthly 'Happy Hours' (where everyone comes together and lets their hair down with games and great food), health and wellness classes (like yoga, Pilates and free health screens), and cultural assimilation classes, as a large proportion of employees are non-local.

## Thinking Purple

One way Yahoo! instils fun and innovation into its corporate culture is by placing great importance on the talent it hires. "A diverse and inclusive environment brings together a variety of talents, backgrounds and experiences, serving as a catalyst for new ideas and innovation within the organisation," says Lim. She believes that these contributions and differences drive Yahoo!'s competitive business advantage, stimulate employees' personal growth and ultimately create success for the company.

Embedding new hires into Yahoo!'s culture and on-boarding them as quickly as possible allows the company to preserve this culture of fun and promote inclusiveness. This is achieved through several ways, including a comprehensive orientation session on an employee's first day and a more in-depth business review and organisational overview two to three months thereafter.

"We also do informal luncheons that get all the new hires for the month together for a casual get-together. The dialogue doesn't stop there—we do regular check-ins with all staff on where they stand and what we can do to 'move their needle' over time," says Lim.

## Purple Goes Global

Yahoo!'s HR team operates across Southeast Asia—so cultural awareness and adjustment is paramount. Each person in the HR team operates with the mindset that no one market is the same, so listening with an open heart and mind takes precedence. It also helps that the HR team itself is made up of different nationalities and experiences, which helps with a diverse approach to decision-making.

"We take into consideration cultural nuances, local practices, traditions and current market data and insights when formulating policies and programmes," says Lim. "Our approach when implementing HR services in each market is a 'localised' one-with support and cost commitment from our global team; we truly need to put ourselves in their shoes and understand the effect of each implemented service."

One such example is the recent rollout of medical insurance coverage that HR localised to suit local practices, needs and market limits.

## Stars in the Making

At Yahoo!, staff are told that they own their own careers. Instead of having them rely on their managers for career direction, empowerment is encouraged. "Every Yahoo! should take ownership by articulating clearly what they envision their careers would look like in the span of short- to medium-term," says Lim. "We constantly give priorities to our existing talents for lateral moves and promotions."

Yahoo! also has a robust learning and development strategy in place to instil leadership readiness within the entire Yahoo! family. 'Leading Yahoos' and 'Managing Yahoos' are two examples of leadership and management development programmes. 'Leading Yahoos' is targeted at leaders, managers and individual contributors in the organisation. It is intended to create alignment across cascading business goals and build accountability for organisational performance and business results. The programme includes content on expectations through Yahoo!'s leadership standards, understanding company/ functional goals and metrics and 360 degree insights into defining strengths, development areas and leadership development plans.

'Managing Yahoos' is targeted at new and newly-promoted managers and is designed to support the transition of employees into managerial roles. The programme content includes effective decision making, hiring skills, coaching and influence as well as an introduction to leadership standards.

Yahoo! has also seen a breakthrough this year in its investments in emerging talents within Southeast Asia. "This group of high-energy talents are singled out and assimilated into a high potential program which we have lined up for them," Lim explains. "They will go through an intensive one-year program which will expose them to multiple facets of the business beyond their scope, and at the same time, prepare them for future roles."

The company also places importance on developing the next generation of leaders through an internship programme. Interns at Yahoo! are not limited to fetching coffee or photocopying hundreds of papers for permanent staff. They are given 'real work' that develops and hones their skills (see boxouts). It's not uncommon to see many interns coming back as full-time employees.

## Recognising Stars

Besides the usual monetary rewards which Yahoo! provides annually and quarterly, HR found that specific and public accolades work best in recognising employees, especially in Southeast Asia. "We have a local recognition program called 'Caught Purple Handed' whereby anyone within Southeast Asia can give out purple hands to someone who's done a great job-big or small- and it's accompanied by a small token of appreciation," Lim says. "In the past, we're given out cinema tickets, coffee vouchers and internal Yahoo! swags."

For group recognition awards within the region, Yahoo! launched 'SuperHeroes' in the first quarter of this year. This quarterly reward program pitches the best team projects against each other and is open to all staff in Southeast Asia. Each voter is given one vote and nominated teams go all out to rally for votes. The winning team gets a cash prize of $5,000 at the end of the quarter.

To encourage employees to think global, an annual global reward programme, 'Super Star', gathers individual nominations around the world and eventual winners are picked by executive-level staff. Every year, 20 odd winners are picked and flown to Yahoo!'s head office in California for a private meeting with the company's CEO, Carol Bartz, and an all-expenses paid trip for the week.

## 5. UNIVERSAL STUDIOS: HR WITH A DOSE OF FUN

"It takes the talents of literally thousands of people to take a theme park from concepts to opening day." So says KB Creative Advisors, the design firm at the heart of the newly-opened Universal Studios Singapore. But opening is only the first step. Now that the rides are in operation, the talent requirements are just as great, if not more so. Keeping the park running like clockwork involves a wide range of people, skills, and talent.

Universal Studios theme parks are frequently lauded as the best in the world—not just in terms of rides, attractions, retail options, and food and beverage, but also in terms of customer service. The newly-opened Universal Studios in Singapore is certainly no different—and the local hiring and training team has made that area a number one priority in all of its induction programmes.

### Key Talents

Universal Studios Singapore, the region's first Universal Studios theme park, employs some 3000 people, of which 70% are local. But it is still just one part of the wider Resorts World Sentosa integrated resort, with the one HR team covering employment issues for all 10,000 staff. It says the theme park staff need to share the same values and commitments as those in other areas of the resort. The HR team therefore looks for people with high levels of passion and motivation to serve, on top of the necessary skill-sets required for each individual Universal Studios role.

Seah-Khoo Ee Boon, Senior Vice President of HR and Training, Resorts World Sentosa, says high energy levels are particularly important for the theme park. Given the nature of the hospitality line, people who are willing to work flexible and shift hours, including weekends and public holidays also make for the most appropriate candidates, she says.

But that doesn't mean it's all casual labour manning the rides and ticket booths. Seah-Khoo says most of the theme park staff are on permanent employment terms, but notes that there are obviously times when temporary labour is also required. "Considering the scale and diversity of our operations in this world-class theme park, we need extra manpower during peak periods, especially over the weekends and public holidays," she says. "We supplement our permanent team, with many casuals and temporary staff, who find this a fun, yet fulfilling, job experience."

Mature workers are also an extremely valuable resource for Universal Studios Singapore. They are encouraged to join the theme park and share their outlook, experience and life-skills with the rest of the team, who, in the case of Universal Studios Singapore, tend to be younger in terms of age. "Their past experiences have been an inspiration to many of the younger team members. Currently, our oldest team member is 73 years old," Seah-Khoo says.

### Long-term Investment

The theme park business is a new one for Singapore, and therefore faces a limited local talent pool. There are only so many people with direct experience and knowledge in opening and running such a multi-faceted hospitality operation. Many of those were based overseas so it is only natural that Universal Studios Singapore employs a number of managers from other theme parks within the group, in particular the Orlando, Florida, Universal Studios theme park.

Seah-Khoo says this experienced team brings "years" of "best-in-class" experience and knowledge. "Staff have certainly benefited from their transfer of knowledge and skills," Seah-Khoo says. That training role is an important part of each management position.

"Our option was to recruit experienced talent from overseas and to put in place a structured training system and processes to facilitate the transfer of skills and knowledge from the foreign talent to our local hires," she said. "To further enhance the transfer of learning, 33 advisors from Universal Hollywood and Orlando arrived a few months before our opening, to provide training and guidance for our team members."

Besides hiring for the right skills, personality and attitude fits, Resorts World Sentosa naturally puts a lot of emphasis on staff training and development. "We are here for the long haul, and we invest in our team members for the long term as well," Seah-Khoo says.

"We have sent more than 200 staff to the Universal Orlando Resort for training for (several) months, with full pay, allowances and accommodation," she said, noting that training should not just be about competency, but rather "excellence" in each job.

### The Road Ahead

Now, less than a year into its permanent operations, Universal Studios Singapore is already looking towards retaining, refreshing and retraining its staff.

As part of its manpower pipeline, the theme park identifies and fast-tracks local team members who have demonstrated good performance. Several staff—originally hired as rank and file team members – have already been promoted to supervisory positions, due to their leadership potential.

"Our priority is to promote and groom our talents from within," Seah- Khoo says.

Besides the cross-departmental transfers that team members can take advantage of, the theme park also has on-going projects with parts of the integrated resort that are still to open. The West Zone, which will boast the world's largest oceanarium – the Marine Life Park, a Maritime Museum and two more hotels, is expected to create another 3000 job opportunities. Seah Khoo says existing team members will have priority to be selected for these new areas.

## 6. UNILEVER-GUNNING FOR REFORM VIA HOLISTIC HR

With a worldwide staff of 250,000 people over six continents, Unilever takes its HR management very seriously. HRM spoke with Unilever Bestfoods Asia President, Tex Gunning, and caught up with his uniquely holistic, community-based approach to human capital management and its role in Unilever's turnaround

Tex Gunning is the head of UBF Asia, a member of the Unilever Group, a US$ 66 billion conglomerate with large market shares in numerous household product lines. Gunning reports to the food division's head, who in turn reports the global chairman of Unilever. However, he is also a rare, humanistic leader in a corporate world full of numbers-obsessed executives, Gunning successfully turned around an ailing Unilever subsidiary while doing his part to change both his executives and the wider world.

From its inception, Unilever was forced to deal with trans-national HR management issues. Born with the 1930s merger of British soap maker Lever Brothers and Holland's Margarine Unie, both companies were already operating in 40 countries. And from the very beginning, Unilever was on the frontier of human capital management. During the Great Depression when workers were very expendable, Unilever placed great importance on employee rights and welfare. In this context, Gunning's human capital and community involvement initiatives are an extension of Unilever's longstanding focus on HR and corporate social responsibility.

## A Holistic, Community-based Approach to HR

Gunning admits that, "Our employees have always been important to us," He adds that, "It is clearly one thing for HR and management to dictate to staff what they should think. It is quite another to empower those staff to truly believe in what you are saying." What makes Unilever's latest chapter, and Gunning's contribution to it, is his holistic approach to energising his workforce towards common goals: product betterment through highly motivated collective thinking.

In Gunning's human capital development model, to create a productive company culture, you first prepare staff for a transformation of values. An accidental result of this process is that staff will improve their character and open mindedness in lockstep with their productivity.

Gunning, who is Dutch by birth, has carried his HR ideals through a trial by fire. Ten years ago he made his name by turning around Unilever Van den Bergh, the company's meat, soup and sauce subsidiary. Unilever Van den Bergh's celebrated transformation under Gunning's presidency eventually inspired a book called To the Desert and Back by Mirvis, Ayas and Roth (Wiley, 2004).

Gunning credits the inspiration for his holistic, yet unorthodox approach to personality traits. "I always have been a truth seeker," he says. "This personality trait has driven my life and my business. I place an enormous emphasis on business and a sense of community."

## Focusing on HR Metrics does not Create New Wealth

An unusually philosophical and existential man, Gunning incorporates humanistic ideals into a communal approach to human resource management. By 'humanistic', Gunning is referring to his HR strategy, which focuses on non-quantifiable, self-motivated community development rather than depending on KPIs or similar metrics. Indeed, Gunning laments that the majority of HR professionals he has met over his 32-year career lacked such humanistic skills. Consequently, "HR tends to be overly focused on brands and money, rather than on people."

Gunning believes that HR directors, like other executives who were trained in today's business culture, are obsessed with extracting value out of singular individuals, stand-alone business units, and fixated on numerical measures. For him, a major blindspot is that those metrics used to evaluate employees or extract value from a business are powerless to create new wealth. "They are not creators," he says, "Growth, which is not as easy as some people think, cannot truly be achieved with a pure focus on numbers and no room for the human factors."

For the growth of companies, generally follows an S-curve shape where rapid early growth tapers off into relative stagnation. For Gunning, the only way to turn an S-shaped growth into a "J-curve" of continuing rapid expansion is by using the company's human capital to differentiate itself into a new burst of growth. And this, in Gunning's opinion, requires a community based approach.

That is not to say that Gunning ignores numerical measures - indeed, he has both faced and been moved by bottom line issues. He describes, with apprehension, one experience he hopes will never have to be repeated. In 1995, severe losses forced him to layoff 700 staff at Unilever Van den Bergh Nederland, "But I promised the staff that me and my management team would not leave the business until we were in growth."

Nor does Gunning's approach focus on short-term results. Unilever Van den Bergh Nederland's recovery was spectacular, and covered in the business press, but it took three years to materialise. Gunning however, perceived the intervening three years as an opportunity to apply his unique human capital management ideas. "I wanted a happy staff, a sense of trust and friendship. I knew that the more we grew this creative community, the more we would grow as a company."

## 7. COMPANY CULTURE: THE KEY TO TURNING S-CURVES INTO J-CURVES

In creating a dynamic company culture, Gunning believes that an HR director's role is to sit squarely at the centre of a contradiction. "There is a fundamental paradox that comes with building a community—the manager wants the community to act as one but then also show all the diversity of the members. Culture is the term given to these relations between different parts of the community—the team members."

For Gunning, to transform a company's S-curve growth path into a J-curve, an HR director must apply non-standard solutions to the "non-orderly" problems which characterise today's business environment. In short, to think 'outside of the box'. "A company can best solve modern business problems by tapping into its collective genius. There are very few leaders good enough or intelligent enough to solve major problems without collective intervention. Besides, why not use all the minds at an organisation's disposal?"

In today's business environment, Gunning's opinions are considered radical but he argues that a consultative, community-based approach draws on all of an organisation's human capital stock and that this naturally leads to bottom-line improvements. As his experience at Unilever Van den Bergh Nederland demonstrated, employee participation in a 'collective mind' produces results that create shareholder value. "People cannot know their business and cannot know the strengths of the team and each other until they know themselves."

## Unusual HR Methods Accepted by Management

Despite initial resistance and heavy cynicism from management, Gunning took his team to a central Asian desert, impoverished regions of India, China and other off-the-track locales. He feels unusual destinations remove executives from their social contexts and these unfamiliar environments induce them to review their life values and see their relationships with themselves and other organisation members in a new light.

Despite management's reservations, their acceptance of such unusual practices shows that to a certain extent, Gunning was preaching to the converted: their acceptance was a symptom of the company's pre-existing soft-skills approach to HR. Gunning's recent transformational journeys have taken Unilever executives to China's Guilin province and the slums of Kolkata (Calcutta). These forays into non-tourist zones grounds his executives and the resulting emotional impact opens them for personal transformation. "People have deep social scripts and masks, this sort of experience delivers a high level of authenticity and trust. Then you are in a position to create an agenda and use your human capital to solve today's non-orderly problems." To deliver a message by such powerful and unconventional means, even to subordinates, takes backing. Gunning has it in his human resources team, led by senior vice president of HR (based in Singapore), Jacqueline Koh. "Our HR is the most essential department and it is not at all difficult for them to see the vision. Different initiatives have a great resonance with HR - the more senior and strategic an HR executive, the more they see the value. Jackie [Koh] is very socially engaged. She truly wants to realise our aspirations through people development."

Finally, just as Gunning seeks to connect executives to their community of employees, he also seeks to connect Unilever to the wider world. A candid comment about the pharmaceutical industry comes from competitive and profit pressures, thereby making some companies hesitate when it comes to sharing their knowledge of life-saving medications with the market-at-large. Gunning is seeing to it that Unilever sets a different example. "With nutrition, we will share everything we know in terms of product development. In fact we have just confirmed our duty to share all our knowledge about nutrition with the World Food Programme and UNICEF."

### People Development

Gunning explains that, "I have a deep realisation that to sustain a business, its mission must have this social angle. Grow your people, then grow your business," he says. He argues that skills development at the individual level is boring—and doesn't contribute that much to the overall development of an organisation's collective culture.

Although Gunning acknowledges training's importance, he believes that HR's obsession with individual training and leadership development is a misguided focus. "It is up to leaders to create space for bringing creativity to fruition. It is very important for leaders to unlock the sense of belonging in an organisation. This is not the typical feeling—most people feel estranged, and that's the problem."

### Holistic HR

Indeed, when he arrived in Singapore nearly five years ago, senior managers warned Gunning that his liberal, collective HRM policy would not go down well with Asians. "This could not have been further from the truth," he counters, "Asian people are conservative when it comes to being open, but they are also very family and communally-oriented. Asians understand the value of the collective better than westerners."

Indeed, Gunning's capacity to adapt an HR policy he developed in the Netherlands to Asia demonstrates the deep connection between his humanistic idealism and bottom line results. He has been able to find a nexus between business, microeconomics, and humanities such as social psychology and existentialism. This is genuinely exceptional since in today's business world, where social paradigms that cannot be reduced to KPIs are considered irrelevant. Indeed Gunning's style may foreshadow a return to unleashing the softer side of the human capital equation.

Ideas have usually outlived their usefulness the moment they are universally accepted. Very few HR directors question individual leadership training, number driven KPIs or talent-based retention strategies that categorise employees rather than unite them into something greater than the sum of their skills. Gunning's successful experiment with collective performance and non-quantifiable factors may yet turn into HR's next big idea.

## 8. PRADEEP PANT, REGIONAL MANAGING DIRECTOR, FONTERRA BRANDS

His journey into Fonterra started when Procter and Gamble bought out Gillette, where he was working. When the acquisition happened, Pradeep Pant, regional managing director, Fonterra Brands, recollects how he sat back and had a long and deep conversation with himself on what he wanted to do next. The options, he says, were many. He could have moved over to "the other side" or looked at different career options for himself. In the spectrum of possibilities was Fonterra. He tells us why he chose it.

"I met a few organisations in the process. And the thing that fascinated me about Fonterra was that working with Fonterra, you represent not only a company, but a country as well. Fonterra contributes to about 8% of the GDP of New Zealand. If we don't do well, the country suffers. The second thing is that it has a unique model. In most agri-based products, the middle man makes all the money. In this case, the farmers own the company. And the third thing which sealed the deal for me was that Asia was the growth region," recalls Pant.

Beyond that, he says, the people and 'can do' Kiwi culture played an important role in his decision. "The Kiwi spirit came through pretty clearly during my talking with the people I met, which is a very 'can do' kind of a spirit. It means to intellectualise a problem to a certain extent, get to a point, take a decision and then go do it. That's my style. I like doing that. And all these things came together."

### Coming on BOARD

Another factor that truly impressed Pant was the action-oriented work philosophy which Fonterra demonstrated right at the start of his interaction with the company and maintains to this day. "I went to Auckland for a day- and-a-half session with them. What happens in these sessions is you meet a bunch of people and they say, 'we'll get back to you-you think about it and I think about it, and we'll come back after three weeks.' It's a pretty drawn out process."

With Fonterra, however, it was different. "I went in, met a couple of guys. I had dinner with the boss. Next morning, I had breakfast with the Finance Director who wasn't there the earlier day. We chatted over breakfast and the HR director came over to say 'here's your offer letter' and I loved that, because here were guys who were talking business. It was fantastic, and I have not been disappointed, because the spirit is real. It wasn't a thing that was put on to bring someone into the organisation. That's truly the spirit of the organisation here. There's a very strong action orientation."

However, he is quick to point out that by an action-oriented work philosophy, he doesn't imply that there is no planning or that there is anarchy. "I'm not saying that this is anarchy and people are doing cowboy stuff. That's not true, but an action orientation-especially in a growth region like Asia which is the locomotive of the organisation, in terms of future growth—is a very good work philosophy."

## Not a Bed of Roses

Despite that, the role was not was not a bed of roses, when Pant took over the reins of the Singapore business. "The business existed in Singapore and it was running. But the challenges as I landed were of two or three kinds. The first and big challenge was that some of our operations were what we define as 'leaking buckets'. They were not doing well; profit was seeping out and they needed a fix immediately. And that came on my radar as the number one item. Until you stop the bleeding, you can't really start looking forward." As well, talent shortage was a big crisis at the time, he recalls. "Lot of positions were open. My finance director was planning to leave, I didn't have an HR director, and I needed someone to run the Middle East and China operations."

For the first two or three months, he focused completely on fixing the leaking, and on the other hand making sure that Fonterra got people on board at a very aggressive pace. And the great thing was, he say—amidst a lot of recruitment, some positions were filled from within the company itself. "We looked at our own talents and we made a few outside recruitments, some of which we managed to do directly by contacting people ourselves, and we managed to pull these guys on board. Once the staffing and the leaking were more or less patched up and rolling, we started looking forward." But at the time Fonterra overall was in the process of changing and defining its long-term strategy. "You can change your tactics, but your basic strategic direction can't keep moving, because otherwise you create instability in the core business. So the organisation itself in the previous couple of years had been busy defining its overall strategy, its brand strategy and within that, I had to define a very clear strategy for Asia-Pacific."

Fonterra Brands Asia needed to address a few basic questions, he says. "Why are we here? We believe in 'double or nothing', because if this is the growth engine, the locomotive of Fonterra, we have got to work at a pace where we can double the business in a three-year period. It's like a triangle—on one side, you need clearly defined business strategy and business model, on another, you need standardised and unified processes and systems. But then what drives everything is the organisation's structure and people. What makes the difference between a good organisation and a great organisation is the people. That's the base and that's the only asset in the company whose value will appreciate with time."

### The People Challenges

The people challenges in Fonterra, Pant recalls, were not uncommon but were multifaceted. "There were lots of holes in the organisation. And I'm talking about the short-term challenge! There were some people who had the capability but were in the wrong roles. And there were people in the organisation who did not have the basic competence required to handle those kind of assignments."

So what did he do to cope? "We did an analysis of the markets and a similar analysis of the people—who are our stars, who are the guys who would drive the business forward in the short and medium-terms, who are the people who are good, probably right guys in wrong roles and who are the people we need to change? Then we went about doing it.

The first step was to communicate and let the people understand clearly where we wanted to go, what were the marching orders and what we wanted happening in the organisation. Then I started by catching the key leaders and making sure those roles are filled, and where needed, we changed the people. We asked a couple of guys to go."

Once the leadership team was in, the whole process started cascading down through the whole organisation, Pant says. "The mistake some people often make is taking potshots into different parts and different levels of the organisation. For me, the focus was to get the leadership team right. I have a full deck of my leadership team now with no holes. These were the talents who went out and got their leadership teams together. When the cascade started going down and fixes started to become visible-including the systems, processes, basic strategies—we went out and put our vision on the map.

### 'Double or Nothing'

"Today if you talk to anyone, they know why it is so. It's not enough to tell people 'what'. You have to tell them 'why'. I know I can't win this battle alone by trying to fight in every war. It's my leaders, who in turn have their functional leaders, their leaders who will win this battle for us."

### Empowerment is the Catch Word

Pant believes that for leaders to go out and hit the bulls-eye in a cut- throat market, empowerment is the catchword. But one needs to be careful. "First, there has to be a very clear communication of what you want to achieve."

Because if you just say, 'hey you have the power to do what you want', it's not enough. So, a very clear direction on where the organisation is going, what's it trying to achieve and why must be given. Second, you can't empower people who don't have the ability. So, it's making sure that the leadership right across has the basic fundamental capability of being able to understand what is being said and is able to execute what needs to be done.

"The third thing that you need is a control mechanism. Once in a while you'll find that because you empowered someone and the marching orders were not clear, or capabilities didn't exist, wrong decisions were taken." It's here that a balancing mechanism is required, he says—one which does not constrain people and leaves room for flexibility.

"Implanting an adequate amount of metrics in the system which will tell you whether the ship is going in the right direction or not is important. Also, it is important for people to understand that you have to work in a matrix way. You can't work anymore by just saying, 'This is my piece of turf...keep out!' He explains that this has been a big cultural change for Fonterra."

"People are beginning to understand that you no longer work for people, but with people. That's a massive change in a company that was very linear before. Today's work environment demands that everyone works in concert.

Imagine you are a part of a huge orchestra and what I am doing is conducting it. But if the saxophone decides to go on its own and play something else, it won't be music anymore, it'll be cacophony!"

## 9. THE RIGHT FIT AT ZAPPOS

Not many companies can boast that they get tour visits to their offices, but Zappos Family of Companies can. The US online shoe retailer receives as many as 2,000 curious visitors per month at its warehouse and offices and rumour has it that some of these onlookers include celebrities and record producers.

Founded in 1999 by Nick Swinmurn, the Zappos Family has come a long way from its humble beginnings to becoming a well-known name among American consumers. It all began with Swinmurn unsuccessfully trying to find a pair of shoes for himself, even online. The desire to find the right pair eventually led him to start an online shoe business, Zappos.com. By 2009, the organisation had grown and joined global online retailer, Amazon.com Inc. and last year the organisation was restructured into 10 companies under the Zappos Family of Companies unit.

Zappos Family is fast gaining a reputation not only for having great customer service but particularly for being a good employer.

### Fitting into Zappos' Shoes

Earning a reputation as a good employer is no mean feat and the organisation's quirky and open culture has helped to achieve this. This culture took some time to develop but it has now become a part of everyday work practices for all Zappos Family employees.

Hollie Delaney, director of HR at Zappos.com. says that the organisation needed to define itself and the people who would work for it, and this definition came in the form of the 10 core values (see sidebox). "Our 10 core values are our foundation and our guide in making decisions," she explains.

Some of these values may seem a tad silly to people outside the organisation—they include "Create Fun and A Little Weirdness" and "Deliver WOW Through Service"—but the organisation has proven that such values work for its employees.

The values came about not just from a management decision but also from a consensus among employees. The organisation's CEO, Tony Hsieh, developed a long list of values (from observing best work behaviours of employees) and sent it to the entire company for feedback. These responses were eventually summarised into the 10 core values a year later.

"The company culture is based on these values," explains Delaney. "It is a culture where you are encouraged to be yourself; people respect each other and each other's ideas; and you are empowered to make the right decisions and use your best judgment." These values are so vital to the organisation's work practices and culture that new hires have to sign a core values document to state that they understand the values and would abide by them.

Moreover, for the organisation to live by its values, it needed to ensure that it found the right type of employee. "Our culture is our biggest asset and we want to make sure that the people working for us really understand and believe in what we are doing and where we are going," states Delaney.

Zappos has a vigorous interview process that is a combination of both technical and culture-based screening in order for the recruitment managers to determine if the candidate fits the team technically and especially culturally. Applicants are subjected to open-ended questions based on the 10 core values and are also given a tour of the company. The interview assessment along with the "feedback we receive from all the employees that the candidate comes into contact with helps the recruiters make their decisions," she notes.

In fact, the organisation goes to great lengths to secure an employee that would be the right fit. Zappos practises the Offer, which consists of giving new hires a significant sum of money (it starts at $2,000 and increases to $3,000, and eventually to $4,000) a few weeks into their training period. To some, this might be a strange practice but the organisation assures that it helps to find committed employees. So far, less than 3% of employees have taken up this offer and then left, while the company maintains a low voluntary turnover rate of 7%.

Recruiting the right people is just the first stage in perpetuating a collaborative and convivial culture. The organisation also ensures that it communicates and encourages its corporate culture through various means such as the Ask anything newsletter and the Culture book.

For the monthly newsletter, employees submit questions on an internal site and relevant department heads respond to them, which is then published for all employees to read. Also, the annual Culture book has answers from all employees to the question: "What does Zappos culture mean to you?" Praise or otherwise, Delaney states that the answers are published as they are, except for changes to grammar or spelling.

## Development for the Long Haul

As an online retail business, serving and handling customers well on the phone is imperative for Zappos and 40% of the company's headquarters are made up of call centres. In order to serve its customers properly, the organisation has comprehensive customer services training for its employees.

Zappos Family has a dedicated team of call centre representatives, known as the Customer Loyalty Team (CLT), but it is serious about training all its employees in customer service. No matter the position, all employees go through four weeks of call centre training (not many organisations can boast this, but the CEO has undergone this training too) and another week of warehouse training. During the training, employees learn to make mock calls and eventually make real calls with a trainer. "They learn how to use our systems, learn about our culture and core values, and get some time to practise their skills before moving into their regular jobs," explains Delaney.

As being part of a CLT is demanding, Zappos maintains an "80:20" rule to prevent burnout of their employees. For 80% of the time CLTs are to be available or on-call, while during the rest of their work time they attend development training programmes or technical seminars. Also, CLTs spend at least 50 minutes a day writing greeting notes for customers.

The organisation has several other learning and development programmes to develop its employees. Various departments have progression plans for employees and learning expectations are laid out so that they can progress to another level. A Pipeline team, a training department within Zappos Family, provides optional classes for employees to learn new skills as well as the organisation's history and culture.

Some of the classes include using Microsoft office programmes and public speaking. There are even customised classes to help support a department's progression plans for their employees.

Besides development programmes, the organisation has an interesting way of keeping track of the development of its employees. It has an annual culture review comprising behaviour-based questions related to the core values. Delaney, however, points out that the culture feedback is not the same as a performance appraisal. This culture review is meant to show the strengths and weaknesses of employees in the core values and how they can better themselves in areas that need improvement.

Delaney adds that the Zappos Family believes that performance reviews should be done more than once a year, which is why it does not conduct traditional performance reviews. However, the onus is on the managers—they are expected to meet with their employees to give regular performance feedback. "Some managers meet weekly or bi-weekly while some have a monthly performance discussion. The HR team works with the managers to help ensure that employees get regular performance feedback."

## Receiving Personal Recognition

Creating a personal emotional connection, or otherwise known as PEC in Zappos Family, with its customers as well as its employees is vital for the organisation. Consequently, the organisation has several programmes to engage and reward its employees.

The organisation has a HR team dedicated to coordinating various events and functions to motivate employees called the P.E.A.C.E (Programs, Events, Activities, Charities, and Engagement) team. Quirky moniker aside, the P.E.A.C.E team also keeps track of employees' personal events such as birthdays and even wedding anniversaries, and sends out cards.

Zappos has a Wishez programme, under which employees can submit a wish on the organisation's internal site and other employees can grant this wish. Wishes on the list have included Christmas cookies to even a car being granted.

Employees can award their co-workers with one $50 cash bonus per month as a way of thanking them for their help or what Delaney says, when they are "wowed by them". The HR sends a monthly newsletter to the entire organisation to show who received these bonuses and why.

Furthermore, managers can present their employees with Zollars, as a way of recognition. Employees can use these Zollars (fake money that comes in several denominations) to purchase Zappos products such as T-shirts and other merchandise in the company store. Managers get these Zollars from HR. There is also a Master of WOW programme, under which employees can nominate another co-worker to win a prime parking spot and a free car wash.

The organisation encourages the practice of ensuring that employees feel empowered, and the ZFrogs programme helps in this instance. Employees participating in this programme can pitch ideas that are evaluated by an executive team. If their idea is selected, the employee can take time off from their everyday role to work on making this idea into a reality.

Ultimately, Zappos Family is interested in maintaining its culture and taking care of its employees. Delaney states that the challenge for the organisation is to "sustain and grow the culture" while also ensuring that employees can pursue their passions.

# Glossary

**Absenteeism**

Failure of an employee to report for duty. He or she may face disciplinary action for not being present at the workplace at scheduled times.

**Ageing Population**

The number of older employees are more than younger ones.

**Applicant Tracking**

Action taken by organizations to monitor the process of recruitment from the time the application letter is received until the recruitment file is closed.

**Apprentice**

A beginner or a novice at work. Sometimes a beginner undergoes and internship. In certain cases, a novice is someone who is undergoing skill training at a certain trade such as a mechanic or technician.

**Arbitration**

The situation where a third party makes a binding decision in a dispute between two parties. An instance of this is when an industrial tribunal makes decision in a dispute between employees and their employer.

**Audi alteram partem**

Latin maxim that means "hear the other side." In simple language, this means giving adequate opportunity to a person to respond to any allegation made against him or her. This is an equitable principle. This means being impartial in order to be fair and just.

**Automatic progression**

This refers to the giving of regular salary increments that are not tied to performance.

**Base Salary**

Standard salary paid. Sometimes called "basic salary", it is the basis in the calculation of allowances and benefits.

**Benchmarking**

The act of identifying best practices that make competitors' products better in quality. The products are either goods or services.

**Benchmarking Human Resources**

The act of identifying other organizations' human resource "best practices" that contribute towards obtaining, producing and maintaining better-quality employees. These practices are the ones that contribute positively to the success of organizations.

**Benefits**

These are rewards or compensation paid in-kind (that is, non-cash) such as life insurance and annual leave. Benefits are given as a method of motivating employees.

**Benefits Administration**

Management of financial rewards given in kind for the purpose of achieving a certain objective such as employee motivation.

**Bonus**

A reward, usually financial in nature, given after a target is achieved. Performance bonus is an example. Contractual bonus is not tied to any target.

**Bottom line**

The final financial result such as profit after tax. The listing in this HR glossary will include other terms as and when necessary.

**Career**

Career includes all the jobs a person had held during his or her working life.

**Career Development and Planning**

This is an act of a person to realize his or her career goals. This also refers to an employer's plan to develop the potentials of employees as a form of strategy to motivate and retain employees. Organization may do this under its succession plan.

**CEO (Chief Executive Officer**

The CEO is the top executive in an organization, ultimately responsible for its success. Alternative titles include Managing Director and Executive Chairman.

**Changing Role of Human Resources**

This refer to the new role that human resources—that is, workers—play in helping organizations to achieve their overall goals. They are treated as assets, not liabilities. Some organizations had accepted that human resource is their most important asset.

**Closed Shop**

The situation where an employer will not hire or cannot engage a person who is not a member of a certain union.

**Coaching**

A management development approach where the manager helps an employee to find solutions to his or her work-related problems and implement them.

**Collective Bargaining Unit**

This is the section in an organization assigned with the important task of negotiating, concluding collective agreements with unions, and to effectively manage such agreements.

**Compensation**

The pay given to employees for work done. Sometimes benefits are given in addition to payment of salaries.

**Competency-based Human Resources**

This is the method of managing the skills and knowledge of employees for the purpose of performing the job to the required standard. This involves training activities intended to improve the knowledge, skills, abilities and behaviors of an individual. It is related to knowledge management. This type of organizational culture encourages learning among employees. And employees must continue to learn for as long as they are working. Some writers refer to it as "competency-based training". This is so because the training given is intended to enhance employees' competencies or to provide them with new competencies in order to perform the job better.

**Collective Bargaining**

Process in which management representatives and union representatives meet to negotiate an employment agreement.

**Common Law**

Called "case law", this is the type of law developed by the court system. It is binding like enacted laws.

**Competitive Advantage**

Something that distinguish organizations from others in superior performance. These include competent people.

**Consultancy**

Services provided by someone who is an expert in a certain field to help organizations to formulate improvement plans.

**Core Competencies**

The skills and knowledge that every employee within a certain group must possess such as problem-solving skills by managers.

**Federal Employment Laws**

These are the laws governing employment enacted by a federal legislature.

**Federal Labor Laws**

Federal-enacted regulations that govern workplace conditions and usually impose minimum terms and conditions of employment. These regulate employer-employee relations.

**Focus Groups**

Groups of employees brought together to discuss or provide data on topics concerning HR.

**Functional Competency**

The skills, knowledge and experience required to perform a specific job.

**Goal**

This has the same meaning as target or objective or aim. It is something desired by an individualor an organization such as high productivity.

**Grievance**

A dispute between parties such as an employer and a union.

**HR Associations**

HR Associations are bodies the memberships of which comprise of HR services-based organizations and HR professionals.

**HR Automation**

HR Automation refers to the use of computers in managing employee matters. An example of this is human resource development (HRD) system, and payroll system.

**HR Information System**

HR Information System (HRIS, in short) is defined as "the use of computers in generating timely and relevant information to assist decision-making."

**HR Outsourcing**

HR outsourcing occurs when an organization asks an external organization to manage certain activities under the HR function. Recruitment is one example.

**Incentive**

An incentive is a reward given when a specified objective is achieved. For example, bonus is given if the company's revenue exceeds a certain level.

**Industrial Relations**

The relationship between employer, unions, government and industrial tribunals. Entities and their respective roles are emphasized.

**Information**

Data that have been collated and processed to convey a certain message. Manipulation of data to make it useful is usually done by using computer software. The HRIS is one.

**Intelligence Quotient (IQ)**

This is the level of an individual intelligence. The IQ test measures a person's ability to reason.

There is an over-emphasis on IQ. Some argue that Emotional Intelligence is more important.

**Intranet**

A network of computers enabling employees in an organization to communicate with each other, or to enable employees to communicate with management. This is one of the methods adopted by organizations to attain a paperless working environment.

**Job Analysis**

Investigation into the duties and responsibilities of a job, the required skills, abilities and knowledge required to perform the job well.

**Job Assignment**

This is a specific task that an employee is required to do and to complete within a given period of time.

**Job Description**

This is a written statement of the duties and responsibilities of a job holder, how he or she is to perform them, and where and when the job holder must perform them.

**Job Design**

The various elements of a job.

**Job Enrichment**

Job enrichment is an aspect of employee motivation where the job is made more interesting and challenging. This makes the employee more satisfied as he feels that his or her contribution is valued.

Allowing employees to make day-to-day decisions in matters relating to their job, especially in routine matters, is an example of job enrichment.

**Jobs**

Works that exist in an organization. Jobs also refers to all the works that a person had held that make up his or her career. Some organizations sometimes define the tasks carried out under a particular position as "jobs".

**Job Specification**

The qualifications, skills, competencies and knowledge required of a person to effectively perform a job. Job specification describes the person, not the job. Sometimes job specification is mistaken as job description.

**Job**

This is a group of tasks that an employee perform to help an organization in achieving its objectives. These are the tasks that an employee is required to perform usually on a daily basis.

**Know-how**

Knowledge and skills of a person.

**Knowledge Management**

This is a systematic way in the provision, enhancement and utilization of the knowledge of employees or knowledge that resides in the entire workforce.

**Labor Laws**

Labor laws are laws governing aspects of labor or employment such as working conditions, minimum terms and conditions of employment. These laws indicate the parameters under which either employer or employee are allowed to act.

**Labor Relations**

Labor Relations is understood as being the same as industrial relations. It refers to the relationship between the management of an organization and workers and their unions.

**Law**

Law consists of both the written and unwritten law governing every aspect of human life. Most of these are intended to regulate human behavior including at the workplace.

**Leadership**

The ability to guide, to motivate, and direct other people in order to achieve a common objective. Leadership assumes that there is followership defined as "the ability to follow a leader." It is usually compared to "managing" usually defined as achieving an objective through the utilization of other people's abilities and efforts. A leader is more than a manager.

**Learning**

The act of continuously improving one's knowledge, skills, and capabilities.

**Line Manager**

A manager who is authorized to manage and direct employees within a specific job function.

Examples are a marketing manager and a production manager

**Nemo iudex in causa sua**

This is a Latin maxim that means that there is no person who should be a judge in his or her own cause. For example, a manager who has made a complaint against an employee cannot take part in whatever capacity in deciding the matter. The least appearance of bias must be avoided.

**Notice**

The time period given when an employee goes for voluntary separation.

**Novice**

Someone who is not yet skilled in a certain trade. Some use the word "apprentice, beginner, or inexperienced".

**Open Office Concept**

This can refer to a manager's open system of managing people, where he or she is open for discussion at any time. This also refers to the new office set-up where people including executives work within their own respective cubicle. Even senior people are not accorded the privacy of a room.

**Optional Retirement**

The age at which employees can choose to retire and still enjoy retirement benefits. The age differs from country to country. In some countries, the terms and conditions for male and female employees may differ.

**Organizations**

Corporate bodies that have existence apart from the people who manage them or own them. Companies, government agencies and voluntary bodies are examples.

**OSHA Compliance**

The requirement for organizations to adhere to occupational safety and health regulations. Failure to comply results in penalties. In Malaysia, it is OSHA. Other countries use different names. The Australian equivalent is Occupational Health and Safety (OHS).

**Partners**

Individuals who have agreed to use their resources, skills and efforts to carry out activities to achieve certain objectives, usually financial in nature.

When used in HR, the word "partner" refers to the Human Resource Manager, HR professionals or employees or workers in general as "strategic partners" of their organization.

The use of this word is not without criticism. If HR becomes partners of the organization, employees will not like it and unions are not too happy about it, too.

**Performance**

The act of carrying out a certain activity or the result of that activity. For example, HR performance refers to the results of the activities of the workforce based on defined standards and measures.

**Performance Appraisal**

A system for determining how well employees are performing their jobs, communicating that information to them and making plans to improve their performance.

**Performance Gap**

This is the difference between the current competency level and the required competency level.

**Performance Management**

Taking action to improve performance of employees, every unit or department and that of the organization by linking or aligning their objectives.

It covers HR activities such as job design, recruitment, training and development, performance appraisal, and the reward and incentives system.

**Performance Measures**

These are indicators that targets are being achieved and to what extent. Sometimes they are referred to as "key performance indicators or KPIs."

**Performance Standard**

The benchmark against which organizations measure performance.

**Personnel**

A member of the workforce.

**Personnel Management**

Carrying out activities related to the personnel function that focuses on the individuals and activities and not on the overall strategic role of the department.

**Planning**

Systematic way to accomplish a defined goal.

It involves preparing a step-by-step plan of action intended to accomplish certain defined goals.

**Pro-active**

Taking action in advance in anticipation of what may happen to avoid or reduce negative effects.

**Productivity**

Output of either goods or services divided by the inputs required to produce that output.

**Promotion**

The movement of an employee to a higher position in an organization either vertically within the same department or diagonally to another department.

**Reactive**

Taking action after a problem has happened. This is the opposite of "pro-active." This can have disastrous consequences. By then, it is too late to take action except to carry out damage control.

**Recruitment**

Recruitment refers to the activities carried out by the HR department to identify and employ the right person for the right job.

**Re-deployment**

The placement of an employee to a certain job or location.

**Reliability**

The extent of consistency and dependability. This can refer to people, team, tool, process, system or method, among others.

**Retention**

With reference to employees, keeping them in service through proper planning and offering the right set of incentives.

**ROI of Human Resources**

A measure on the return from employees taking into consideration all their skills, capabilities knowledge, and qualification.

**Telecommute**

To telecommute means to work from home. A genuine employment contract exists except that the employee is allowed to work at home, putting in the same number of hours.

It is agreed that there is problem of supervision. There is not way that the employee is actually doing the job.

One way of ensuring that the same amount of work is done is to assign tasks that require completion within a specified time limit.

**Trainer**

A person who has the expertise and competence to help other people acquire certain types of skills necessary in the effective performance of their duties.

Every manager, such as the HR Manager, and supervisor is expected to train subordinates.

**Training**

Training refers to activities intended to develop and improve an employee's skills and to add to his or her knowledge of the job. The main purpose is to help the employee perform his or her job to the satisfaction of the employer.

**Training Needs Analysis**

This is the determination of the types and regularity of training needed by each employee in an organization and the skills needs of the organization.

**Underwriter**

A person or organization that ensures money will be available to pay for losses that are insured. An insurance company can be considered an underwriter.

**Union**

Workers who organize a united group, usually related to the kind of work they do, to collectively bargain for better work conditions, pay or benefit increases, etc.

**Unjustifiable dismissal**

Firing an employee in a way that the courts do not find justifiable (i.e. unfairly or in violation of the employment contract).

**Viral Marketing**

Any marketing technique that induces people (or web sites) to pass on a marketing message to other people or sites, creating a growth in the message's visibility and effect. A classic example of this concept was Hotmail whereby each email sent via Hotmail included Hotmail's own advertisement in the footer ("Get your Free Email....").

**Virtual HR**

The use of various types of technology to provide employees with self-serve options. Voice response systems, employee kiosks are common methods.

**Voluntary Benefits**

Benefits that are paid for by the employee through payroll deductions.

The employer pays for administration. Examples of these benefits include life insurance, dental, vision, disability income, auto-insurance, long-term care coverage, medical supplement plans and homeowners insurance.

**Wage drift**

The difference between basic pay and total earnings, due to a variety of possible factors such as overtime, bonuses, gender, age and performance.

**Whistle blower**

An employee who publicly reveals wrongdoing taking place within his/her company. Whistle blowers are protected from retaliation by the Protected Disclosures Act of 2000.

**Work-life Balance**

The attempt to balance work and personal life in order to have a better quality of life. A person with a balanced life is an asset to his or her business, as he or she experiences greater fulfillment at work and at home.

**Work/Life Employee Benefits**

Work/Life benefits are "non-traditional" employee benefits that assist employees in managing their lives. Employers purchase these services from vendors and they are offered to employees as benefits. These services can make the difference in attracting and retaining employees. Common life management benefits include: child and elder care referral services, employee assistance program (EAP), concierge, legal assistance, and emergency back-up childcare.

**Workforce Planning**

The assessment of the current workforce in order to predict future needs. This can consist of both demand planning and supply planning. Many e-recruitment software providers include modules for workforce planning.

**XML and HR-XML**

Extensible Markup Language. A common system used for defining data. Unlike HTML, XML is not a fixed set of elements. XML allows information creators to apply descriptive markup (or "tags") around each discrete element of data. The HR-XML Consortium strives to spare employers and vendors the risk and expense of having to negotiate and agree upon data interchange mechanisms on an *ad-hoc* basis. By using XML, the Consortium provides the means for any company to transact with other companies without having to establish, engineer, and implement many separate interchange mechanisms.

# Index